Performance Interventions

Series Editors: **Elaine Aston**, University of Lancaster, and **Bryan Reynolds**, University of California, Irvine

Performance Interventions is a series of monographs and essay collections on theatre, performance, and visual culture that share an underlying commitment to the radical and political potential of the arts in our contemporary moment, or give consideration to performance and to visual culture from the past deemed crucial to a social and political present. *Performance Interventions* moves transversally across artistic and ideological boundaries to publish work that promotes dialogue between practitioners and academics, and interactions between performance communities, educational institutions, and academic disciplines.

Titles include:

Alison Jeffers
REFUGEES, THEATRE AND CRISIS
Performing Global Identities

Marcela Kostihová
SHAKESPEARE IN TRANSITION
Political Appropriations in the Post-Communist Czech Republic

Jon McKenzie, Heike Roms and C.J W.-L. Wee (*editors*)
CONTESTING PERFORMANCE
Emerging Sites of Research

Jennifer Parker-Starbuck
CYBORG THEATRE
Corporeal/Technological Intersections in Multimedia Performance

Ramón H. Rivera-Servera and Harvey Young
PERFORMANCE IN THE BORDERLANDS

Mike Sell (*editor*)
AVANT-GARDE PERFORMANCE AND MATERIAL EXCHANGE
Vectors of the Radical

Melissa Sihra (*editor*)
WOMEN IN IRISH DRAMA
A Century of Authorship and Representation

Brian Singleton
MASCULINITIES AND THE CONTEMPORARY IRISH THEATRE

Performance Interventions
Series Standing Order ISBN 978–1–4039–4443–6 Hardback
978–1–4039–4444–3 Paperback
(*outside North America only*)

You can receive future titles in this series as they are published by placing a standing order. Please contact your bookseller or, in case of difficulty, write to us at the address below with your name and address, the title of the series and the ISBN quoted above.

Customer Services Department, Macmillan Distribution Ltd, Houndmills, Basingstoke, Hampshire RG21 6XS, England

Performance, Politics, and the War on Terror

"Whatever It Takes"

Sara Brady

palgrave
macmillan

First published 2012 by
PALGRAVE MACMILLAN

Palgrave Macmillan in the UK is an imprint of Macmillan Publishers Limited, registered in England, company number 785998, of Houndmills, Basingstoke, Hampshire RG21 6XS.

Palgrave Macmillan in the US is a division of St Martin's Press LLC, 175 Fifth Avenue, New York, NY 10010.

Palgrave Macmillan is the global academic imprint of the above companies and has companies and representatives throughout the world.

Palgrave® and Macmillan® are registered trademarks in the United States, the United Kingdom, Europe and other countries.

ISBN 978–0–230–23490–1

This book is printed on paper suitable for recycling and made from fully managed and sustained forest sources. Logging, pulping and manufacturing processes are expected to conform to the environmental regulations of the country of origin.

A catalogue record for this book is available from the British Library.

A catalog record for this book is available from the Library of Congress.

10   9   8   7   6   5   4   3   2   1
21   20   19   18   17   16   15   14   13   12

Printed and bound in Great Britain by
CPI Antony Rowe, Chippenham and Eastbourne

To Kevin

Contents

List of Illustrations

Preface

14 July 2011. I'm watching the *Colbert Report*, and Stephen is talking about art created by Guantánamo detainees. After running through a delicious mash of graduate school lingo, Colbert concludes:

> surveying their oeuvre, it now occurs to me: could all of Gitmo in fact be just one giant art installation? Take our enemies from the stone-age villages in Afghanistan, fly them halfway across the world and then drop them into an extragovernmental, intraliminal space, neither America nor the battlefield, herein using unchecked executive power in an act of blistering self-critical metarecontextualization. Not to mention some of those guys look like they got wrapped up by Christo. So I say forget Marina Abramovic, forget Laurie Anderson. The greatest performance artists of our generation are these two guys [pointing to image of George W. Bush and Barack Obama].

As usual, Stephen Colbert has a point. His observation nods to an outer layer of a massive onion – one whose layers peel back one after the other to reveal performances that are local and global, scripted and impromptu, puppet-like and political. The summer of 2011 is no doubt one all about political theatre of a particularly self-conscious and peacock-feather ilk. In the wake of the Arab Spring, the summer that has followed has been highlighted in the United States by floods and tornadoes, heatwaves and stalemates. Responses to these events show over and over again that performance is indeed a key term for the twenty-first century, as Jon McKenzie argues.[1] We live in a mediatized era in which politicians are performers, and the best one wins: the one who can raise the most money, and persuade enough voters where reality lies. Same-sex couples can get married in New York, while the Governor of Texas plans his "Response: A Call to Prayer for a Nation in Crisis" for 6 August 2011. Truth has so very little to do with anything, as the Murdoch/News Corporation phone-hacking scandal has so aptly proved. The "debt ceiling" crisis in the United States has shaken an already frightened global economy while millions of vulnerable people face starvation and death in Somalia.

In the early twenty-first century, politics is performance and political theatre is all but irrelevant. What is "posturing" when realities are created through the public performances of politicians and pundits? In a July 2011 public conversation with Wikileaks founder Julian Assange, Slavoj Žižek addresses this point, debunking the title of "terrorist" given to Assange by others, and questioning exactly in what context "terrorism" exists:

> What is your, under quotation marks, "terrorism" compared to the terrorism which we simply accept, which has to go on day by day so that things just remain the way they are? That's where ideology helps us. When we talk about violent terrorism, we always think about acts which interrupt the normal run of things. But what about violence which has to be here in order for things to function the way they are? So I think, if – I'm very skeptical about it – we should use – in my provocative spirit, I am tempted to – the term "terrorism," it's strictly a reaction to a much stronger terrorism which is here. So, again, instead of engaging in this moralistic game – "Oh, no, he's a good guy," like Stalinists said about Lenin – "You like small children. You play with cats. You wouldn't" – as Norman Bates says in Psycho, "You wouldn't hurt even a fly." Now you know. No, you are, in this formal sense, a terrorist. But if you are a terrorist, my god, what are then they who accuse you of terrorism?[2]

A "terrorist" like Julian Assange exemplifies the power of information in the twenty-first century. Using the term "political theatre" is moot because all politics is theatre, and some may say that's always been the case. And yes, power has always stood behind the scenes in politics; however, the "show" of the politician bolstered up by corporate interests has reached new levels, especially in the case of US President Barack Obama. Obama is an extreme example of this new type of politician, with a 2012 campaign that has raised $86 million in the second quarter of 2011 – more than any politician in history.[3] Politicians are now only worth their weight in performance. So are television pundits. Acting skills reign supreme: while reality stars strive to keep looking like they are *not* acting, television pundits and politicians aim to reach a level of naturalism that Stanislavsky's students could only dream of. Therein lies the "hope" of the Murdoch phone-hacking debacle: if the mess is not contained, the curtain just might be lifted.

Anthony Weiner, the New York member of the US House of Representatives who fell from grace after tweeting images of his underwear, had his own curtain lifted in the summer of 2011. Weiner, who was a rising star on the US "left," sits on the opposite spectrum from the untouchable Obama – closer to Bill Clinton. Clinton's 1990s nemesis, former US House Speaker Newt Gingrich, got away with indiscretion while professing morality in the Clinton impeachment hearings. In the same public conversation with Assange, Žižek refers to Gingrich as the "scum of the earth" for going after Clinton during the Monica Lewinsky scandal while not just cheating on his wife, but asking her to sign divorce papers while she was in the hospital. When Žižek calls Gingrich the scum of the earth he is not simply speaking of him as a hypocrite. He is touching on the profound importance of the suspension of disbelief in politics, especially that of the US right.

Gingrich cheating on his wife while going after Clinton in the Lewinsky scandal points not simply to hypocrisy. It touches on the double in politics: performing one idea while actually supporting its opposite. This is what Žižek is talking about when he says "ideology appears as its own opposite."[4] It can be as simple as the "Clean Air" act or as complex as calling the United States a democracy while holding Bradley Manning in solitary and bombing the shit out of Libya. It's about trying to save taxes on corporate jets while cutting social "entitlement" programs. It's about hydraulic fracturing, or "fracking," the method now being used throughout the United States and internationally to recover natural gas and oil. The effects of fracking on humans, animals, and communities are turning out to be devastating. Ideology rears its ugly head in a scene from Josh Fox's documentary *Gasland*, in which a man demonstrates how he can light his tap water, contaminated by local fracking, on fire with a lighter. Even the occurrence of several earthquakes in Arkansas has led to fracking as a possible cause – and even Fox News reported on it.[5] But politicians and corporations insist fracking is an answer to foreign oil.[6] The politicians' performances reign supreme because they make people believe that all these acts (of terrorism?) are patriotic.

It's a kind of denial. It reminds me of the Mafia, of the essence of corruption – of the criminal who can go to church on Sunday. It's what enables Christopher, the infamous soldier of the *Sopranos*, to tell his uncle Tony Soprano that his girlfriend Adriana ran out on him when in fact she was taken to the woods and shot after Christopher revealed to Tony that she became an FBI informant. The problem is that there is always rot in hypocrisy, denial, and corruption. In theatre, however, cruelty and catharsis can happen precisely because of the form's purity, which lies in the agreement by the audience and actor to make believe. There is murder and vengeance in pure conscience in the theatre. The opposite is the camouflage of reality, the construction of the matrix, whatever you want to call it. The black magic of theatre? Politicians use theatre to bad ends – they use something good for evil. Isn't that wrong and rotten to the core? My argument here is less about moralizing than it is about maintaining a critical standpoint.

As the debt ceiling crisis has unfolded, critics and fellow politicians have referred to the Republican–Democrat failed negotiations as "political theatre." The mayor of Braddock, Pennsylvania, John Fetterman, told television host and comedian Bill Maher: "It's all bullshit political theatre [...] it's all posturing."[7] Economist Michael Hudson argued that the "crisis" around the debt ceiling is an "artificial" one, created and supported by the financial sector. President Obama, according to Hudson, has "gone along" with a "charade" to the detriment of the majority of the US population.[8] In his floor speech on 26 July 2011, Republican Senator John Boozman described the strained negotiations as "political theatre." But for me none of these examples qualify as political theatre. Unless one considers political theatre to be akin to what Richard Schechner calls "dark play" – the kind of performance in which not everyone knows there's a performance – a play – going on. If the "crisis" is artificial – if Obama held up a charade – then we're all inside a theatre, but the audience doesn't know it. The actors – politicians – are on stage, performing, and "we" are sitting in plush, red velvet seats. But we aren't aware of the proscenium.

A funner, less harmful political theatre does, however, exist these days. Politicians like Gingrich and Weiner have actually created viable scripts for performers – and this time I mean real performers, like actors and comedians, to rehearse. In a mini new wave of verbatim theatre, John Lithgow performed Newt Gingrich's 18 May 2011 press release (a melodramatic reaction to what the Gingrich campaign perceived as unwarranted and repeated attacks on the former US Representative) on the *Colbert Report*.[9] Just a few weeks later, the text of Anthony Weiner's embarrassing "sexts" proved so irresistible to Bill Maher that he enlisted Jane Lynch to come on his show *Real Time* to act out, word-for-word, the trashy-sexy messages. Both performances were delightful – in much the same way verbatim theatre is loved – because the audience *knows* that the text is "real." *These* are examples of a reincarnation of political theatre.

So this is why I wrote this book. Because I do believe that it's important to appreciate the variety of performances on offer in live and mediated contexts. The collapse of politics and theatre can be best identified and analyzed by scholars of performance. The field of performance studies has long argued for the study of actions that occur outside of conventional theatre spaces. Coupled with that challenge is the – yes, political – imperative to recognize performance when we see it. That is the only way forward.

Performance, Politics, and the War on Terror: "Whatever It Takes" offers a look at theatre and performance as events that occur both within as well as outside the aesthetic frame. The study begins and ends with the US presidency, focusing throughout on the equal attention paid by both administrations to the performative in the political realm. Chapter 1, "Bushismo," analyzes the brazen political performances of George W. Bush and how, through a particular arrogance, he forged a so-called global war on terror. The second chapter, "Protest Visible and Invisible" is a comparative study of civilian and military activism in the Vietnam era and the post-9/11 decade that pays particular attention to reconstructing the live political spectacles disappeared by the Bush-era media. Chapter 3, "War: The Video Game," examines the concepts of 'war' and 'gaming' both on several levels – as a metaphor; as simulation; as therapy; as training; as recruitment; as play; and as reality. The fourth chapter, "Torture: Simulated and Real" looks to the field, the screen, and simulation to argue that in the case of torture, 'fiction' and 'reality' often blur. Finally, Chapter 5, "Obamania," considers the way in which the same tool used by Bush – performance – offered change, hope, and belief, but has more effectively secured a status quo.

Sara Brady, July 2011

Acknowledgments

Many people inspired, encouraged, and helped me as I embarked on the research and writing of this book. I presented several parts of the project at a number of conferences, and received invaluable feedback from many colleagues, especially those in two ASTR working sessions: "Amerika: Theatre and the Kafkaesque American Cultural Landscape" convened by James Harding in 2007; and "Power and Performance: War on Stage" convened by Jenna L. Kubly and Kimi D. Johnson in 2010. I would like to thank my friend, colleague, and former teaching assistant Gabriella Calchi Novati for her support. My students at Trinity College Dublin taught me as much as I could teach them and more in my class on performance and politics. The book would not be nearly as fun to read without the images that many photographers and artists allowed me to reprint in these pages; thanks to Trevor Paglen, Jeff Busby, Walter Garcia, Lovella Calica, Joseph DeLappe, Paul Kawika Martin, and others. I am appreciative of those who agreed to talk with me about their own work, including Evan Knappenberger, Steve Powers, and Maboud Ebrahimzidah. I am also grateful for the assistance of the following people: Amy Heller from Milestone Films; Geoff Millard, Chair of Iraq Veterans Against the War's National Board of Directors; Lynn Estomin from Warrior Writers; Jessica Shaefer at Creative Time. Paula Kennedy first expressed interest in my idea and I would like to thank her for her patience and encouragement. Series editors Elaine Aston and Brian Reynolds supported the project throughout the process. Benjamin Doyle at Palgrave offered solid guidance as I completed the manuscript. I'd also like to thank Penny Simmons for her helpful suggestions and support while preparing the manuscript for publication. Finally, I'd like to thank my family and friends for their love and support, and especially my parents Mary and Tom Brady for always encouraging me to pursue work that made me happy.

1
Bushismo

[T]here's no question about it, this act will not stand; we will find those who did it; we will smoke them out of their holes; we will get them running and we'll bring them to justice. We will not only deal with those who dare attack America, we will deal with those who harbor them and feed them and house them. [...] Make no mistake about it: underneath our tears is the strong determination of America to win this war. And we will win it. [...] They will try to hide, they will try to avoid the United States and our allies – but we're not going to let them. They run to the hills; they find holes to get in. And we will do whatever it takes to smoke them out and get them running, and we'll get them.

George W. Bush, 15 September 2001[1]

It is difficult to imagine how any democracy can avoid being corrupted when war becomes the foundation of politics, if not culture itself. Any democracy that makes war and state violence the organizing principles of society cannot survive for long, at least as a democratic entity. The United States descended into a period in which society was increasingly organized through the production of both symbolic and material violence. A culture of cruelty emerged in the media, especially in the talk radio circuit, in which a sordid nationalism combined with a hypermilitarism and masculinity that scorned not merely reason but also all those who fit into the stereotype of other – which appeared to include everyone who was not white and Christian.

Henry Giroux[2]

1

Bushismo

The OED defines *machismo* as "strong or aggressive masculine pride." Taking a cue from the Spanish, I define the term *Bushismo* as the particular "strong or aggressive" pride associated with former US President George W. Bush: privileged, powerful, certainly trying, if not succeeding, to be masculine, and fiercely – stubbornly – proud. Pride, in the case of George W. Bush, was created and maintained in live and mediated performances, forging a large-scale performative environment. This chapter considers the social-political-economic arena of the Bush II years and his many performances as well as his figure in representation. Bush performed many times; the soundbites are all on youtube.com of the famously not-brilliant US President displaying, well, *Bushismo* of all colors. Some of my favorite examples are quips like, "Too many OB-GYNs aren't able to practice their love with women," or the "Tennessee saying" he butchered in September 2002: "Fool me once, shame on [...] shame on you. Fool me... You can't get fooled again!"[3] Bush's ever-present grin and the almost agitated state he seemed to perpetually occupy made for comedy, yes, but these brief acts need to be understood within the wider performative milieu they occupy.

Aside from the fact that Bush had his own brand of charisma, his own Bushisma, he was just one politician in a long line of public speakers spouting prepared, and sometimes improvised, political remarks. This category of performance is what Richard Schechner calls "make-belief" – that is, acts in which the audience are supposed to believe that what they are seeing and hearing is real (as opposed to the "make-believe" of the theatre); that what is happening before them is perhaps controlled, and yet somehow spontaneous and meaningful.[4] That most political functions and appearances are just the opposite – well-planned, rehearsed, and organized examples of performance if not "theatre" – may or may not be lost on the viewer. The soundbites are performances that occur within a larger context involving the speechwriter-playwright, the Secret Service-stage managers, the advisor-dramaturges, and the campaign manager-directors. Since Aristotle's *Rhetoric*, political performance has been studied. The fields of history, political science, and communication studies have long paid attention to political speeches and appearances. In comparison, theatre and performance studies scholars have only just begun to explore the performativity of politics from their unique perspective.

The concept of performance provides a lens through which to analyze specific acts, events, objects, and behaviors. Performances occupy a continuum on which artistic/theatrical events fall alongside everyday activities.

Richard Schechner's comparison of the "make-believe" of theatre and the "make-belief" employed in the context of a political candidate who campaigns with the intention to convince voters of her integrity offers a useful way to understand how the category of "performance" can include more than just theatre.

Performance studies scholars in recent years have looked at political performances from several perspectives, from the very specific to the more general. Tim Raphael, for example, focuses on the career of a particular politician: Ronald Reagan. Raphael has written about Reagan's "brand," developed through his television appearances in the 1950s for General Electric. He suggests: "To fully appreciate the legacy of Reaganism requires recognizing the capacity of corporate capitalism and mass-mediation to shape the body politic through the body electric."[5] Reagan's "body electric" served as a performative conduit through which the rhetoric of progress and the free market fused with the charisma of a popular political figure.

Casting a wider net, Diana Taylor draws on the intersections of performance, theatre, art, politics, and protest, using sites of performance throughout the Americas. In an editorial for the journal *e-misférica* she offers a close description of the performance of someone who could be any major politician:

> A well-rehearsed politician stands elevated on an elaborately crafted stage in a huge auditorium, delivering an impassioned speech to delegates and supporters. The adoring wife and children look on. [...] Those present as "live," embodied spectators see most of the proceedings on huge monitors. [...] For distant spectators who watch the proceedings on television, the delegates, stage hands, and hecklers inside, and protestors outside, become performers, a part of the show they see. For them, the event is further mediated by professional spectators, those expert commentators who evaluate the efficacy of the performance. Does it motivate and persuade spectators? [...] At the bottom of the screen, an information loop encourages viewers to participate actively by emailing their reactions to the designated website. [...] A successful performance turns spectators into voters and donors, whether those spectators are embodied (live), or the product of the 'live' transmission that creates spectators everywhere.[6]

The picture is a familiar one, especially during campaign season. Taylor asks, "So why do we care about performance? Because our political leaders do. They are ever more radical performers."[7]

Like Raphael's detailed analysis of Reagan's "body," Taylor draws attention to the relevance of performance studies to studies of political behaviors. To consider politicians as radical performers is to understand their actions in a context that fuses aesthetics with efficacy. In a similar vein, Richard Schechner comments on the collapse of art and politics, as exemplified by the "radical" performances of the Nazi Party. Nazi performances such as the Nuremberg Rallies of the 1920s and 1930s reveal that "it's not possible to sift out 'art' from 'politics.' The two are profoundly intermeshed then and now – as the mobilization of public opinion (directly or via media) constitutes a decisive base of political, military, state, and economic power."[8] In juxtaposition to performances by "legitimate" politicians, the actions of terrorists, as Schechner points out in his essay "9/11 as Avant-Garde Art?" also function in art-like ways. Schechner frames 9/11 as an event that exemplifies Antonin Artaud's theatre of cruelty, which offers the possibility of a "mass spectacle" that agitates "tremendous masses, convulsed and hurled against each other."[9] Noting Artaud's stipulation that such spectacle must remain within the confines of theatre and not real life, Schechner adapts Artaud's theory to a contemporary context, in which "the walls between the real and the virtual have crumbled, the theatrical and the actual have merged."[10] In this setting, the terrorism of 9/11 "works like art more on states of mind and feeling than on physical destruction. Or, if you will, the destruction is the means toward the end of creating terror, which is a state of mind."[11] Keeping in mind the close association between the *affect* produced by terrorists and politicians, I would like to chip away at the in-between of politics and performance: the unseating resemblance to theatre, and the undoubtedly real effects wrought by some such "performance."

The big picture

The political rally, speech, endorsement, or appearance is always a blip on the political radar; it's always one stop on the campaign trail and one small part of a larger political-performance environment. What is produced by this "larger" environment is sometimes tangible – the Patriot Act – and sometimes intangible – the Cold War's "fear," Carter's "malaise," or Obama's "hope." The rally boosts donations, the campaign succeeds, the politician gets the vote, and upon inauguration it's not just about Bush, it's about The Administration. The Kennedy Administration evokes a different feeling than the Nixon Administration and the Bush Administration (is supposed to) evoke(s) a different "feeling" than the

Obama Administration. This intangible realm of feeling, zeitgeist, or political capital operates on a massive scale, especially in the post-9/11 context. Within a couple of hours, everything "changed." I place quotes around the word because I would argue that the tangible change – the loss of lives and the buildings, the damage to the Pentagon, the temporary economic blow – has less to do with the intangible "change" through the mediatization of the events and the social-cultural-political arena in the United States and abroad than one would expect. What, for example, would have happened if the perpetrators had been portrayed as "criminals" instead of "terrorists"? A reality constructed not around a criminal justice reaction but a military one so quickly set in that it is difficult to even contemplate what a legal prosecution might have looked like.

The warpath begun immediately after 9/11 that led to the invasion of Afghanistan, and eventually Iraq, was enabled by the public feelings that essentially supported Bush in all his endeavors. The intangible during these years were backed by fiction: fake yellowcake and a constructed connection between Al Qaeda and Iraq. Instead of rational thinking and hard facts, there was conjecture with little critical viewpoint. These developments were supported by corporate news whose reporter-entertainers repeated the same scripts again and again. The public followed with varying levels of support. There were moments of dissent, such as Congress Member Barbara Lee's 14 September 2001 speech on the House floor in opposition to Bush's resolution to use force against the 9/11 perpetrators.[12] There were many protests before, during, and after the invasion of Afghanistan and later Iraq, which I discuss in Chapter 2. There were awkward moments like Michael Moore's Oscar speech, discussed further below. There were also key moments of consent, from Bush's speech on the evening of 11 September 2001, to his approval ratings, which spike at 9/11 and the invasion of Afghanistan before beginning a descent with a small gain upon the invasion of Iraq and his re-election. The Bush victory against Senator John Kerry in 2004 was an astonishing moment for many and yet was the direct result of how political performances successfully instilled a fear and paralysis in the American constituency – the American audience – that displayed an almost textbook example of a dysfunctional family. Especially to the rest of the world, Bush was like the abusive father whose children will not expose him. The day after the election the *Daily Mirror* described the results as a "disaster" with the following front-page headline: "How can 59,054,087 people be so DUMB?"[13] The American people seemed to be in some sort of denial that things can be wrong enough to make a change that resembled the association of the abused with the abuser. Overall, there was an inability – a refusal – to believe that, in the face of no WMD and no association between Saddam Hussein and Al Qaeda, the guy in charge got it seriously wrong.

Bush's performances

George W. Bush did not come into power with a powerful mandate; the 2000 election did not yield a clear winner and led to a major lawsuit in Florida that reached the US Supreme Court in *Bush v. Gore*. On 13 December 2000 Al Gore gave a concession speech and in January 2001 Bush was inaugurated. Much of the beginning of Bush's presidency is now famously insignificant. It was not until the morning of 11 September 2001, when Bush sat in on an elementary class in Florida while two planes crashed into New York's World Trade Center, that his first of many memorable performances occurred. The performance, during which Bush is informed by an aid of the second plane crashing into the South Tower, has had many afterlives. Like the images of the events of 9/11, the several-minutes clip has been replayed in a variety of contexts, including an adaptation in the film *Scary Movie 4*. The "pet goat" clip is often juxtaposed as a perversely calm moment of inaction by Bush with the horrible violence of the planes crashing into the Towers and the Pentagon. Bush's actual acts of that morning constitute a live performance that has disappeared – behavior that famously can't be reversed. The video record of these acts was meant at the time as a documentary record of a presidential visit: a significant photo op, but not meant at the time to be a major piece of history. The copies of this video and the editorializing of what occurs on tape constitute Bush in representation and can only ever be analyzed retroactively. Most replays stress the length of time for which Bush sat and participated in the class reading exercise while it was becoming increasingly clear that the there was a major national crisis going on. Michael Moore's *Fahrenheit 9/11*, for example, shows a clip of Bush sitting with Moore's voice narrating the amount of time passing in an attempt to reveal Bush's negligence and ineptitude as a world leader.

The moments immediately following the terrorist attacks were apparently fairly chaotic for Bush as well as Cheney and the rest of the Administration, with Cheney being moved to a safe place and Bush's plane flying nowhere. It was not until later that day, when Bush had some more control over the situation, that he was able to appear on television with relative confidence. A State of Emergency was declared. New York was in turmoil with missing person flyers covering street signs, building walls, and subway stops and volunteers rushing to the scene to help. Bush made relatively brief comments that evening, and on the following Saturday he issued a double message that resonated for years afterward. In a press conference at Camp David on 15 September 2001, Bush was asked by reporters: "how much of a sacrifice are ordinary Americans going to have to be expected to make in their daily lives, in their daily routines?"[14] The question made sense. Bush talked of a war being waged by "barbarians" against the US. Travelers were stranded at airports; there was great fear of public places like malls and urban centers; there were bomb scares for days after; indeed, for the weeks following the terrorist attacks, the government didn't have to instill fear in Americans. The images of 9/11 achieved that goal – as Schechner notes, the terrorists had successfully caused destruction that created terror as a state of mind. With what could only be a sort of desperate political move with more than a touch of mixed messages, Bush assured the audience that:

> Our hope, of course, is that they make no sacrifice whatsoever. We would like to see life return to normal in America. But these people have declared war on us and we will do *whatever it takes* to make sure that we're safe internally. So, therefore, people may not be able to board flights as quickly. Our borders are tighter than they've ever been before. We've taken a variety of measures to make sure that the American people are safe, just as the Attorney General spoke about.
>
> But we hope, obviously, that the measures we take will allow the American economy to continue on. I urge people to go to their businesses on Monday. I understand major league baseball is going to start playing again. It is important for America to get on about its life. But our government will be on full alert and we'll be tracing every lead, every potential to make sure that the American people are safe.[15]

Bush declared a war, demanded readiness from "everyone who wears the uniform," while communicating a message of the maintenance of normalcy. Pacifying the American people would have to work because the State of Emergency would be the new normal for an indefinite amount of time. Standing next to Attorney General John Ashcroft and Secretary of State Colin Powell, Bush answered the press's last question:

> Q[uestion]: How long do you envision–
> *The President*: The definition is *whatever it takes*.[16]

Figure 1.1 President George W. Bush clears brush on his Prairie Chapel Ranch, 9 August 2002, in Crawford, Texas. Photo by Eric Draper. Courtesy of the George W. Bush Presidential Library.

What followed was more like sheer nerve. On Monday 17 September 2001, Bush told reporters: "I want justice, and there's an old poster out West... I recall, that said, 'Wanted, Dead or Alive.'"[17] Rupert Murdoch-owned newspaper the *New York Post* ran a cover on 18 September 2001 designed like an old-fashioned "Wild West" wanted poster that read: "Wanted Dead or Alive: Osama bin Laden for Mass Murder in New York City." Like much of Bush's perceived persona, the "Wanted" comment performed a hopeful version of a tough, rancher type. George W. Bush promoted himself as an everyday guy who could talk to anyone. Like Reagan before him, he also donned a cowboy hat more than once, and he famously spent as much time as possible on his Crawford, Texas "ranch" (Figure 1.1). But Bush's seemingly brave and brazen attitude had very little supporting evidence. The Crawford property, purchased in 1999, was more a vacation home than any sort of working ranch; his "Western" persona also didn't hold up well: former Mexican president Vicente Fox told the *Daily Telegraph* that Bush had literally backed away from a horse Fox invited Bush to ride.[18] Bush delivered a televised speech a few days later with resolute nerve, naming Al Qaeda as responsible and targeting the Taliban:

> Americans are asking "Why do they hate us?"
>
> They hate what they see right here in this chamber: a democratically elected government. Their leaders are self-appointed. They hate our freedoms: our freedom of religion, our freedom of speech, our freedom to vote and assemble and disagree with each other.[19]

The "they" was supposed to be taken as "the terrorists"; as "Al Qaeda," and, by association, "the Taliban." Bush's "they," however, cast a dangerously wide net. In light of the Arab Spring that took place a decade later, his 2001 conflation of "terrorists" and political activists reads more than a bit oversimplified:

> They want to overthrow existing governments in many Muslim countries such as Egypt, Saudi Arabia, and Jordan. They want to drive Israel out of the Middle East. They want to drive Christians and Jews out of vast regions of Asia and Africa.[20]

By choosing not to proceed with an investigation of 9/11 that would be based in criminal justice, Bush needed to build into his rhetoric a justification for war, and democracy fit the bill. He focused on ensuring the continued American "way of life":

> These terrorists kill not merely to end lives, but to disrupt and end a way of life. With every atrocity, they hope that America grows fearful, retreating from the world and forsaking our friends. They stand against us because we stand in their way.[21]

Bush further associated the terrorists responsible for 9/11 with the legacy of twentieth-century atrocities, with a quick return to the idea of making war:

> We have seen their kind before. They're the heirs of all the murderous ideologies of the 20th century. By sacrificing human life to serve their radical visions, by abandoning every value except the *will to power*, they follow in the path of fascism, Nazism and totalitarianism.

And they will follow that path all the way to where it ends in history's unmarked grave of discarded lies. Americans are asking, "How will we fight and win this war?"

We will direct every resource at our command – every means of diplomacy, every tool of intelligence, every instrument of law enforcement, every financial influence, and every necessary weapon of war – to the destruction and to the defeat of the global terror network.[22]

But style was key, and Bush prepared the American people for a new era, the global war on terror. Contrasting the coming war to what was perceived at the time to be the most surgical military operation to date, Kosovo, Bush used the political capital at hand and predicted what eventually ensued: significant loss of life and unending conflict:

Now, this war will not be like the war against Iraq a decade ago, with a decisive liberation of territory and a swift conclusion. It will not look like the air war above Kosovo two years ago, where no ground troops were used and not a single American was lost in combat.

Our response involves far more than instant retaliation and isolated strikes. Americans should not expect one battle, but a lengthy campaign unlike any other we have ever seen. It may include dramatic strikes visible on TV and covert operations secret even in success.[23]

One of the most significant lines of Bush's speech was yet to come, however: the drawing of a line in the sand, the "us" and "them," the "fuck-you" to the world that defined US foreign policy for his entire administration:

We will starve terrorists of funding, turn them one against another, drive them from place to place until there is no refuge or no rest.

And we will pursue nations that provide aid or safe haven to terrorism. Every nation in every region now has a decision to make: *Either you are with us or you are with the terrorists.*

From this day forward, any nation that continues to harbor or support terrorism will be regarded by the United States as a hostile regime. Our nation has been put on notice, we're not immune from attack. We will take defensive measures against terrorism to protect Americans. Today, dozens of federal departments and agencies, as well as state and local governments, have responsibilities affecting homeland security.[24]

Jon McKenzie provides an astute analysis of Bush's 20 September 2001 speech, focusing on the President's citation of Nietzsche's "will to power" and his "either you are with us or the terrorists" ultimatum:

The President's "either/or" ultimatum divides the world in two: an us and a them, freedom vs. tyranny, good vs. evil, democracy vs. the will to power. It imposes a difference and also demands a decision. In a word: this is a test, a global test of democracy's performance in a new world order. With this test, President Bush effectively challenges the nations of the world to perform – or else. Either governments perform in accordance with this "war on terrorism" or they may face the power of US high-performance weapon systems. We can read this decisive and divisive test as the speech act's intended illocutionary force.[25]

Bush's statements, McKenzie argues, are performative in the Austinian sense, creating recognizable sides in the so-called war on terror. For McKenzie, this declaration was a test; or, it created a global test site, demanding that every nation in the global community submit to the United States' wishes. He proposes:

What effects might his performative have on solidifying the emerging performance stratum, that new world order, that Empire, that Integrated Circuit which proudly proclaims itself to be democratic – and in which the United States is variously cast as the supreme hegemon, its top executive, or its reluctant yet forceful policeman.[26]

The "emerging performance stratum, that new world order" McKenzie describes is for me the widest net cast; it makes up the outside layer of political performance that I am addressing in my study. That evening "Bushismo" covered the new world order.

Henry Giroux describes the social/political/cultural/economic shift that subsequently occurred in the United States: "War gained a new status under the Bush administration, moving from an option of last resort to a primary instrument of diplomacy in the war on terror."[27] Bush moved swiftly from the position of an unimpressive first year in office to one capable of testing the outer limits of executive power. He accomplished this through performance in front of a camera – a performance whose significance lies not in its content as much as its context. His televised speech was a key "national" moment – who *wasn't* watching? The text of the speech can be studied in such detail years later in part because of the massive audience tuned in on that night. Ironically it did not occur on the mass scale that 9/11 did, but the live, shared experience of Bush's 20 September address to the nation makes its language all the more significant.

Truth, "truthiness," and the fake

In addition to Bush's brief speech on the evening of 11 September 2001, his "smoke them out" talk on 15 September, and his war drumbeat on 20 September, the terrorist attacks of 11 September 2001 elicited an incredible number of immediate political/governmental responses, including the State of Emergency proclaimed by the President, the Patriot Act, and the invasion of Afghanistan. These actions need to be considered alongside the *cultural* responses of Hollywood and the mainstream media, including the "Beverly Hills Summit," which I discuss in Chapter 4, at which Bush advisor Karl Rove outlined ways in which the television and film industry could support White House policies. These political-cultural responses cultivated, in the months after the 9/11 attacks, a reliance on performance by politicians and the media. Within this performative environment, the "feeling" or "appearance" of truth – what *Colbert Report* host Stephen Colbert ironically calls "truthiness" – became more important, concrete, and more "real" than any sort of verifiable truth. Although there are countless examples before and after 9/11 of this kind of information manipulation, the connection between Saddam Hussein and Al Qaeda and the presence of WMD in Iraq best exemplify "truthiness" as used or abused, especially by the US government and the Bush Administration in the post-9/11 era.

Political and international studies scholar Stuart Croft describes this construction of "truthiness" as a "decisive intervention" through which a "new common sense" was co-produced by both governmental and cultural institutions.[28] For art historian Dougal Phillips, the "screen" is a key figure in the Bush administration's production of reality:

> The White House real appears to be very much predicated on a *libidinal investment in the screen*, an unconscious investment which is revealed

by the Bush administration's reliance on rhetoric and imagery to show the world the way they wish it was.[29]

The Bush White House enjoyed uninhibited access to the US audience via the "screen" immediately after 9/11. The ability to produce and manipulate information to the public became particularly relevant in the 18 months that passed, and a case for the Iraq War developed. Several investigative journalists have traced the contrived relationship between regime change in Iraq – a plan already in the works – and the threat of Al Qaeda and the events of 9/11.[30] Bush conflated Al Qaeda and Saddam Hussein on 25 September 2002, claiming that "you can't distinguish between Al Qaeda and Saddam when you talk about the war on terror."[31] Condoleezza Rice told CNN's Wolf Blitzer that, despite the lack of any concrete evidence, Saddam Hussein was pursuing nuclear weapons and "we don't want the smoking gun to be a mushroom cloud," a line that became salient through multiple plays on entertainment-news programs. It was Colin Powell's UN address in February 2003 that sealed the Iraq deal for many. Powell detailed evidence that Iraq was not complying with UN resolutions, that the country pursued nuclear weapons, and that Saddam Hussein had connections to Al Qaeda. Powell's performance relied on his perceived integrity and authority. When, in February 2011, it was revealed that much of the information was not only false, but the source known as the "Curveball" had been pressed to repeat inaccurate information, Colin Powell criticized the CIA and the Pentagon for not providing reliable intelligence.[32]

The UN speech exemplifies how the "screen" functions. Phillips argues that real and metaphorical screens provide the means with which political power can process and produce information for the public, which in turn creates meaning around such information:

> I refer here not only to the screen in the televisual sense, but to a more expansive notion. Along with the well-known televisual elements of the contemporary geo-political scene – the Hollywood-designed briefing room, the Fox News agit-prop and the like – we can also include the fantasy object of the SDI missile screen, the defense initiative force-field intended to girt the United States, protecting it from intercontinental harm. Further, there is a privacy screen (or veil) set up around the operations of the Administration through the workings of spin doctors, who spin a kind of information web, serving as a screen in the sense of the semi-permeable apparatus which lets some things through but traps others.[33]

The "screen," therefore, is strategically placed for the performance of politics. Dougal Phillips compares moments that speak to this difference, a difference between the credulous and the critical.

> The existence of competing phrase regimes for the constitution of "realities" continues to play out, in everything from the reserves and prices of oil to the pinning of villainy on various nefarious characters in the Mid-East and Pakistani scene. What this linguistic play ultimately reflects is that we are witness to transparently discordant versions of "reality" in the current geo-political scene, and that the establishment of power is often taken hostage and radically subverted by the uncontrollable powers and failures immanent to language and representation.[34]

Phillips juxtaposes phrases such as George W. Bush's 1 May 2003 "Mission Accomplished" statement with Saddam Hussein's claim from the courtroom in July 2004 that he was the "President of Iraq," describing Hussein's performative as a form of "wresting control of the phrase-universe." Similarly, he cites 9/11 hijacker Ziad Jarrah's claim to passengers over the PA system that he was their "captain."

In her essay "The Year of the Fake," Naomi Klein addresses the disturbing conflation of facts and fiction. Klein traces the great heights reached by the "fake" in 2003:

> a year that waged open war on truth and facts and celebrated fakes and forgeries of all kinds. This was the year when fakeness ruled: fake rationales for war, a fake President dressed as a fake soldier declaring a fake end to combat and then holding up a fake turkey. An action movie star became governor and the government started making its own action movies, casting real soldiers like Jessica Lynch as fake combat heroes and dressing up embedded journalists as fake soldiers. Saddam Hussein even got a part in the big show: He played himself being captured by American troops.[35]

Klein covers the notorious "fakes" surrounding the Iraq war that were in part facilitated by the openness of public opinion to information traveling through screens. The Bush Administration lied in its justification for invading Iraq, Bush announced that the war was over in a staged moment that even he admitted later was overdone, and troops didn't enjoy the well-decorated roasted turkey platter held up by Bush in his surprise Thanksgiving visit to Iraq. Jessica Lynch, the 19-year-old private whose rescue from an Iraqi hospital was not only staged but falsely documented, corrected in a television interview allegations that she suffered gunshot wounds and was mishandled by Iraqis. Klein notes the power of the fake: "The real Jessica Lynch – who told Diane Sawyer that 'no one beat me, no one slapped me, no one, nothing' – has proven no match for her media-military created doppelgänger, shown being slapped around by her cruel captors in NBC's movie, *Saving Jessica Lynch*."[36]

Michael Moore's Oscar, or, the invalidation of the political

There was something in the air in 2003, something that let the screen flow with false information and a belief in "truthiness" – in a truth desired. In the first moments of the Iraq War a strong sense of consensus – in spite of massive global disapproval – permeated the US landscape. Visual culture scholar Nicholas Mirzoeff describes in *Watching Babylon* the discomfort that those opposed to the war faced, as what looked like a quick reprisal of Gulf War I ensued. Mirzoeff characterizes the images of and about war as weapons themselves that deny reaction. "War images seem to be, like the stealth bombers, hard, sharp-edged and opaque, designed to evade all forms of radar, physical and cultural. Their immunity to criticism is in part a function of their sheer proliferation, especially in times of political crisis."[37] There are some key moments during this time period that, when analyzed as performance, reveal an enormous amount about the larger public-political-performance arena in the United States at the time.

One such moment occurred when the documentary filmmaker Michael Moore accepted the Oscar for Best Documentary 2002 at the Academy Awards Ceremony in Los Angeles. The timing was ripe: the awards were held on 23 March 2003, just days after the 20 March invasion of Iraq. Michael Moore's 2003 Oscar speech is a perfect, 45-second example of a spontaneous performance protest that stirred the pot in sensitive ways. Unlike a politician, who stays within the perceived rules of public speaking, Moore stepped out of genre and out of context. His film *Bowling for Columbine* (2002) had been nominated for Best Documentary. He described years later in an interview how he felt waiting in the audience for the announcement to be made. He recalled telling his fellow nominees: "'Eh, listen, if I win, I'm probably – I can't like thank my hairdresser. You know, I'm going to have to say something.'"[38] Moore further describes with humor the mental battle he experienced with social and cultural norms about what is "appropriate" to say not only in public, but at the Oscars:

> I'm in this like out-of-body experience, getting up out of my seat. [...] I'm walking up to the stage, and it was like, you know, the two voices that are in Gollum's head in Lord of the Rings. You know, I had that – it was like – you know, like one voice was saying, "Oscar! Precious! Precious Oscar! Just thank your agent and the people, the little people who brought you here, and leave the stage!" And the other voice was going, "No, there's a war on! You have to say something! You have to!" "No, no! Don't listen to him! Don't listen! No! Oscar! Precious!" "No, Oscar bad! Bad Oscar! War going on!" And it was like this fight going on in my head for like the thirty seconds it takes to climb the stage.[39]

Faced with what he perceived as a moral dilemma, Moore had to decide finally whether to use the circumstances of a prominent Hollywood live audience and a television audience of millions to say what he thought about what was going on in Iraq. And he did:

> [W]e live in fictitious times. We live in a time where we have fictitious election results that elects [*sic*] a fictitious president. We live in a time where we have a man sending us to war for fictitious reasons, whether it's the fiction of duct tape or the fictitious of orange alerts. We are against this war, Mr. Bush. Shame on you, Mr. Bush! Shame on you! And any time you've got the Pope and the Dixie Chicks against you, you're time is up! Thank you very much![40]

The Oscar music came up, and Moore was literally silenced. He was not the only nominee that night to acknowledge that the war was underway, but he was the only one to issue direct opposition. The live audience booed – although Moore points out that they came from the back where the producers, sponsors, and agents sat, not where the Hollywood stars were seated – and there was *anger*. Anger that he spoke out of turn? Anger that he drew attention to what was going on in a country on the other side of the world? Anger that he broke the rules of Oscar etiquette? Anger that he spoke out against the President? All of it. Moore was quickly ushered offstage. His comments were extremely unpopular. At the time, mainstream news and pundits were mostly for the war and the public was waiting for the military to report on "where" the WMD were. News of the Oscars reported on Michael Moore in a negative way.

Michael Moore has remained a controversial figure – he, like the more recent figure of WikiLeaks's Julian Assange, exists in the public realm as both myth and liar, truth-teller and uppity whiner, hero and shameful embarrassment. These political-performative characters can be lots of things, but never neutral. Bush's own performances similarly follow a path of bias and power – albeit in a very different way.

The real, and fear: 2004

Fakes abound from 9/11 through 2003, but 2004 was different. There was the announcement that former professional football player Pat Tillman, who abandoned a million-dollar salary and family to fight for his country in Afghanistan, was "killed by enemy fire after courageously charging up a hill to protect his fellow Army Rangers."[41] Within a month the story was exposed as false; Tillman had in fact been shot by friendly fire. The inability of the "fake" to stand up and the return of the Real continued throughout the year. In late April *60 Minutes II* featured photographs of abused prisoners at the Abu Ghraib prison. In early May journalist Seymour Hersh published a detailed report in *The New Yorker* magazine. Revelations followed of mistreatment and torture of detainees at Guantánamo and other black sites. Phillips's argument that the "screen" constructs preferred "realities" while also always providing a membrane vulnerable to the Real rang true in 2004. Referring to Baudrillard's idea of "the pressurized fuselage system of the West," Dougal Phillips writes:

> These pinpoint attacks come in the form of the leaked torture photo on the global TV screen, the single terrorist slipping through customs and borders, the missile that the force field misses, the single airborne Anthrax particle. So the libidinal investment in the screen as defense against the real carries with it a sense of security but a false sense of *protection.*[42]

"Reality," "truth," and meaning are not the only by-products of this screen. For Mark Danner, the "pinpoint" to the Real quickly folds into the "growth industry" of scandal:

> Revelation of wrongdoing leads not to definitive investigation, punishment, and expiation but to more scandal. Permanent scandal. Frozen scandal. The weapons of mass destruction that turned out not to exist. The torture of detainees who remain forever detained. The firing of prosecutors which is forever investigated.[43]

Danner describes scandal as a form of information manipulation that doesn't just release preferred narratives through a membrane and keep out others; rather, it establishes a loop. Frozen scandals

> metastasize, ramify, self-replicate, clogging the cable news shows and the blogosphere and the bookstores. The titillating story that never ends, the pundit gabfest that never ceases, the gift that never stops giving: what is indestructible, irresolvable, unexpiable is too valuable not to be made into a source of profit. Scandal, unpurged and unresolved, transcends political reality to become commercial fact.[44]

Danner argues that the twenty-first-century scandals differ from those of the past in their unending circulation. Watergate, for Danner, is a scandal to think on with nostalgia because it had a clear before and after.

In addition to scandal, it is important to note the role of fear in the post-9/11 construction of political realities. Fear was also delivered via the semi-permeable screen. With a public plugged into a preferred reality that connected Iraq and Al Qaeda, believed that the rest of the world was behind the United States, and remained invested in the idea that "freedom" and "democracy" relied on "victory" in Afghanistan and Iraq, fear could be – and needed to be – produced and maintained. Through a variety of performances – from US President George W. Bush's State of the Union addresses, to the Department of Homeland Security's terror alert system – ranging from "green" or "low" to "red" or "severe" – a culture of fear developed in the United States that opened the door to a justification of pre-emptive attack on Iraq, bolstered support for regime change, and contributed to Bush securing a second term. Even in the face of the stunning revelations of the spring and summer of 2004 such as the Abu Ghraib scandal and the waterboarding of several detainees, "torture" was a non-issue in the 2004 presidential election. Scandals froze, and fear reigned. It is important to establish this performative context in which the "war on terror" evolved because it serves as a foundation from which to investigate, as I do in subsequent chapters, specific sites of performance, from performance art and documentary theatre to military training exercises.

The blank slate

The reliance by politicians on performance was most certainly not a post-9/11 innovation. There was, however, a particular moment that occurred with the "event" of 9/11 within which there existed the *perception* of an *absence* of a *script* to follow. Naomi Klein describes this idea of the absence of a script, or an empty space, using shock as both an object of study and a metaphor. She describes shock as a time when we lose our narrative/history – we (that is, the victims of shock) are a blank slate. This void produced a need for creativity – an opening for improvisation in the wake of 9/11. As I discuss in Chapter 4, this need led the military and the CIA to representation – to television, to film, to pop culture, to fiction – for ideas with *results* performed in the "field." Live performance in "real life" was, in such contexts, based in "art." These sites of performance trouble any definition of the term that relies on artistic representation. Performance studies – which argues for the understanding of behaviors outside of the conventional theatre as constituting "performance" – therefore offers a particularly relevant perspective on the making and remaking of political and cultural realities in the post-9/11 era.

This is why it is appropriate for a performance studies scholar to look at the war on terror. I suggest that instead of analyzing politics through a traditional political science, sociological, or even communication studies model, a look at politics through the aesthetics of performance will reveal more about the effectiveness of politics. I would further argue that the *application* of creative narratives and theatre in place of policy and protocol necessitated by the perceived void left by 9/11 has contributed to devastation in the name of "freedom" and "democracy." I do not wish to take a moral high ground, but on the level of analyzing performance, the war on terror was clearly sold by George W. Bush and other performing politicians from Tony Blair to Colin Powell, bought by audiences, and carried on through a status quo established in the process. Giroux describes this progression:

> War was no longer the last resort of a state intent on defending its territory; it morphed into a new form of public pedagogy – a type of cultural war machine – designed to shape and lead the society. War became the foundation for a politics that employed military language, concepts, and policing relations to address problems far beyond the familiar terrains of battle. In some cases, war was so aestheticized by the dominant media that it resembled an advertisement for a tourist industry. The upshot is that the meaning of war was rhetorically, visually, and materially expanded to name, legitimate, and wage battles against social problems involving drugs, poverty, and the nation's newfound enemy, the Mexican immigrant.[45]

Giroux's analysis speaks to the ultimate justification for the global war on terror, supposedly fought around the world, wherever terrorists may be hiding, while simultaneously being fought against sleeper cells in the United States. But the sleeper cell could have anyone as its members, as the whiteness of John Walker Lindh, the "American" Taliban originally from California who was captured in late 2001 in Afghanistan, demonstrated. From the ubiquity of the sleeper cell, it is not a stretch to legitimizing the targeting of any disenfranchised or marginalized population in the United States, such as the Mexican immigrant, as Giroux notes. In his critique of US culture Giroux argues that "Dialogue, reason, and thoughtfulness slowly disappeared from the public realm as every encounter was framed within circles of certainty, staged as a fight to the death." The war on terror made possible a heightened sense of otherness with the cultivation of fear while ignoring the deterioration of society on the ground. A character from the 2009 television series *Southland* captures this simultaneous victimization and invalidation. The show, an attempt at a gritty and realistic take on the police patrolling the city of Los Angeles, features a bus driver who witnesses a gang shooting. When the police question her only to leave in frustration because she won't talk, she stands up and tries to explain to the officers what's at stake. She's lost family members. "Everybody bangs around here. Shoot, we got our own war of terror right here."[46] As contrived as the scene may seem, the bus driver's reaction exemplifies the extent of the "global" war on terror in popular imagination both outside and inside the United States.

Back stage: Cheney's dark side

To understand how the war on terror became so engrained in US culture, it is crucial to return again to the days following the terrorist attacks of 11 September 2001. Less than one week later, Vice-President Dick Cheney explained to Tim Russert of *Meet the Press* how the White House intended to pursue those responsible:

> We'll have to work sort of the dark side, if you will. We've got [...] to spend time in the shadows in the intelligence world. A lot of what [...] needs to be done here will have to be done quietly, without any [...] discussion, using sources and methods that are available to our [...] intelligence agencies if we are going to be successful. That's the [...] world these folks operate in. And, uh, so it's going to be vital for [...] us to use any means at our disposal basically, to achieve our [...] objectives.[47]

Cheney's now infamous response has been investigated by journalist Jane Mayer, whose book *The Dark Side: The Inside Story on How the War on Terror Turned into a War on American Ideals* exposes how ill-equipped the US government was to deal with Islamist extremism. His description of the "dark side" implied the creation of a sort of "back stage" on which the subsequently devised "war on terror" could be prosecuted. The nuclear deterrence scripts memorized by Cheney and his Cold War-era colleagues could not directly apply to the actions of 9/11; however, his "doomsday" expertise came in handy. Mayer describes Cheney as an "unapologetic advocate of expanding presidential power," relating that desire to the *Meet the Press* appearance. "Soon afterward," Mayer continues, "Cheney disappeared from public view. But his influence had already begun to shape all that followed."[48] In the period immediately following 9/11, Cheney's energy would combine with President George W. Bush's "brashness"[49] – his Bushismo – to fill a major void in US intelligence: "The sad secret of the CTC [Counterterrorism Center ...] was that despite the fierce talk, before September 11 the CIA had no spies inside Al Qaeda or the security guard surrounding bin Laden. They had never recruited a single agent inside his network or infiltrated any of his training camps."[50] There was no time to catch up, and there was no place for excuses; instead, key figures in the Bush Administration turned to performance. A narrative was created through the evil-doer Osama bin Laden and his organization Al Qaeda, and the fight against "evil" became the "war on terror." In part this narrative brought Osama bin Laden into being; on the other hand, he was already well-known since his 1996 *fatwa*, or declaration of war against America.[51] Within this performative environment, the historical approach to terrorism, which "treated it as a crime like any other, was inadequate for the post-9/11 world," according to Mayer.[52] The law, therefore, quickly became malleable – less 'real.' Bush's demeanor, on the other hand, became more like 'fiction': "Undaunted," Mayer writes, by the estimated $1 billion cost of supporting the Northern Alliance, "Bush reportedly responded with a line that would later become the unofficial motto of Jack Bauer, the macho terrorist-busting hero of Fox Television's fantasy melodrama *24*." He said, according to Bob Woodward, " 'Whatever it takes.' "[53]

Within this performative landscape the unthinkable became "fact"; the crisis produced by a foreign attack on the US mainland moved Hollywood fiction into reality. Slavoj Žižek observed: "The unthinkable which happened was thus the object of fantasy: in a way, America got what it fantasized about, and this was the greatest surprise."[54] This perceived shift enabled a push for a new paradigm. The idea that 'old' rules no longer applied ("the mood [...] was 'rule-of-law be damned'"[55]) opened space for a rewriting of law and an environment of exceptionalism to thrive.

Naomi Klein's *Shock Doctrine* theorizes such a moment, at which ideas already developed in universities, think tanks, and boardrooms find the ideal entrance – in a seemingly improvisational way – into society, producing major economic, social, political, and cultural change.[56] Klein focuses to a great extent on the disastrous results of imposing post-crisis free market policies; often, however, such movements are accompanied by other political and social shifts.[57] In the case of the United States, drastic gestures began on 14 September 2001, when President George W. Bush issued Proclamation 7463, Declaration of National Emergency by Reason of Certain Terrorist Attacks. The Proclamation has been extended for one year, every year since 2001, most recently on 10 September 2010 because, according to a 2010 White House press release, "The terrorist threat that led to the declaration on September 14, 2001, of a national emergency continues."[58] Giorgio Agamben has analyzed the circumstances of such a "state of exception" in his 2005 book of the same name,[59] in which he continues his response to German legal scholar Carl Schmitt's theorization of the sovereign, initiated in *Homo Sacer: Sovereign Power and Bare Life.*[60] In the current US "state of exception," executive power quashed checks and balances, allowing President Bush to issue orders limiting the rights of both citizens and non-citizens. The 13 November 2001 "Detention, Treatment, and Trial of Certain Non-Citizens in the War Against Terrorism" military order named suspected terrorists as "enemy combatants," a term which limited their right to due process and paved the way for "enhanced interrogation" techniques.

Long before the 'Torture Memos,' and shortly before the November 2001 order, Cheney performed a justification for torture in his insistence on going to the "dark side." After eight years of Bush rule, the Obama Administration struggled under pressure to deal with the legacy of two Bush terms, and the torture debate continued. Alfred McCoy describes the issue as subject to cycles, during which "Congress and the press will conduct a major expose of torture; the public will be momentarily aroused; there will be no sustained investigation, no prosecution, no penalty; [and] the practice will continue."[61] The use of torture post-9/11 presents various contradictions to consider. First, it is not the first era in which the United States has employed torture directly or indirectly;[62] second, the "shadows" only remained unlit for a limited time (albeit enough to cause major damage); third, the concept of torture constitutes an area of performance in its own right. Tracing how the United States moved from a creepy suggestion of the "dark side" to a troubled debate around "enhanced interrogation techniques" reveals that in the midst of nothing – of an empty space – a gloves-off attitude led to an explosion of secrecy and the use of representation to create performances of torture.

Bush in representation from *W* to *Lil' Bush*

It is obvious that representation is key to 9/11. The event was mediated as it unfolded. Richard Schechner writes: "Almost as they were occurring, the 9/11 attacks were marketed as popular entertainment. Representations of the attacks are paradigmatic of the accelerating conflation of news and entertainment."[63] Like other major historical events, 9/11 becomes an essential before-and-after marker of representation. Part of the "after" is a multitude of examples of George W. Bush in representation. Like all US presidents, and like so many major political figures throughout the world, Bush has been a subject of representation from photography to cartoon to film and theatre. What makes the images and performances of Bush particularly interesting has to do with his incompetence (perceived or otherwise) in his powerful role; the inarticulate nature of much of his public speaking; the revelations of so many poor decisions; his insistence on sticking to his story; and his actions as supreme leader of the global community at the start of the twenty-first century. Bush famously offered comedians material that needed no editing. His "real life," or "make-believe" appearances therefore have an interesting co-existence with his figure in parody.

His own live performances folded into the popular imagination as his role as leader of the "free world" became suddenly more visible after 9/11 than before. A global audience watched him speak and move, from his passive silence in the first moments of the attacks to his lukewarm national address on the evening of 9/11 to his brazen speech on 20 September, his State of the Union addresses, his speech just after the first anniversary of the attacks, and most especially his "Mission Accomplished" appearance. On 1 May 2003 Bush flew, in uniform, aboard a Navy jet, which landed on the USS *Abraham Lincoln* aircraft carrier (Figure 1.2). He gave a victory speech in front of a large banner that read "Mission Accomplished." (Figure 1.3). His speech directly linked the Iraq conflict with 9/11. What was just as astonishing as Bush's performed ending to a "war" that had never been officially declared a "war" was the deceptive tactic of the aircraft carrier landscape. The average observer perceived the location to be somewhere in the Persian Gulf; but the Naval carrier was actually floating off the coast of southern California. His act of pure theatre was later criticized for its contrived, and even manipulative nature. His appearances carried a certain significance due to the fact that over his eight

Figure 1.2   President George W. Bush walks with Navy Lt. Ryan Phillips as they depart the Naval Air Station North Island in San Diego for a flight aboard S-3B Viking jet "Navy One" en route to the USS Abraham Lincoln. Photo by Susan Sterner. Courtesy of the George W. Bush Presidential Library.

years in office he famously gave very few press conferences. In addition to his own speeches, and as the national sense of humor that seemed to disappear after 9/11 began to return, George W. Bush began to appear in other representational forms. In American style, he was parodied by comedian Will Ferrell on *Saturday Night Live* from the time of the 2000 campaign through his eight-year reign; James Adomian gave numerous impressions on the *Craig Ferguson* show and a cameo in the film *Harold and Kumar Escape from Guantánamo Bay* (2008). Bush was parodied in even more cartoon programs, from *South Park* to the *Simpsons*, to the British animated show *2DTV* to Comedy Central's *Lil' Bush*, which portrayed Bush as a child whose friends included Lil' Condi, Lil' Rummy, and Lil' Cheney. *Lil' Bush* (2007) crossed the imagined childhood of Bush II as the son of a US President with the circumstances of his own administration with a biting satire that equates the Bush II policies with

Figure 1.3 President Bush gives a "thumbs-up" sign after declaring the end of major combat in Iraq as he speaks aboard the aircraft carrier USS *Abraham Lincoln* off the California coast, 1 May 2003. AP Photo by J. Scott Applewhite.

a misguided, youthful immaturity. Bush's poor approval ratings enabled much of these products of popular culture to flourish while he was still in office. After Barack Obama's election and during Bush's lame-duck period, Will Ferrell revived his impersonation of Bush for a play entitled *You're Welcome America: A Final Night with George W. Bush*, which had a brief run on Broadway in 2009 and was broadcast on HBO.

Next to the humorous depictions of Bush mixing his metaphors and stumbling through rhetorical strategies were several attempts to take Bush on in a serious manner. In November 2002 Alexandra Pelosi's documentary, *Journeys with George* had its TV premiere. Her hand-held camera followed Bush for over a year through his 2000 election campaign. Pelosi caught Bush looking not-so-smart, but she also captured the shift that occurred as Bush morphed from just one of the candidates to a serious contender, and on video this change seems to surprise no one more than Bush himself. The frank clips of Bush with his guard down reinforced his supporter's preference for his everyday-guy persona while affirming for his critics that he had no qualifications for his job. Pelosi's work also bridged a cynical view of Bush with an attempt to present a version of "truth." As the drumbeat for war continued in late 2002, and as the spring of 2003 brought the invasion of Iraq, leading to the failure to locate WMD, the spectacular proclamation of "Mission Accomplished," and the Battle of Falluja, a desire for "truth" developed. With the Abu Ghraib scandal, the revelations of torture, and the Downing Street

Memo, this desire became an obsession for some. A spurt of documentaries arose that included independent films from *Bush's Brain* (2004), an expose of Karl Rove's role in Bush's career, to Michael Moore's critique of the Bush Administration in *Fahrenheit 9/11* (2004), to Public Broadcasting Service's Frontline special *Bush's War* (2008), to *Uncovered: The War in Iraq* (2004), to the *Road to Guantánamo* (2006), to Rory Kennedy's *Ghosts of Abu Ghraib* (2007), to the many videos produced by Brave New Films.

As the Bush era began to wane and the second term drew closer to its finish line, Oliver Stone released the biopic *W* (2008). Stone, a film director known for his commitment to truth but also to visual storytelling, cast Josh Brolin as George W. Bush, the failed businessman and recovering alcoholic. The film received lukewarm reviews, in part perhaps because Bush was still in office and practically a lame duck that fewer people took interest in. But Stone had taken the mystery of how Bush could convince a nation of so many far-fetched ideas and attempted to get to the bottom of his personality. Like many of the contemporary portrayals of Bush, *W* suffered from a feeling that the characters were contrived, played by actors playing real people readily visible to audiences. The search for truth, however, took on a unique flavor in live performance, where the space of theatre offered a particular window on re-establishing a sense of gravity and reality lost in the entertainment-news of mass media.

Documentary theatre: performing "truth," testimony, and evidence

Since 2001, the genre(s) of documentary theatre, verbatim theatre, or reality theatre as such performance is alternatively characterized, has featured a number of investigations into "truth." Documentary theatre attempts to reclaim such truth through "evidence." In her introduction to a special issue of the performance studies journal *The Drama Review* on documentary theatre, guest editor Carol Martin writes: "Its practitioners use the archive as evidence to create a performance of testimony; audiences understand what they see and hear as nonfiction; the actors ostensibly perform 'verbatim.'"[64] While acknowledging the problems inherent in such claims to truth, Martin describes six "functions" of contemporary documentary theatre:

1) To reopen trials [...]
2) To create additional historical accounts [...]
3) To reconstruct an event [...]
4) To intermingle autobiography with history [...]

5) To critique the operations of both documentary and fiction [...]
6) To elaborate the oral culture of theatre.[65]

Martin and others point to the spike in the popularity of documentary theatre in the post-9/11 years as a search for truth and reality in an environment without clear boundaries. Several examples of post-9/11 documentary theatre conform to Martin's "functions" of the genre. Many representative works come from contemporary British playwrights and theatre companies, including David Hare's *Stuff Happens* (2004); Tricycle Theatre's *Guantanamo: Honor Bound to Defend Freedom* by Victoria Brittain and Gillian Slovo (2004).

David Hare's *Stuff Happens* traces the road to the invasion of Iraq. In his author's note, Hare provides the disclaimer: "What happened happened. Nothing in the narrative is knowingly untrue. Scenes of direct address quote people verbatim. When the doors close on the world's leaders and on their entourages, then I have used my imagination. This is surely a play, not a documentary." The premiere of *Stuff Happens* was filled with hype[66] and the play, despite Hare's insistence to the contrary, was essentially criticized as a verbatim piece. The play certainly aligns with several of the objectives outlined by Martin, including the creation of additional historical accounts – indeed, Hare referred to the piece as a "history play." In addition, *Stuff Happens* reconstructed past events, and, in the process, examined the "operations of both documentary and fiction." Hare's imaginings of conversations between Bush and his advisors served to humanize him because Hare attempted to take Bush as seriously as possible. In this respect Hare's play provided a unique perspective since it was so difficult to take Bush's actual live public appearances seriously. However, Hare's play also became one in a list of "political" pieces that was perceived in subsequent years as another biased and boring verbatim piece created for preaching to a converted theatre audience. If *Stuff Happens* relies less on physical space than the psychic space occupied by politicians, Tricycle Theatre's *Guantánamo: Honor Bound to Defend Freedom* and the dance theatre piece *Honour Bound* both exploit the physical space of the infamous prison in an attempt to expose a version of truth.

The US naval base at Guantánamo Bay, Cuba is a liminal space caught between national and political boundaries. It is Cuba, but it is not; it is controlled by the US military, but it is not part of the United States. There is an agreement allowing the United States rights to the location, but Castro's government has famously not cashed the rent checks. Guantánamo became, after 9/11 and the launch of the so-called war on terror, a perfect place to mete out 'justice' beyond the reach of the traditional court system. Even its use as a prison was organized so secretly and swiftly that the management of the site was caught in-between the military, the executive branch, and the intelligence community.[67] Although the US Supreme Court eventually upheld *habeas corpus* for detainees, assuring them a 'place' in the US court system as well as affirming Guantánamo as a US 'space,' issues remain as to what was and is performed there.

Guantánamo became a surprisingly visible 'stage' in itself where power was naturalized. In contrast to former Vice-President Dick Cheney's move to the 'dark side' and the operation of hidden 'black sites' around the world, images of Guantánamo's Camp X-Ray[68] feature bright orange jumpsuits of detainees amid chain-link fences.[69] Performances *at* Guantánamo include those performed *upon* the bodies of detainees as well as those asserted *by* detainees. For example, the use of waterboarding is itself a performance of the "state of exception," which has occurred on Guantánamo's "stage." Detainees have in turn performed acts of resistance against their detention and treatment, including hunger strikes and suicide.

Guantánamo: Honor Bound to Defend Freedom, which premiered in London in 2004, credited Victoria Brittain and Gillian Slovo as playwrights with the additional note: "taken from spoken evidence." This piece of documentary theatre occupies a space between a quest for truth and an exploration of theatrical fiction in order to impact audiences, as well as offering a particular education. In contrast to Hare's unique take on the Bush Administration's road to invading Iraq and the UK government's involvement, *Guantánamo* was performed with an authority more closely aligned with strict verbatim. Actors play the real-life characters of detainees, their families, their lawyers, and politicians using their own words *edited* by the playwrights. Like *Stuff Happens*, however, *Guantánamo* used "evidence" to provide a theatrical experience during which, as Carol Martin describes, "The bodies of the performers as well as the bodies of those being represented [...] are decisive in ways that overlap but are also different from fictive theatre."[70] Although in some documentary theatre the performance is autobiographical – that is, the person performing is the person being represented – more often "documentary theatre is where 'real people' are absent – unavailable, dead, disappeared – yet reenacted."[71] In both *Stuff Happens* and *Guantánamo*, the performance relies heavily on the stage presence of the actor and the success with which the performers can summon within their own bodies and performance a feeling of the truth of those they represent.

Figure 1.4   Honour Bound, conceived, co-designed and directed by Nigel Jamieson; choreography by Garry Stewart. Photo by Jeff Busby.

In its quest for the truth, verbatim theatre, a genre criticized for being a text-heavy project devoid of spectacle and theatricality, can fall short of doing what theatre does best – that is, offering to audiences an experience that *rings* true, that is filled with meaning. Ironically, the hyperrealism of testimony plays can lead to disappointing nights in the theatre for many. The "genre" of documentary theatre has responded to such shortfall, and some post-9/11 performance has taken a cue from verbatim theatre and invested the potential of live, moving bodies as well as technology to offer what would be considered a step away from strict verbatim into an aesthetic of documentary coming into its own. *Honour Bound* (2007), a collaborative effort conceived and directed by Nigel Jamieson for Sydney Opera House and Malthouse Theatre with choreography by Australian Dance Theatre's Garry Stewart, retells the story of David Hicks, an Australian who was captured in Afghanistan in 2001 and detained at Guantánamo Bay from 2002–7. *Honour Bound* is a piece of dance theatre that stages Hicks's experience of imprisonment and its effects on his mind and body through an exploration of the performers' bodies. Instead of relying solely on Hicks's words or the words of others to provide the foundation of the piece, *Honour Bound* mixes the movement of live performers with images and video (Figure 1.4). Hicks

Figure 1.5 Climbing the walls in *Honour Bound*, conceived, co-designed and directed by Nigel Jamieson; choreography by Garry Stewart. Photo by Jeff Busby.

twists in the air down into his cell at Camp X-Ray. He climbs the walls of his cell and the stage, walking Spiderman-like on projections of legal documents (Figure 1.5). Hicks and other detainees repeat stylized movements while the image of George W. Bush describes the enemy combatants held at the prison.

Other key documentary performances took a similar strategy of carefully and creatively approaching "truth" especially in response to the Bush Administration's war on terror. Two pieces produced by the Culture Project in New York City, *A Question of Impeachment* (2007) and *Blueprint for Accountability* (2010), are both representative of an active engagement of a certain theatre community with public discussions of political issues. These events mixed theatre and journalism, offering audiences both scripted and non-scripted performances, panel discussions, poetry readings, and staged scenes. *A Question of Impeachment* focused on the case against George W. Bush and Dick Cheney at the end of their second term, when enough information had been released in the press to take action but politicians lacked the political will. *Blueprint for Accountability* is an ongoing series described by the Culture Project as a "bold new hybrid of investigative journalism and theatre" that addresses different issues around accountability. These events maintain ties to theatre and film, often featuring well-known and established actors, artists, journalists, politicians, and other figures, while demonstrating a freedom from the boundaries of verbatim theatre.

Bush's wikiality

The legacy of the Bush Administration will no doubt be a curious one. The manipulation of facts and the willful ignorance of evidence seemed to go beyond political strategy during the Bush years. 9/11 provided an ideal opportunity to forge a "new common sense" that amounted to a truth based in subjective desire. It is not surprising that the 2000s also witnessed the explosion of reality television, blogs, Wikipedia, social networking, and the extension of "pundit" and "politician" to celebrity and comedian. In these years, a solo performer like Stephen Colbert could fuse comedy with punditry, and whether he is taken seriously or not simply doesn't matter. Similarly, Wikipedia could contain just about any information, and students will cite it in research papers regardless of such unreliability.

The "wiki," in fact, is a term derived simply from the Hawaiian word for "fast" – at least according to Wikipedia (wink). The contemporary idea of a "wiki," as it applies to the digital age, is particularly relevant to the legacy of the Bush era and the idea of Bushismo. The wiki provides a space to make one's own truth. Wikipedia is the internet resource that isn't a "reliable" source – at least that's what teachers tell their students – because anyone can create its reality and its meaning. Anyone can edit, make changes, and so therefore there is no reliability or responsibility. And yet it still becomes the premiere source of information. Its Google search ranking is so high that most search items list a Wikipedia entry first. In the twenty-first century, the first Google result *feels* "relevant," reliable. But it is, in the end, not necessarily "true," not necessarily "factual," and not necessarily "reality." Stephen Colbert pays homage to the form of Wikipedia in his "definition" of "wikiality": "On Wikipedia, we can create a reality that we can all agree on – the reality we just agreed on."[72] The irony is that *from* the unverified truth of Wikipedia comes the interjection of an exposed purported set of "secret" truths from Wikileaks. Further, the status of Wikileaks is surrounded with doubt – it becomes *less* reliable than Wikipedia.

Within this "wikiality" Bush and Cheney, along with their Cabinet members and advisors, may have produced a reality of their own based on inaccurate information, leading to wars of questionable legality and the continued pursuit of free-market capitalism, but their misdeeds similarly do not matter. Bush wrote that although he "didn't like hearing people claim" that he had "lied about Iraq's weapons of mass destruction," the "worst moment of his presidency" was when Kanye West suggested he "didn't care about black people" after the disaster of Hurricane Katrina and its aftermath.[73] Dick Cheney defended waterboarding in an ABC News interview in December 2008, stating he thought it was "appropriate."[74] The questionable activities of these politicians – sought after by events like the Culture Project's *Blueprint for Accountability* have become "frozen scandals," subject not to legal process but to a cycle of inaction that doesn't hide the issues but circulates them repeatedly. In the next chapter I take a particular interest in visuality by focusing on the ideas of visibility and invisibility as they relate to protests surrounding the war on terror.

2
Protest Visible and Invisible

Politics, before all else, is an intervention in the visible and the sayable.[1]

Shannon

Those familiar with the transatlantic route from Ireland to the United States might remember the days not so long ago when a certain percentage of all such flights had to make a stopover at Shannon airport in County Clare. Although negotiations between the United States and Ireland in the 2000s led eventually to virtually no mandatory stops on the Dublin–US route, it was common for frequent fliers to sometimes not even realize their flight would have to make a landing on the Irish west coast before heading across the Atlantic. I found myself on one such itinerary in the summer of 2005. The airlines seemed to hide the stopover, characterizing the service as "nonstop." Annoyed beyond recognition that I hadn't noticed how late my flight would arrive in New York (which would have tipped me off to the Shannon stop), I spent the descent cursing those US–Ireland bilateral aviation agreements. As we landed and began to taxi toward the terminal, I noticed an unmarked jet on the tarmac. Immediately my petty annoyance changed to curiosity, because Shannon is used by the US military as a stopover. Rendition flight? I wondered.

I de-planed and followed the rest of the crowd made up of baffled Americans weary for home and Irish tourists excited for an American adventure. Nobody seemed to care much about the hour-or-so delay inside the Shannon terminal except me. Out of routine, I walked a circle around the duty-free shop, found nothing of interest, and headed for the small cafeteria inside the waiting area. That's when I noticed the group of soldiers. I knew upon seeing them that they must have been the passengers on the unmarked plane and that indeed there had been no extraordinary rendition... today (and I doubted there would be in broad daylight but one never knows). This was just the usual stopover, the kind that had been landing for years. As an international airport set on the far western end of Europe, Shannon played an important role in the development of long-haul travel in the post-World War II era. The airport opened the first duty-free shop in the world in 1947 and was once a fueling station for the Russian airline Aeroflot.[2] Although Shannon has long been used as a stopover for US military aircraft carrying personnel, its use since the March 2003 invasion of Iraq has been most noticeable with several hundred thousand soldiers passing through each year since the start of the war.

It was a group of such soldiers, on their way to the Middle East, that I spotted during my 2005 layover. In uniform, they dotted the waiting area in clumps, talking and laughing, playing videogames on hand-held devices and comparing their duty-free purchases. There was a particularly boisterous group near me who were telling jokes and laughing. They looked like a high school clique, with beefy guys chatting up slender, good-looking young women. I found their socializing bizarre because I didn't think I would feel like joking around if I were going to Iraq or Afghanistan. I tried to ignore them even though they fascinated me. Were they on their first deployment? Third? How old were they? Was this the first time they had ever left the country? Left home? They looked very, very, young. I looked around the rest of the waiting area, searching for their superiors. A group of men who still looked young, but older than the in-crowd, sat on the opposite side of the area looking serious. I glanced back and noticed one young woman who sat between myself and the cool kids – I hadn't noticed her before. I was stunned by her stillness and silence. She sat motionless and without the company of a book or magazine, earphones or hand-held. She seemed to just be thinking. I found her contemplation profound. She had little interest in the cool kids, and in fact, she clearly did not appear to have been a cheerleader or a prom queen from any stereotypical representation of teenage-hood that I could make out. What fascinated me most was that at first she was invisible to me – she was drowned out by the louder, fun-going soldiers. But as I now tried not to stare, her presence – her *visibility* – was utterly clear, and filled with meaning. Her visible presence symbolized for me – whether it was her real situation or not – the cost of war in the United States. She seemed to already be missing family, maybe children left behind. She seemed to know either what she was getting into, or at least had an idea that it was not going to be fun. Her uniform reminded me that this was her job, not an act of patriotism or heroism.

Shannon airport is a site of visibility and invisibility. It is located in a neutral country, Ireland, that involves itself in the war-making of another country, the United States. Its neutrality is visible and its bias is invisible. The US military personnel that wait in its terminal can be seen, and yet the CIA personnel, private jets, and very possibly human cargo that also land and takeoff from Shannon are most decidedly unseen to the duty-free shop and travelers like me. And yet they are made of real stuff – as evidenced by the research of protest group Shannon Watch and others, who carefully document flight plans and aircraft identification information.

This chapter is about visibility and invisibility, presence and absence, embodiment and exclusion. I am interested in the constant tension between the visible and the invisible. The visible is only so if acknowledged and the invisible only needs to *not* be acknowledged. I first explore this tension through the idea of "secrecy" and move to the idea of "protest." Just as secrets play with materiality and ephemerality, protests engage with embodiment and exclusion. Protests are performative. They make visible the invisible; they expose the secret; and they recontextualize that which power renders "natural." In this analysis I consider the visible protests that met the start of the Iraq War in 2003 and the process through which these acts were made invisible. Tracing the success of war on terror rhetoric through the use of performance as a tool to cultivate cultural fear, I examine to what extent performances in protest of the invasion of Iraq beginning in late 2002 and continuing through the present day have been made virtually invisible by major media outlets. My analysis pays particular attention both to the performative use of the military uniform in protest as well as the ways in which camouflage, the basis of military uniform design, serves as an organizing concept for the points of connection among secrets and exposure, visibility, and invisibility, protest and acquiescence.

Theorizing secrecy

In his book *Blank Spots*, artist and radical geographer Trevor Paglen describes his investigation of the United States' secret world. Maps, he notes, are supposed to cover ground – but they also conceal spaces. Paglen argues that the "black world" – this series of unmapped sites of power – can be found worldwide, "from secret prisons in dusty Afghan hinterlands to ice-encrusted radomes near the North Pole, and from remote eavesdropping stations in the Australian outback to makeshift camps and dirt landing strips in South American jungles."³ He recounts sitting for hours in different locations, including a Las Vegas hotel room, in order to "render visible the invisible" – to photograph the comings and goings of government employees who "spend their days working in the defense industry's deepest recesses" throughout the southwestern United States.⁴ In addition to the physical spaces that become hidden from plain sight, it is the intangible qualities of this world that concerns Paglen: "[T]his black world is more than a collection of places. It is an economy of secret dollars, a world of security clearances and secrecy oaths, code names and classifications tucked away in archives larger than the nation's greatest libraries."⁵ The black sites constitute an alternative geography that indeed exists to many – Paglen notes that "approximately *four million* people in the United States hold security clearances to work on classified projects in the black world."⁶ The secret world has been around for a long time, but former Vice President Dick Cheney's call to the "dark side" in 2001 served to boost funding and support for its expansion. Paglen analyzes the construction of the black world in order to make sense of the secret prisons and even secrecy as an idea. "[W]hen we think about secrecy," he writes:

> it's helpful to think about it in terms of geography, to think about the spaces, landscapes, and practices of secrecy. We live in a world that can often seem supremely abstract, ungrounded, and confusing, especially when it comes to matters of politics and notions of democracy. I think that trying to understand secrecy through geography helps make the subject more real. Thinking about secrecy in terms of concrete spaces and practices helps us to see how secrecy happens and helps to explain how secrecy grows and expands."⁷

The materiality of that which is secret relies on its ephemeral existence – its absence from the map – and yet it *must* have substance. Smoke and mirrors – performances – are used by politicians and media to avert the eye, overlook the map, keep walking, keep driving, keep shopping, keep moving. Performance Studies scholar Diana Taylor calls this "percepticide," a self-blinding. "The 'war on terror,'" she writes, "produces public percepticide."⁸

Jacques Rancière describes this denial of visibility: "The essence of the police lies in a partition of the sensible that is characterized by the absence of void and of supplement."⁹ His theory of political action speaks to the dual focus of this chapter on secrecy-invisibility and openness-visibility.

Figure 2.1 Trevor Paglen, *Morning Commute* (Gold Coast Terminal), Las Vegas, Nevada, Distance ~ 1 mile, 6:26 a.m. Courtesy Trevor Paglen.

The "police" in Rancière's logic is not just the NYPD or the LAPD, but the larger intertwining figures that maintain order and essentially keep the public in place. Rancière's police, then, maintain secrecy by acting like it doesn't exist – by insisting on "the absence of void." Paglen's work to document and collect evidence of the void attempts to work against the "police" by "insisting on the black world's materiality."[10] The geographies produced by Paglen's images (see Figure 2.1) carry out Rancière's idea of politics. "The essential work of politics," Rancière explains, "is the configuration of its own space. It is to make the world of its subjects and its operations seen. The essence of politics is the manifestation of dissensus as the presence of two worlds in one."[11] Paglen writes: "Geography tells us that it's impossible to take something that exists and make it nonexistent at the same time." Paglen uses geography to perform Rancière's dissensus.

Paglen's art constitutes protest against secrecy. His visual images should be considered as documentation of the performances he undertakes against secret spaces: driving the circumference of a restricted area; waiting for days in a hotel room with a radio and telescopic lens; camping out on a hilltop with a telescope. In Paglen's performances, black sites *are* the power to make black sites. Work like "Morning Commute" contrasts with other representations of black sites in popular culture. Instead of capturing the creepy absurdity of UFO chasers and bizarre experiments, Paglen chooses to visualize the mundane walk along a tarmac – life as experienced by the real people who operate within the secret world. In contrast, the 2010 television series *Rubicon*, featured on the AMC network, is filled with maps. Set in a spy firm in New York City, *Rubicon* follows the mystery of an intelligence analyst as he navigates the secret world and its betrayals and dangers. Instead of the disappeared and redacted maps of Paglen's research, *Rubicon*'s set had walls covered with maps of the world. The offices of the "American Policy Institute" or API, where the protagonist works, contain maps with labels tracking the movement of suspected terrorists. The analysts that comb through data in their map-covered New York City conference room are introduced later in the series to a black site. In Episode 8, the analysts are abruptly escorted by CIA agents on a long-haul flight to a secret prison, where they are charged with aiding the interrogation of a terrorist suspect. The episode points to the haphazard approach of the US intelligence and military communities while serving as a justification for the existence of secret prisons and the black world by building the suspense of a "threat." In a Kafkaesque sequence of events, the "kidnapped" analysts have no idea where they are as they struggle to investigate the case, instruct interrogators on what to ask for, all the while experiencing a fatigue that parallels the detainee's mistreatment.

The characters in *Rubicon* correspond to the people Trevor Paglen photographed in "Morning Commute." On television, these people learn the hard way that the maps that are crucial to their daily analysis, which is really the project of ongoing construction of the secret world, mean nothing in the face of the performance of the ticking-bomb scenario. Once the "terrorist" (who is only a satellite photograph to the analysts back in New York) becomes materialized in a cell, the secret world is hidden even from the analysts, and the effort to extract information perceived to be inside the "terrorist" wields absolute power. Trevor Paglen already knows this, and his work, for which he takes real risks in the real world by coming close to the legal limit of proximity to secret sites, constitutes a protest against such power.

Cultivating fear: reconstructing post-9/11 performances of dissent

> Political demonstration makes visible that which had no reason to be seen; it places one world in another – for instance, the world where the factory is a public space in that where it is considered private, the world where workers speak, and speak about the community, in that where their voices are mere cries expressing pain.[12]

Dozens of post-9/11 protests that have taken place around the world have received – especially in the case of US media – either little, no, and/or inaccurate coverage. Journalist Bill Moyers said of the October 2007 protests:

> Last weekend more than 100,000 people turned out in 11 cities across the country to protest the occupation of Iraq, in Los Angeles, San Francisco, Seattle, Chicago, Philadelphia, Boston, New York, among others.
>
> Yet based on the miniscule amount of coverage the mass protests afforded in the mainstream media, it was as if the demonstrations never happened.[13]

Protests against the wars in Afghanistan and Iraq – as is the case with much political action in public spaces – are regularly erased by mainstream media outlets, making the events invisible. The large-scale, live events that began soon after 9/11 were diminished by other more "successful" performances surrounding the war on terror, including Bush's 12 September 2002 address to the UN General Assembly; his January 2003 State of the Union speech; Colin Powell's United Nations speech in February 2003; and others. Political demonstrations that work to expose the illegality of the war in Iraq or the unwinnable quagmire of Afghanistan are consistently and effectively made invisible by the effects of percepticide. Diana Taylor first developed her idea of public self-blinding in the context of her research on Argentina's Dirty War, when violence in public was both seen and not seen by spectators: "Spectacles of violence rendered the population silent, deaf, and blind." In the light of day, people were shown state violence in the form of harassment, arrest, kidnapping, and the "disappearing" of fellow citizens:

> The military spectacle made people pull back in fear, denial, and tacit complicity from the show of force. [...] The military violence could

have been relatively invisible, as the term 'disappearance' suggests. The fact that it wasn't indicates that the population as a whole was the intended target, positioned by means of the spectacle. [...] To see without being able to do disempowers absolutely. But seeing, without the possibility of admitting that one is seeing, further turns the violence on oneself. Percepticide blinds, maims, kills through the senses.[14]

The acute nature of people being swept off the street while shouting their own names seems to not correspond to the war on terror as experienced in the psychic and physical spaces of mainstream United States. It does, however, speak to the rounding up of suspects in the wake of 9/11 that was at times arbitrary and even reckless, as well as the acts of "extraordinary rendition" carried out by the US government which sent dozens of detainees to secret locations to be tortured. The potential for these acts derives from the contemporary state of exception existent not only in the United States but in the "black world" and other sites where foreign governments are complicit with the United States. The Patriot Act, the infamous torture memos, the State of Emergency, the warning system, and most especially the 2001 designation[15] of detainees as "enemy combatants" without due process.

Still, percepticide is what the US public suffers from in the post-9/11 era. The public is self-blinded and refuses to see the erosion of civil rights, the cost of permanent war, and the reality of violence both committed by and victimizing military, paramilitary, and civilian populations. The lack of coverage of protests is just one example of how denial operates in the context of the global war on terror. Protests against the wars in Iraq and Afghanistan can be dismissed as revivals of Vietnam-era demonstrations, events separated from the present by the end of the Cold War, the Reagan years, the rise of the free market, the explosion of information technology, and the first Gulf War.

But protests occurred. Since 9/11 dozens of major protests have been held all over the United States and all over the world, with turnouts matching and often exceeding those of the resistance to Vietnam. The irony is that the power of the protest exists through live performance. Protests, therefore, are best understood as part of the "repertoire," the realm of embodied knowledge. However, they are inadequately relegated to representation and entry into the "archive," the documentation left behind the live performance. I use these terms "archive" and "repertoire" in the sense that Diana Taylor explains them: the archive being made up of "supposedly enduring materials (i.e., texts, documents, buildings, bones)" versus the "ephemeral of embodied practice/knowledge (i.e., spoken language, dance, sports, ritual)."[16] Anti-war protests work toward their objectives through presence and visibility, but without the creation of documents, even more of their meaning dissipates after the event. Subsequent political action might attempt to create new events in the reconstruction – using the archive – of past protests in an attempt to open new space of live performance that can have effect.

Protest began soon after 9/11, when the Bush administration quickly started planning retaliatory action in Afghanistan. Initially fuelled by the anti-globalization movement, protests were held just weeks after 11 September 2001 on 29 September in Washington, DC and San Francisco with a clear message against an invasion of Afghanistan. Describing the actions in Washington, DC *Democracy Now* reported that protestors near the Capitol building "carried flags that read 'Destroy imperialism, not Afghanistan,' and 'Food and medicine to the people of Afghanistan and Iraq' and 'We do not support your war'" while being "swarmed" by police on motorcycles and in helicopters. "The air was filled with the acrid smell of pepper spray," requiring some protestors to be treated. A dozen protestors were arrested.[17] Protests around the United States and in Scotland, Germany, Australia, and India followed.

By the fall of 2002 the Bush administration began a rallying cry for war in Iraq, and major demonstrations were held on 26 October 2002 in protest against the ongoing war in Afghanistan and possible invasion of Iraq. The biggest event in Washington, DC saw as many as 100,000 protestors, while cities around the world, including Rome, Berlin, Copenhagen, and Tokyo, held demonstrations that coincided with the Washington march. The failure to accurately and thoroughly cover these events has been studied by the non-profit research website Media Matters. In response to media coverage of the 12 September 2009 "March on Washington" organized by conservative activists, Media Matters compared front-page coverage by several national newspapers of the two events. What they found was that although the 2009 protests saw a lower turnout of 60,000–75,000, newspapers gave the conservative demonstrations "more prominent placement" than the 2002 antiwar protest:

> The *Washington Post* and the *Los Angeles Times* featured articles about the September 12 protest on their front pages, after the *Post* had provided only a photo of the Iraq war protest on its front page while printing its article on C1 and the *Times* had provided its only coverage of the Iraq war protest on page A17; The *New York Times* and *Houston Chronicle* both put photos of the September 12 protests on

their front pages after providing no front-page coverage of the 2002 Iraq war protest.[18]

Similar patterns of media coverage followed the protests that continued through the invasion of Iraq and after. Major demonstrations were held on 18 January 2003 in Washington, DC, San Francisco, Tokyo, and Cairo, but saw limited coverage in mainstream media. The 15th of February 2003 was declared a global day of protest called "The World Says No to War," with large-scale events in several cities, including London, Barcelona, Rome, New York, Calcutta, Baghdad, Sydney, San Francisco, and Damascus, among other locations. The actions proved to be the most significant in history, with "[a]t least 30 million people demonstrat[ing] in national capitals, large cities, small towns and rural villages around the world."[19] According to one of the day's organizers, United for Peace and Justice, the New York City event gathered 500,000 participants to a rally in front of the United Nations.[20] CNN, in contrast, reported numbers between 100,000 and 375,000.[21] By downplaying numbers and invalidating the significance of the actions, the echoes so common in contemporary mass media were not heard.

Noam Chomsky offered some insight into the comparison of current war protests and Vietnam-era demonstrations:

> [M]y view, which is not the standard one, is that the antiwar movement is far stronger now than it was in the '60s. In the 1960s, there was a point, 1968, '69, when there was a very strong antiwar movement against the war in Vietnam. But it's worth remembering that the war in Vietnam started – an outright war started in 1962. [...] Protest was zero, literally. I mean, it was years before you could get any sign of protest. [...] [C]ompare Iraq. There were huge protests before the war was officially launched.[22]

The legacy of the 1960s–70s protests against Vietnam obviously laid the groundwork for the action taken in an effort to halt the invasions of Afghanistan and Iraq. Sidney Tarrow distinguishes the Iraq War protests from past movements in three ways: first, "[t]heir vast geographic reach"; second, "[t]he enormous numbers of participants they attracted, many of them with little previous experience of contentious politics"; and finally, "[t]heir coordinated transnational nature."[23] These actions have continued with anniversary protests marking the March 2003 Iraq invasion and yet they are not "news." The concentration of media ownership and the increasing influence of television advertising on news programs has continued to redefine news, blurring the line between information and entertainment. Another 2009 Media Matters study exemplifies the bias so famously denied by Fox News:

> A Media Matters review of Fox News' coverage of demonstrations prior to the April 15 tea parties found that the network did not offer similarly promotional coverage of anti-war protests or other demonstrations in support of progressive positions. Instead, the network's hosts, contributors, and guests often attacked participants in those protests.[24]

Ignoring antiwar protests – relegating them to invisibility – is just one way in which mass corporate media shapes public perception, encouraging percepticide along the way. The bombardment of the visual in entertainment-news – the circulation of useless images and narratives about celebrities, serial killers, and kidnappings – creates performances of known scenarios that leave viewers hanging on plot for minutes, hours, and days until the next story comes along. Self-blinding, therefore, has more to do with seeing and following the distraction than *not* seeing at all. It is in these circumstances where the corporate media *are* Rancière's "police": "police interventions in public spaces," he argues, "consist primarily not in interpellating demonstrators" in the Althusserian sense, "but in breaking up demonstrations."[25] Yes, the police physically broke up the demonstrations in February 2003 in New York, but Fox News also tells the public what to do. Politics, for Rancière,

> consists, before all else, in recalling the obviousness of what there is, or rather what there is not, and its slogan is: "Move along! There's nothing to see here!" The police is that which says that here, on this street, there's nothing to see and so nothing to do but move along. It asserts that the space for circulating is nothing but the space of "moving-along," of circulation, into a space for the appearance of a subject: the people, the workers, the citizens. It consists in re-figuring space, that is, in what is to be done, to be seen and to be named in it.[26]

News, therefore, becomes more "political" than ever – the dissemination of information to the public, once considered a public good, becomes an interjection into a continuous loop of entertainment, of plot.

The lack of coverage can go both ways as well. Geographers Don Mitchell and Lynn A. Staeheli published a 2005 study of protest permits in the United States, comparing two demonstrations that took place in 2002 in Washington, DC. For the first event, a rally with an attendance of up to 100,000 in support of Israel, the geographers could find no evidence that "a protest permit was applied for or granted"; nor is there any "record of a police presence at the rally."[27] In contrast, a protest during the same month of 2002 *against* the IMF/World Bank meetings held in April in Washington was met with both delays in its application for a permit as well as a strong police presence and control over where protestors gathered and moved. Police even "infiltrated protest groups and masqueraded as protestors during the marches."[28] Mitchell and Staeheli argue that the permit system for protests in the United States has changed drastically, especially after 9/11, making the permit system less and less neutral to content. The refusal of a parade permit in New York City for the 15 February 2003 demonstrations against the invasion of Iraq exemplifies for Mitchell and Staeheli this shift away from precedent. They observe that on the one hand, "the legal incorporation of dissent has been accomplished by constructing spatial strategies that have had the effect of routinizing protest," while, on the other hand, "protestors have broken out of the routine," ignoring permit requirements. "Dissent," they write, "has become resistance."[29]

Uniforms and resistance

Antiwar protests in the post-9/11 era have resembled Vietnam-era actions, but have evolved as information technology and social networking have become increasingly part of everyday life and, especially, organized resistance as exemplified in the 2011 protests throughout the Middle East. Unrest in the Middle East has also made clear that dissent can indeed spur change for better or for worse. Democracy, as experienced in the United States, has gotten used to protest – it has become "routinized" and to some extent completely ineffectual. The inability for social protest to truly have any effect in mainstream US perceptions needs to be understood in the context of social disobedience in the 1960s. Whereas the performances of the civil rights movements and antiwar demonstrations operated with a quality of being "once-behaved," in a manner related to the Happenings that began in the 1950s, contemporary protest can be easily dismissed as restoring 1960s behavior. Protest in the 1960s brought at least a sense of newness, which is not to say that protest was a new phenomenon, but it disrupted the post-World War II collective complacency. There was a shock value in burned draft cards, long hair, and the recontextualization of military uniforms that can no longer affect mainstream culture.

In many ways performances by veterans of Iraq and Afghanistan relate closely to those of the Vietnam era, especially protestors who perform soldier identities while producing resistance to military action. These identities merge in a work of "reality theatre" created by the German/ Swiss collective Rimini Protokoll. Their piece *Resist, Refuse, Rebel*, performed in 2007, featured two Vietnam vets wearing the uniforms of Iraq/Afghanistan deserting soldiers as they lectured on the history of opposition to military service. *Resist, Refuse, Rebel* speaks to the power of costume in the context of the military uniform. To what extent does such "wearing" give resisting soldiers more authority (or authenticity)? How does such adornment – as well as the removal of the uniform – interact with the "telling" such soldiers perform?

A history of resistance in uniform: *Resist, Refuse, Rebel*

Formed in 2000, Rimini Protokoll claim to go beyond "documentary theatre" to create "reality theatre" in which no "actors" are used; instead, "real" people "play" themselves. Stefan Kaegi, who is Swiss, met Germans Helgard Haug and Daniel Wetzel while studying at Geissen University. Rimini Protokoll describe their works as "theatre ready-mades" in which "people who are alien to theatre productions but [who ...] are the experts on perspectives on reality come to serve as suppliers of materials and as actors"; these nonactors "are Ready-Made presenters for the stage."[30] Kaegi explains Rimini Protokoll's lack of interest in talented but conventional actors: "Why should we look for such actors if we have people who tell us their stories? What draws us away from actors is the fact that they would never bring us across such stories."[31] The group finds that the "experts" who express interest in their projects – by responding to the collective's advertisements or otherwise coming in contact with the artists – offer ways into realities they and their audience might otherwise never know. Daniel Wetzel distinguishes "experts" from "amateurs," as some critics have called Rimini's performers: "for us they are experts: on the one hand because they know something we're interested in, or because they embody a certain part of society, a certain profession, or a certain competence, which has molded them, which informs their thinking and even the way they look."[32]

In *Resist ...* two members of VVAW, Dave Blalock and Darnell Stephen Summers, use military uniform in a way similar to the 1971 Winter Soldier investigations, which included veterans testifying to atrocities, and yet distinctive in the veterans' attempt to perform resistance to military hegemony (Figures 2.2 and 2.3). Cast members from Rimini

Figure 2.2   Darnell "Stephen" Summers and Dave Blalock in *Resist, Refuse, Rebel*, part of the Dictionary of War Project, Berlin, 2007, http://www.woerterbuch-deskrieges.de/en-dict/concept/Resist-Refuse-Rebel.

Protokoll's production of *Wallenstein*,[33] Blalock and Summers offer in *Resist* a lecture-demonstration on the history of military resistance, which ends with an anti-war rap and a virtual flag burning. *Resist, Refuse, Rebel* is one of many 'definitions' constituting the Dictionary of War, a mixed-media project launched in Germany in 2007.[34] Originally performed by Summers and Blalock on 24 February 2007, *Resist, Refuse, Rebel* defines each of the three terms through a history of US resistance to war and military service. Beginning with an example of 1787 when George Washington "crushed a rebellion of soldiers in the Continental Army and ordered them executed by "their own unit,"[35] Summers and Blalock cover resistance in all the major US conflicts. The performance features interviews with conscientious objectors and their lawyers, video footage of protests such as Dave Blalock's megaphone speech along the walls of a US military confinement facility in Germany, and images of deserting soldiers, including Jeff Patterson, who sat on a military runway in Hawaii "refusing" to deploy to Saudi Arabia in 1990.

The performance has no refined production values. The tone is informal. The performers, as they begin, can't be heard and need technical

Figure 2.3   Darnell "Stephen" Summers and Dave Blalock in *Resist, Refuse, Rebel,* part of the Dictionary of War Project, Berlin, 2007, http://www.woerterbuch-deskrieges.de/en-dict/concept/Resist-Refuse-Rebel.

assistance to get their audiovisual aids hooked up and microphones on. The stage is black and bare except for a desk with a laptop and a large projection screen. Each of the two men stand with cordless microphones, taking turns lecturing. The men, both long-standing members of Vietnam Veterans Against the War, appear in partial military uniform. Both men wear their hair long. They stumble through the lecture from memory and refer occasionally to notes on the table. Darnell Summers performs a rap called "You Been Took," written in 1990 by G.I. Jack from Stop the War Brigade. The rap condemns military recruitment: "I guess I had stupid on my face/ [...] The wool is off my eyes/ and now I realize/ There was nothing but lies/ [...] So when you raise your right hand/ give him a look/ the finger/ and then book/ before you get took." It is not until the end of the piece that Darnell Summers informs the audience that the uniform he wears, which has so far appeared as almost a stereotype of the protesting Vietnam veteran, is actually a uniform once belonging to a contemporary US soldier. Like all the uniforms Summers wears in performance, he explains, this one was given to him by a soldier about to desert. Dave Blalock ends the piece by entering a virtual flag-burning website visible on the screen backdrop and burning two virtual flags.

Summers's strategy conforms well to Rimini Protokoll's stated intention to contrive situations that will allow the spectator to experience reality in a new way. Director Stefan Kaegi explains that they want to create "the feeling for the spectator that all that he [or she] has discovered, he [or she] has discovered for him [or her]self."[36] Patrice Blaser describes Rimini projects as "all about drawing attention to other aspects of reality [...] by suddenly discovering something that has always been there, but remained unnoticed in everyday life, and is made visible only now, with the help of that special gaze that one has when one observes in an art-context."[37] The "reality" of *Resist, Refuse, Rebel* therefore challenges the "fictional" space of the theatre. The resistant presence of non-actors in the theatre space attempts to disrupt the conventions of traditional representational theatre. The political potential of these works, I believe, is in the sort of Brechtian "series of interruptions"[38] that occur through the "stumbling and awkward"[39] presence of the performers. Daniel Mufson writes: "There's a clumsiness, a reluctance, a frankness that permeates the performances; we're always beholding humans, rather than people representing humans."[40] Such acts, like the work of performance and body artists, creates an uneasiness in the audience member in its refusal to allow for a delineation between artist and subject, actor and character, reality and theatre. We are asked instead to interrogate reality. Like camouflage, we have been deceived; things are not as they seem, making what has been revealed – the source of the uniform – resonate more deeply in the spectator. The audience is left with the verbal/textual lessons offered in the lecture and the embodiment of that counter-narrative in the re-used uniform.

Uniforms and camouflage: discipline/deception

Military uniforms have gone through centuries of evolution influenced by function, fashion, and politics, from brightly colored, formal-ceremonial, identifiable garb to khaki and camouflage by the twentieth century.[41] Camouflage is interesting in its own right as a form used by the military. Its formal development by the militaries of a number of countries at the beginning of the twentieth century was enabled by hiring artists to design and paint uniforms as well as ships, submarines, airplanes, tents, tanks, and other military property.[42] Art was deployed in the attempt to conceal; camouflage served a type of naturalization. Through matching – mirroring – camouflage would do what flora and fauna "naturally" do: produce the pattern/image of the surroundings in order to hide a particular entity. Camouflage also served to confuse; British World War I battle ships were painted in a modernist "dazzle" fashion that served not to make the ships invisible, but to distort their images in an attempt to prevent enemy ships from accurately predicting location. More recently, the suicide attacks by Afghan insurgents "disguised" in Afghan army and police uniforms have reminded the world of just how effective camouflage's deception can be.

Camouflage's artistic origins and simultaneous obsession with presence and invisibility has grown into an interactive relationship with fashion, while the form remains a distinctive marker of military identity. Originally an innovation of hunting traditions, camouflage became relevant to modern warfare as military technologies improved. Throughout the twentieth century camouflage developed through the work of artists. "France led the way in the employment of camouflage artists to disguise weaponry in the First World War."[43] Artists simultaneously responded to the functional military creations with artistic works incorporating camouflage, such as the British surrealist Roland Penrose, who photographed his car painted with a camouflage pattern as well as his stylized military uniform designs.[44] Pablo Picasso once took the credit for military camouflage, claiming the Cubists created it, but he never worked, as many of his contemporaries did, for European armies.[45] The design elements of camouflage make any attempt to find an "origin" of camouflage difficult; it is a concept that has always been applied in both art and non-art contexts, and can be traced to ancient practices such as Native American hunting strategies that use animal skins as disguises.[46] The use of camouflage was extensive throughout World War II, but after that the US military dropped the patterns in favor of solid neutral colors. The Vietnam War saw a resurgence in camouflage, in part because the lush landscapes in which combat occurred required it. The contemporary explosion of camouflage in popular imagination and material culture, Tim Newark explains, happened first as a response to the use of uniforms in protest by Vietnam veterans. He cites Pierre Buraglio's *Mondrian Camouflaged* (1968), which covers a Mondrian grid with camouflage pattern, as an example of camouflage becoming "a new symbol of the militarism crying out to be subverted in anti-military protest art."[47] In the decades that followed camouflage rose to the status of kitsch, from its use as costume by Public Enemy and the Eurythmics, to runway designs, to kids' lunchboxes and toddler clothing.[48] Although traditional patterns are still used in the military of most countries, the use especially by the United States and British military of 'dot matrix' or digital patterns on combat uniforms came around the same time that war itself became digitized at the end of the twentieth century. Camouflage has therefore always had meaning in the real world, occupying physical/visual space while existing as something mediated, conceptual, and metaphoric.

The performance artist Coco Fusco has explored the multiple meanings of camouflage in her 2006 pieces *A Room of One's Own* (see Figure 4.5) and *Operation Atropos*. Fusco's performances investigate the question "What does it mean to have female soldiers, acting at the behest of the US government, use their sexuality as a weapon against terrorism?"[49] The project, which includes a performance-lecture given by Coco Fusco as a female interrogator (*A Room of One's Own*) and a documentary based on Fusco's training with a former military interrogator (*Operation Atropos*), premiered in 2006 and toured extensively, culminating in the 2008 publication *A Field Guide for Female Interrogators*.[50] José Muñoz describes the use of camouflage in *Operation Atropos* as a performance that "folds back the conceptual camouflage that the state produces."[51] In the performance of *A Room of One's Own*, Fusco "briefs" the audience while managing the interrogation of a detainee in another room with CCTV. In her desert fatigues, Fusco plays the part of female US military power, nodding to the roles that women from Condoleeza Rice to Lynndie England have played in the war on terror. It is a performance that intentionally clouds fiction and reality just as camouflage does:

> Rather than denouncing this performance of power, Fusco hijacks power's groove, occupying it with a critical difference that denaturalizes the government's ideological camouflage. There is a lot of camouflage in *Operation Atropos* and *A Room of One's Own*. It is important to remember that this specific mode of patterning – theatre – was invented to mirror the natural world. Its effects are meant to be naturalizing. Fusco's performance enacts a kind of hypercamouflage by pushing camouflage's process of naturalizing. The nation's performance of the state of exception, its current Middle East policy, and even its use of words like "liberation" and "freedom" are ideological disguises that are meant to be taken as natural. In an effect that can be described as neo-Brechtian, Fusco's art interrupts this deployment of mass camouflage.[52]

Using the 'as if' of theatre, *A Room of One's Own* harnesses the audience's willingness to believe for a time that the uniform worn center stage signifies authority and that the person in it inhabits the validity necessary to manipulate, contort, *torture*, the mind-body of another. The performativity of this particular military camouflage uniform blurs costume and authority with little in the way of irony to explore a larger point about the role of power in the context of female sexuality.

Wearing and telling: Vietnam

Active and discharged military personnel have long used military uniform to enact a variety of "soldier" identities while producing resistance to military action. These actions can be best understood with a historical consideration of military uniforms and subversion, including camouflage and its relationship both to deception as well as art. In such contexts, military uniforms take on performative power. Performance-protest in uniform both engages with and challenges the categories of "art" and "life," at times deliberately straddling representation and reality. It is important to acknowledge camouflage's significance in the history of military protest. As a form of concealment intended for deception, camouflage theoretically lends itself to the subversive material that it became over time. Concern with regulating who wears military uniform and in what context has been of concern in the United States in particular since at least World War I.

Although generally forbidden by federal law in 18 U.S.C. 702, civilian wearing of military uniform is allowed under special circumstances by 10 U.S.C. 772, which states in part:

> (f) While portraying a member of the Army, Navy, Air Force, or Marine Corps, an actor in a theatrical or motion-picture production may wear the uniform of that armed force if the portrayal does not tend to discredit that armed force.[53]

In general, however, Sections 771 and 772 specify that other than the clothes they are discharged in, military personnel are not allowed to keep or wear uniforms – especially in public circumstances – unless that person comes under one of the exceptions such as the above concession for theatre and film. This is of course why, in the late 1960s as service members began to protest the war in Vietnam, the use of military uniform in such protests became so important. By marching in their fatigues, the antiwar movement gained political capital. Coupled with the civil rights movement of that decade, the subversive and irreverent costumes defied authority and demanded change. Isolated incidents, such as

the court-marshalling of Lt. Susan Schnall, a navy nurse, for protesting against the war in uniform and distributing antiwar leaflets from
a plane in 1968, became the beginning of a movement deliberately
invoking uniform as a political statement.

In 1970, the *Schacht* case confirmed restrictions on the wearing of
military uniforms, while ruling that the "actor" exception needed to also
protect first amendment rights. Daniel Jay Schacht was convicted in 1968
for violating 18 U.S.C. 702 as a result of dressing in uniform for a protest
"skit" performed on the morning of 4 December 1967 in front of the
Armed Forces Induction Center in Houston, Texas.[54] Schacht appealed,
lost in his Court of Appeals case, and the matter reached the US Supreme
Court in 1970. In his opinion, Justice Black inadvertently made a case for
unconventional theatre, site-specific performance, and poor theatre:

> Certainly theatrical productions need not always be performed in
> buildings or even on a defined area such as a conventional stage. Nor
> need they be performed by professional actors or be heavily financed
> or elaborately produced. [...] Here, the record shows without dispute
> the preparation and repeated presentation by amateur actors of a
> short play designed to create in the audience an understanding of
> and opposition to our participation in the Vietnam war.

The issue at hand was whether the protest was "theatre," and Black's
opinion argued that the protest was indeed a type of theatre. As theatre,
the event fell under the exception specified in 10 U.S.C. 772. However,
the problem of language arose: 772 states that although uniform could
be used in a theatrical production, it could only be legal if "the portrayal
does not tend to discredit" the represented armed force. The *Schacht*
decision found this part of the exception as a potential violation of the
first amendment:

> An actor, like everyone else in our country, enjoys a constitutional
> right to freedom of speech, including the right openly to criticize the
> Government during a dramatic performance. The last clause of 772 (f)
> denies this constitutional right to an actor who is wearing a military
> uniform by making it a crime for him to say things that tend to bring
> the military into discredit and disrepute.

The majority opinion struck the last words of clause 772 (f), overturn-
ing the Court of Appeals decision to confirm Schacht's conviction
and essentially allowing for a protestor to wear military uniform.

The dissenting opinion considered the key issue to be about theatre. Justice White wrote:

> The critical question [398 U.S. 58, 70] in deciding what is to count as a "theatrical production" ought to be whether or not, considering all the circumstances of the performance, an ordinary observer would have thought he was seeing a fictitious portrayal rather than a piece of reality.

White felt that "this question seems eminently suited to resolution by the jury" – a statement that echoes to some extent Schechner's distinction between what "is" a performance and what is not. In other words, what both judges point to is a discomfort with the fine line between theatre and reality, and as long as protest remains in the realm of not-reality, it can exist. Performativity, of course, fundamentally clashes with such a conception, and the effectiveness of protest, ironically, relies on such a clash in order to *affect* an audience.

As White suggested, and as the student of performance knows, the line between theatre and not-theatre is not always so clear. One such example marked a key turning point in the anti-Vietnam War movement. Consisting of testimony voluntarily given in a Detroit hotel by Vietnam veterans shortly after the revelation of the My Lai massacre in 1971, Winter Soldier was organized by Vietnam Veterans Against the War (VVAW). Winter Soldier became a controversial event that complicated the already waning support for military occupation in Vietnam. The transcripts were later entered into the Congressional Record and discussed during the Fulbright Hearings of the same year. A subsequent documentary (1972) showed the testimony footage, which provided a forum for veterans to embody an identity as 'soldier' while confessing to, and documenting, actions committed that amounted to war crimes. "Winter Soldier" referred to eighteenth-century radical Tom Paine's characterization of the American Revolution: "These are the times that try men's souls. The summer-soldier and the sunshine patriot, will, in this crisis, shrink from the service of their country; but he that stands it *now*, deserves the thanks of man and woman."[55] In 1971, antiwar veterans saw themselves as the "new winter soldiers" who "hoped to end the Vietnam War by exposing US war crimes." The purpose of multiple testimonies in a concentrated time and place was to "show that 'My Lai was not an isolated incident,' but 'only a minor step beyond the standard official United States policy in Indochina.'"[56] Many, but not all, attending veterans – those who testified and those who listened – wore

all or part of their service uniforms. These 'costumes' used in performance allowed both for evidence to become not just oral, but physical.
Military uniform provided validation that revealed the disjunction in
the Vietnam conflict between justified war and senseless violence, aggression, and a conflict of choice instead of necessity. Winter Soldier remains
a performance that can be analyzed on several levels: as a performance of
testimony; as a documentary of that live performance; and as a script –
a bridge – for its revival in the early twenty-first century by Iraq and
Afghanistan veterans.

Wearing and telling: Iraq and Afghanistan

The work of Iraq Veterans Against the War (IVAW), an organization that
both continues the work of VVAW while constituting a sort of sequel
for the post-9/11 global war on terror, held a revival of the 1971 Winter
Soldier in 2008. The more recent Winter Soldier began with an event
at the National Labor College in Silver Spring, Maryland in March of
2008. Subsequent gatherings occurred in various locations around the
US (Figure 2.4). Soldiers have testified, in front of the Congressional

Figure 2.4 Iraq War veteran Seth Manzel testifies about the torture of Iraqi
detainees during the Northwest Regional Winter Soldier Hearings, Seattle, May
2008. Courtesy of Bob Haynes/IPS.

Figure 2.5 Still from *Winter Soldier,* www.wintersoldierfilm.com. Courtesy of Milliarium Zero and Winterfilm Collective.

Progressive Caucus, about not only the atrocities witnessed in Iraq and Afghanistan, but also about insufficient supplies, mental health problems, and other war-related issues. Winter Soldier qualifies as a performance of testimony, a type of theatre in the sense that its 1971 'script' was revived in 2008, and a piece of documentary performance in which "telling" becomes a performance of self – a performance of "soldier" (Figure 2.5)

Post-9/11 uniform protests

Other post-9/11 military protests using the uniform have had a variety of specific concerns, including religion, immigration, sexual preference, and the military's stop-loss policy. A naval chaplain was convicted in 2006 of "disobeying an order by appearing in uniform" during a news conference "held at the White House to protest a Navy policy requiring nondenominational prayers outside of religious services."[57] Shortly after the 2010 Arizona law passed requiring immigrants to carry proof of status with them, CNN reported on Pfc. José Medina, a Mexican-American Army medic, who joined a vigil in protest of the law in "Army fatigues and a beret" shortly before deployment to the Middle East.[58] West Point graduate Dan Choi has become infamous for his use of uniform in protest against the military's "Don't Ask, Don't Tell" policy, most recently when he chained himself to the White House fence in April 2010.[59] Others have taken the uniform off in order to change its original function. For the War Experience Project, uniforms have become canvasses to be painted on by veterans and those interested in "public dialogue on warriors' terms" during painting workshops and a touring exhibition.[60] Combat Paper is a similar project focused on making paper out of uniforms. Co-founder Drew Cameron explains:

> The story of the fiber, the blood, sweat and tears, the months of hardship and brutal violence are held within those old uniforms. The uniforms often become inhabitants of closets or boxes in the attic. Reclaiming that association of subordination, of warfare and service into something collective and beautiful is our inspiration.[61]

Both the War Experience and Combat Paper have positive missions concerned with opening lines of communication and maintaining healthy relationships among veterans and the public. Two other projects that I turn to below in detail find through performance a much more confrontational stance: *Operation First Casualty* and the *Watchtower Protest*.

Operation First Casualty

To mark the fourth anniversary of the war in Iraq, members of the post-9/11 incarnation of military resistance, Iraq Veterans Against the War (IVAW), staged their own 'reality theatre' in the streets of Washington, D.C. Called *Operation First Casualty*, the protest/performance involved soldiers wearing their own uniforms[62] patrolling the streets with imaginary guns and civilian volunteers on hand to be stopped, arrested, thrown to the ground, and generally treated the way Iraqis are treated "in country."[63] The event was later remounted in New York City, San Francisco, Hartford, CT, and Denver. One of the performers, Adam Kokesh, explains what took place:

> [I]t has long been said that the first casualty of war is the truth. So what we did was conduct a mock combat patrol through the streets of Washington, DC, in order to bring a small part of the truth of the

Figure 2.6   Photo of *Operation First Casualty* by Lovella Calica.

occupation home to the American people and give them a small sense of what it's like to have squads of men in uniform, with rifles, although we were simulating them of course, running around the streets of their city.[64]

Like *Resist, Refuse, Rebel*, Operation First Casualty deliberately played with the line between reality and fiction, war and peace, life and art (Figure 2.6). Organizer Geoff Millard warned:

This is a serious event and will put our experiences front and center, as the nation has never seen. It will be intense and treated like a military operation though we will use NO WEAPONS WHAT SO EVER! OFC will be staged in full military uniform but we must always remember that it is a non-violent protest aimed at resurrecting our first casualty.

OFC will be mentally stressful and may trigger a lot of PTSD so I would ask anyone who reads this to think long and hard before signing up. We will however be conducting a Vets 4 Vets that evening.[65]

Although Millard's warnings seem valid enough – especially his disclaimer about PTSD – the performance itself had a double effect. Video footage of the events expose the challenges of this kind of protest – in each city, the quiet, smooth, synchronized jogging of the patrolling soldiers with well-mimed guns seems to penetrate the peaceful city space. The image of them moving is, however, familiar in the post-9/11 era of militarized civilian life in the United States. Still, the silent patrolling seems more effective than the jarring yells of the soldiers and respondent screams of the civilian volunteers. At these moments, the mostly white volunteers shout things like "Iraq for Iraqis! US out of Iraq," and they sound almost ridiculous. The spectator/viewer, if she hasn't already, begins to notice how many photographers are following the soldiers and how the piece isn't even a good example of theatre. According to the photo blog Zombietime.com, at the San Francisco event "[p]hotographers far outnumbered the protesters. There was a great deal of overly dramatic screaming and shouting as the soldiers ran back and forth abusing the prisoners."[66]

Although Zombietime exemplifies the extreme cynicism one might develop around such a political/antiwar protest, others found the performance more compelling. Describing the New York OFC,[67] Stephen Duncombe writes:

> The performance is simple, and powerful. A platoon of soldiers in battle fatigues carry out missions in a US city that might happen on any day in Iraq: patrolling a street, coming under fire, arresting suspected "bad guys," and breaking up a street demonstration. The soldiers don't carry guns; using their hands instead they let the viewer imagine what would be there. Counter to more traditional protest models, these activists don't tell the spectators what to think with placards or convince with broadsides; they draw people into an experience and try to make it "real" for them.[68]

Duncombe describes the New York OFC as an "ethical spectacle," or:

> a spectacle that adheres to principles that most progressives hold to: democracy, egalitarianism, community, a belief that the future can be better than the present, and, perhaps ironically, a fealty to reality.[69]

Duncombe requires that such actions have certain characteristics: they must be *participatory*; *open*; and *transparent*, or "a spectacle that people know is a spectacle and that is not mistaken for reality." Further, these performances "must also be rooted in the *real*: a performance of reality rather than its replacement." Finally, the ethical spectacle "should represent a *dream* – something that we know isn't real but that motivates us nonetheless."[70] Duncombe's ethical spectacle sets itself apart from the fiction of theatre – and as a performance "rooted in the real," it is interesting to note that this street performance in military uniform would be illegal under the federal law discussed above that bars the use of uniform outside of service *unless* in the context of "theatre." Indeed, the "law" got involved when Adam Kokesh, a US Marine, had his honorable discharge revoked after he was seen protesting in uniform. The Washington event happened to be covered by the *Washington Post* and upon his picture being printed taking part in the "street theatre," Kokesh found himself under investigation by the Marines. Threatening to revoke his honorable discharge, Marine investigators told Kokesh he had broken several rules, including wearing uniform during an antiwar demonstration and "making statements characterized as 'disrespectful' or 'disloyal.'"[71] In cases like Kokesh's, visibility becomes meaningful as it exceeds theatre. If these protests were perceived solely as inhabiting the fantasy of theatre, they would be easier for authorities to accept and easier for the public to dismiss. *Operation First Casualty* doesn't just make visible a scene from the theatre of war in a public place, but moves through one space in order to conjure another.

Evan Knappenberger

In a similar attempt to bring forth a scene from the theatre of war, Evan Knappenberger simulated the nearly 100 days he spent in a tower while serving in Iraq:

> Standing Tower Guard on a 6′ scaffold at the Federal Building in downtown Bellingham, Iraq Veteran Evan Knappenberger, 1st BDE, 4th Infantry Division, started a weeklong vigil on June 1st to draw attention to the US military STOP-LOSS and INACTIVE RESERVE policies, which he submits are being used as a substitute for conscription in a political war.

> I spent a year in Iraq. I pulled 97 nights on tower guard, explained Knappenberger. Many of the friends I served with have completed their contractual obligations to Active Duty. Now, they're being sent back to Iraq for their third or fourth tours. Some soldiers are getting called up after living years of civilian life. Stop-loss is an unethical policy.[72]

Figure 2.7   Evan Knappenberger simulates his watchtower duty, Washington, DC. Photo by Evan Knappenberger.

Instead of a space for surveillance, the 'theatrical' tower Knappenberger constructed in Bellingham, Washington, became a place to both allow audiences to share an experience of war as well as to discuss the issues surrounding war (Figure 2.7). Knappenberger's eight-day protest focused specifically on the US military's stop-loss policy, through which personnel who have fulfilled their service contracts are redeployed without consent.[73]

Knappenberger has very specific ideas about the use of military uniform in his protest. I corresponded with Evan, and asked how he thought the uniform functioned as part of his performance. He replied:

> To me the significance of using the uniform is to degrade it. For nearly four years, the uniform ruled my life and every move. Long after I stopped having nightmares about combat, I am still having nightmares about being in the wrong uniform somewhere. My goal in life is to see the end of the standing military. In order to accomplish this, it is necessary to utilize all the tools at our disposal, necessitating a further cultural revolution. I think the peaceful culture of the future will look back on all types of uniforms as archaic, authoritarian and demeaning. By using the uniform in a social protest situation, my main goal is to demonstrate the pain and violence associated with the uniform; to change the meaning of a uniform in the eyes of the participants and audience.

Knappenberger also touched on the performativity of the military uniform:

> The town I live in is fairly quiet. When a military uniform is worn, it changes the social dynamic drastically. It polarizes people along the peace/war dichotomy and becomes a weapon against the culture of the peace side. By wearing the uniform, at first I felt like I was striking a blow against the military culture.[74]

Knappenberg's actions not only expose that which is usually invisible – that is, the everyday life of military personnel stationed thousands of miles away from its sponsoring nation. By engaging with the height of his tower, Knappenberger calls attention not only to the implications of surveillance on a culture far removed from the mainstream United States, but also to the tedium and boredom that mark long stretches of deployment. Just as *Operation First Casualty* moves through one urban space to engage with another, Knappenberger's *Watchtower* simulates deployment while creating a symbol for the assumed authority of the United States' role in the so-called war on terror.

Conclusion: uniform protest on video and in games

The form that the military protest can take has evolved in the post-9/11 environment. Soldiers in Iraq and Afghanistan have downtime and access to portable electronic devices that make the experience in the theatre of war different from previous conflicts. Soldiers not only play games in their "downtime," but also create videos. Some of these videos have served as blogs, offering a space for soldiers to vent their frustrations. Once accessible online, these clips can be viewed by family and friends at home, viewers with the same (or opposite) views, as well as their superiors. I discuss some of these videos in Chapter 3 as protest-messages for audiences *outside* the theatre of war. Just as the use of military uniform in live protest, such videos blur the line between protest and service. A particular soldier identity – one not obedient but antagonistic and frustrated – can be portrayed and sent "home."

Some post-9/11 protests have not bothered with video but instead have used digital gaming to produce visibility. Upon the third anniversary of the war in Iraq, digital media artist Joseph DeLappe logged onto the free online US military video game *America's Army* and began a protest that intertwined notions of visibility, embodiment, context, performativity, and protest. By logging in, DeLappe became a player in the game, which means he became virtual US Army personnel, in uniform/costume. His US Army uniform was pre-determined by the structure of *America's Army*, which creates US military identities for all players. As US soldiers, all players fight an enemy constructed by the US military as "generic" terrorists in an effort to avoid ethnic stereotyping: "They're white guys with blond hair, they're African Americans, they're Hispanics, they're Asian, they're everybody and they're nobody."[75] This "unreal enemy" is, according to Robertson Allen, still very much "an internalized other that cannot exist without the presence of the American soldier as well." So, in US military virtual uniform, facing "enemies" who also see themselves as wearing US military uniform, Joseph DeLappe began to name names (Figure 2.8). In chronological order, DeLappe typed the name, age, service branch, and date of death of US military personnel killed in Iraq via the text messaging feature that broadcasts to all users – without firing his gun: "I stand in position and type until I am killed. After death, I hover over my dead avatar's body and continue to type. Upon being reincarnated in the next round, I continue the cycle."[76] As of 15 June 2009, DeLappe had entered the names of 4002 of the 4313 total US military personnel killed in Iraq. At the time of writing, in March 2011, this number has risen to 4439 – and does not include Afghanistan deaths or casualties from the United Kingdom and other nations' forces.[77]

DeLappe's protest is performative and site-specific. He describes his "online gaming intervention" as "not only a way of remembering," but

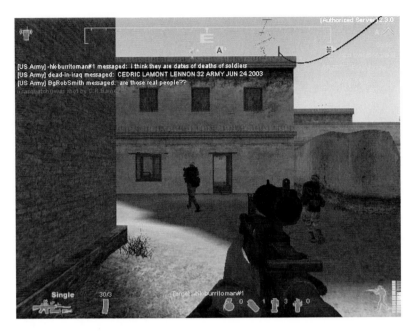

Finger 2.8 Screenshot from Joseph DeLappe's *dead-in-iraq* (2006–ongoing). Courtesy Joseph DeLappe.

also a way of "bringing reality into the fantasy." As Irene Chien writes: "In real warfare, death is the ultimate irreversible horror, the horizon of finitude. But in video games, death is a core game mechanism that is infinitely repeatable."[78] Dying is an essential part of gaming: "Figuring out a game requires discovering through trial and error what actions get you killed, so dying again and again is key to progressing through the game." Chien's analysis of "death scenes," a kind of "machinima," or film clips of videogames placed *in* videogames can be seen almost as a complementary performance to DeLappe's perpetual naming of names: "Death scenes turn the repetition of death into a ritualized pleasure of offering an instant replay of you getting killed, often aestheticized by slow motion and multiple camera angles."[79] Here repeatability and interruption are key: "Although death must be continually repeated to attain mastery of the game, it also threatens mastery at each repetition because it interrupts the flow of gameplay and communicates failure."[80] Similarly, death interrupts *dead-in-iraq* because DeLappe, as a "neutral visitor" who does "not participate in the proscribed mayhem,"[81] repeatedly dies, forcing him to wait and start up the game again to continue his protest.

An art professor at the University of Nevada-Reno, DeLappe displays screen captures on his *dead-in-iraq* page that document the performance and give the viewer a sense of the range of reactions the user of "dead in iraq" gets during *America's Army* missions. Some players are curious; one asks: "dead in iraq, are you enlisted? reserve? have you been to Iraq?"[82] Others are annoyed, frustrated, or angry at "dead in iraq"'s persistent messages listing the names of deceased soldiers: "dead in iraq shut the **** up!" DeLappe has in fact been "voted off the game" by fellow players when he is deemed to not be following *America's Army*'s Code of Conduct. However, as he explained in an interview, "A lot of times I'm completely ignored."[83] The performance is just one of DeLappe's many new media projects that are not made for the gallery space; rather, they are "always highly specific and responsive to their respective locations. His online site-specific art is therefore a performative act of intervention into digitalized quotidian existence."[84] DeLappe makes the familiar strange by disrupting context in everyday environments. His *dead-in-iraq* project is also nicely sustainable because he has not violated any copyright law; nor can it be considered hacking.

Although it differs greatly from Vietnam-era protests such as the 1967 "Stop the Draft Week," during which draft cards – perceived as critical to protest under conscription – were destroyed or returned to authorities, *dead-in-iraq* can be understood within a larger history of war protest. Dean Chan points out that the performance-protest "is part of a lineage of protests that involve the symbolic invocation and naming of the war dead," from "the 'Naming of the Dead' public ceremonies in 2004 organized by the International Stop the War Coalition,"[85] to ABC's primetime news program *Nightline* making the controversial choice to read the names of Iraq and Afghanistan casualties.[86] *Dead-in-iraq* is clearly a contemporary protest that engages the new media resources of the twenty-first century to enact performance in everyday digital culture. By using the "official game of the US Army" as a site of performance – a site within which the "civilian" can play "soldier" for free, anytime, anywhere – *dead-in-iraq* speaks to the increasingly blurred distinction of "war" and "peace," "soldier" and "civilian." In the next chapter I will further explore the militarization of US society, the collapse of "war" and "game," and the role of technology in the "perpetual" war on terror.

3
War, the Video Game

I enter a dark room that feels like a tiny cinema with one wall lit with the visual of a brown, barren, mountainous landscape. I am bombarded by the sounds of shooting guns and helicopter blades. An average-height female active military recruiter tells me to "shoot at the enemy." "How will I know who the enemy is?" I ask her (loudly). "You'll know," she says calmly. "Just shoot at all of them." Then she walks away. I step up into a Black Hawk helicopter, sit on a stool in front of a gun perched on the side of the open aircraft. It's like a scene from *Black Hawk Down*, with the multi-screen display moving so that I feel like I'm really up in the air in the helicopter, ready to shoot at "targets," or get shot down. The terrain isn't Somalia though. I try to figure it out – but there are no specifics – the landscape is generic, looking like everywhere and nowhere: Afghanistan, Bosnia, Nevada, Australia? I give up. I shoot at the moving images on the multi-screen display. I am stunned by the jolt and feel amazed at how "realistic" it feels. But then I catch myself: realistic? How would I know? I've never fired a machine gun before. I shot at the screen, but to be honest I could not tell whether the video was actually responding to the virtual shots or not as they were supposed to. At the end of what seemed like a long five minutes, a message appeared: "Mission Accomplished," the screen told me. Then: "What is your mission?"

This is not war. This is War, the Video Game. I'm not in Afghanistan, but in a mall outside Philadelphia. I'm at the Army Experience Center.

"War is culture"

When soldiers refer to action as being like a video game, as they frequently do, it is not a metaphor. By turning the diverse aspects of foreign life into a single narrative, the counterinsurgent feels in

65

control of the situation as if a player in a first-person-shooter video game. The commander thereby feels himself to be in the map, just as the game player is emotively "in" the game.[1]

This chapter engages the concepts of war, games, and performance in order to analyze how certain military performances enable long-term counter-insurgency culture. I first consider the breakdown between war and peace as well as war and game, in order to prepare for a discussion of the military-industrial-entertainment complex and its crucial role in what has become a new technological age of the militarization of culture. I then examine several examples of the "loop" I perceive existing between play and combat. The first example concerns the Army Experience Center, located in the Franklin Mills Mall in Pennsylvania, where visitors aged 13 and older can (after showing photo ID for registration in a database maintained by the US Army) surf the internet, play videogames, and "experience" military simulators (specifically, Apache and Black Hawk helicopters and a Humvee). Repeat visits are encouraged – leading ideally to enlistment. The second example examines *Virtual Iraq* and *Virtual Afghanistan*, adaptations of the video game *Full Spectrum Warrior*,[2] which are used to treat post-traumatic stress syndrome (PTSD) in veterans. These examples will be analyzed with consideration of the intersections among play, performance, games, counter-insurgency, training, and therapy in order to make sense of the "war" in "culture."

Undercover at the Army Experience Center

Opened in August 2008, the Army Experience Center was a 14,500-square-foot multimedia, multipurpose facility with more than one express mission. For critics, it was a sinister, long-term move by the US military to build up a healthy population of potential recruits. For the Army, it was an educational facility – with an added benefit that recruiters happened to be there. The nature of the double-sided mission is not hidden. On the AEC's "About Us" section of its website, the Army offered a convoluted narrative of the Center's origins:

> The US Army needed an innovative way to communicate its mission, values, resources and career opportunities to a new generation of Americans on a local level. The Army Experience Center (AEC) now serves as a twenty-first century destination for people to get accurate information about the Army directly from the source. Conceived and built over a ten-month period in the Franklin Mills Mall in Philadelphia,

the [...] technology and education center is fast becoming a model for Army recruiting nationwide. Touch screen kiosks, state-of-the-art presentation facilities, community events and high-action simulators are just a few of the AEC features helping to shatter outdated stereotypes and start new career conversations.[3]

The overt focus on "education" with a secondary, almost convenient by-product of "recruitment" created, for detractors, subtle and deeply problematic coercion. Pat Elder, a leader of the movement to force the military to close down the AEC, explained, "I think the military knows full well what it's doing. I think their intent is to indoctrinate children at the youngest age and for me it's outrageous because much of the American public is complacent and quiet."[4] Elder's comments reminded me of what Richard Schechner writes about war in *Performance Theory*: "It's not nice to think of war as a kind of hunt-and-destroy sport, but that's how colleges teach it and one way recruiters sell it."[5] This chapter is about both the use of performance by the military to sell war to potential recruits and its reliance on performance to train and heal the soldiers – "warriors" – those recruits become.

After hearing about the Center, I had to "experience" it for myself. So, on a cold day at the end of December 2009, I drove with a friend down to somewhere-outside-of-Philadelphia, Pennsylvania to the vast shopping mall. There had been a significant snowfall in the Philadelphia area just before Christmas; the massive parking lot was littered with huge piles of snow. As we drove through row after row of empty lot, I started to get the feeling that this mall had seen its heyday. We parked on the edge of the maze of buildings, adjacent to a department store that lay vacant with its own vast empty parking area. On this sunny, bright, and bitterly cold day, the Franklin Mills Mall was a run-down mess: a relic of the day when outlets were actually stores that sold seconds, imperfect goods, and overstock items from famous designers at discounted prices. Now the outlets that still exist in the mall are mostly satellite stores for brands owned by big corporations stocked with lower-quality merchandise just for the outlets at prices lower than "retail." It was difficult to even find goods that were "seconds" or "imperfect." They were all perfect, and they were Hilfiger or Guess or whatever – just not what you pay more for in Bloomingdales.

My companion and I walked through the mall. Franklin Mills is a long, one-story shopping endurance experience. We parked on one end, unsure of the Army Experience Center's location. We found out the long way that the AEC was located at the other end. The mall space itself is a long, ongoing line of stores. There are sections: orange, red, blue – and you walk from section to section hoping that one day you'll get to the end. The way *to* the AEC was actually fun; we stopped in lots of stores: bargains galore. I'd nearly forgotten what I came for when I saw a large, glass-walled shop up ahead on the right. In big block silver letters it read "Army Experience Center." It looked like someone's mission control – large flat-screens, dozens of computer stations, and a few official-looking people standing around looking busy. Across the way there was a Dave & Busters arcade/sports bar and a skateboard park, both of which, incidentally, were far more crowded than the Center.

We made our approach. I decided, suddenly but firmly, to go undercover.

Several staff, dressed in black shirts with AEC logos, stood at and around the circular reception area, which allowed for people to approach on foot from the front and at the back served as a sort of bar, which, on this occasion, was being used by the logo-shirts (who, we discovered, were active military personnel) who were eating their lunch from the nearby food court.

"Hi," I said to the man who came around the front of the reception counter to greet me. "What *is* this place?" As I waited for his spiel, I gazed up at five large flat-screen monitors above him. Alternating displays showed ads for the video game *HALO 3* and the opening hours and upcoming events at the AEC. The man at the counter was very friendly. He was not in the army (I asked). He told us that the AEC was a place where people can come and "learn more about the Army." In fact, he told us, "It's the only one in the world." I slipped at that point and said, "Isn't there one in London?" (which there is – it's called the Showroom and it's located in a mall in Dalston outside London[6]). "I'm not sure," he said.

He told us more about the AEC. "It's not a recruitment center. It's for kids who think they want to join the army but they come here to find out for sure." Hmph. He pointed out the water, Gatorade, and Red Bull for sale, and then generously offered us a tour with an active duty personnel who, I gathered, had already finished his lunch. The soldier had been in Afghanistan.

We embarked on our tour through the Center, passing the off-limits "training" room that looked very mission-control-like, through the many computers with Aeron chairs and flat-screens lining the walls, in front of which reclining media chairs held a handful of 20-something males playing NFL videogames *(were their significant others shopping? I wondered)*. The videogames available to play in the AEC include Playstation and other brand games. There are regular video games (like sport and other "nonviolent" games) mixed in with (official) military games and/or violent or combat-related games. There were only about three teenage-looking males in the AEC that day, no females. There was no admission fee, but everyone was required to register with photo ID in order to use the Center's facilities, which include three life-size simulators: a Hummer, a Helicopter (Black Hawk) and another Apache (Helicopter). I was given an AEC membership card that allowed me to login to one of the computers. Facility employees could therefore monitor my usage as I played video games, surfed the internet, or "experienced" one of the simulators.

Our soldier showed us one of several "Career Navigators" at the side of the Center. These large flat-screen touch displays were virtual learning stations for the Army. They had Google maps customized with the locations of "all the Army bases around the world," in an effort to help interested ... youths (above 13 per AEC rules)? Army enthusiasts? Potential recruits? *see* where they might get to work? We moved around the globe and were able to view bases in Hawaii and Europe. Nothing in Ireland, where I lived at the time, not even at Shannon – where all Middle East bound military stopover.[7] I asked the soldier about this. "No, nothing is listed in Ireland. But I stopped there on my way to Afghanistan." Shannon isn't a "base" after all. I noticed the rest of Europe didn't seem to have as many bases there as I thought the United States had; some had a different icon (which the soldier informed me are considered "camps"). But when we got to Africa, I knew something was up. There were very few bases – and even the Middle East was sparse. "Oh, not *all* of the bases are on here," he explained. *Hmph.*

I moved over to the Caribbean, looking for dream locations to be based. "What's this one?" I tested him. "Guantánamo Bay," the soldier smiled. "That's Puerto Rico," I said. "It is?" "Yeah," I replied. I was confused because there was only one base listed in Puerto Rico. But I was so shocked that he didn't know which island was Cuba that I moved the Earth with my finger to the left. "*That's* Cuba," I said as I zoomed in on the neighboring island. "Well, that won't be listed there much longer," he said. "Huh?" Again, confused. "Well, they are shutting it down." "The prison, you mean." "Yeah, Guantánamo Bay," he replied. "Yeah," I said, "but the *base* will still be there." "No, I don't think so." Hmphhh. "Do you really think they will leave their interests in Cuba?" I said, and sensed my cover slipping. "Um... well, I think they are shutting down the whole Guantánamo." I tried to make light of things. "Well, Castro never cashed the rent checks anyway." He didn't know what I was talking about.

Moving right along. My companion wanted to know if he could start a new career with the Army and the soldier was happy to oblige. Exiting from Google Maps, he brought us to another program that listed in touch-screen, visual format the many categories of careers one can pursue in the Army. From public relations representative to mechanic, we were tempted by pictures of happy military helping one another and other people. My companion picked engineering. "This is what you can do as an engineer in the Army," the soldier told us as he brought up a long-list of things one can do, none of which included the things I suspect one really needs to do if they are in the twenty-first-century Army. I didn't pay any attention and touched "Compensation." I was curious. "Ah, pay. That depends on your education level," our soldier told us. "Here is your basic compensation" (something like $17,000/year) "and then your allowances and skill-related compensation" (which brought the total to a whopping $30,000-something/year figure). "And this is before taxes?" I asked. "I think so, but you get more money the more education you have." To get said education, he went on, the Army will give you (depending on your state) in the ballpark of $5,000 per year toward school.

The soldier showed us the room with the Apache simulator. Young men were using the "ride" and firing very loud guns. When our soldier friend opened the door to the room, the sound of the guns was even louder. I asked the soldier if the sound bothered him, "Because," I told him, "that sound bothers me and I've never been to Afghanistan." He smiled and led us to the next simulator room, then, pausing before he opening the door, he turned to me. "Yes, it does."

We walked into another dark, but this time quiet, simulator room. The Humvee (Figure 3.1). "It's out of order right now," he told us. "How similar are these simulators to the ones that the Army really use?" I asked. At first he enthusiastically told us how similar they were; then, as if he took a second look at them he said, "well, but not really. The buttons on the simulators don't all work and there would be more of them." At that moment I realized that the simulators here in the AEC were not simulating combat, but instead mimicked the simulators used in Army *training*. For this soldier, the presence of the simulators reminded him not of combat at all, but of the machines he used in his own active duty training. In fact, the best simulation performed at the AEC is its re-creation of a television or movie set – along the lines of *CSI* or *24* – with strategic lighting, hi-tech gadgets, and glass walls – a hyperreal performative environment.

After going through the Army Experience Center – after investigating "undercover," of playing "dumb," after looking at the computer monitors

Figure 3.1 A Humvee simulator at the Army Experience Center, Philadelphia, Pennsylvania, 2 September 2008. Photo by Carrie McLeroy (SMC – Army News Service). Photo courtesy of US Army.

where I could check my email or play *HALO 3*, after watching the bored 20-something men play American Football videogames alongside other 20-something men play violent army games, after getting dizzy on the simulator, after walking by the lit-up office where the recruiter-staff were working, after having a moment of feeling a bit in awe of my country's military might, my friend and I were ready to go. We scraped ourselves out of the Aeron chairs, said goodbye to the 20-somethings, and headed for the exit. As we did, we passed the main sitting area of the Center where the active military personnel we saw earlier were sitting on the sofas. What I found most interesting was that they weren't playing *HALO 3* or *America's Army* on the big screen hung in the front of the lounge area. They were playing, with great intensity and concentration, *Guitar Hero*. They were playing together – like a band (2 guitars, a woman on drums). I reminded myself that this was not a recruiting center.

And yet it was. The AEC was staffed with 20 recruiters. Although I was introduced to the space by the man at reception as a "safe place for kids to come" and play video games and surf the web for free, in particular because, "Philadelphia is not the safest place you know," there was not much getting around the reality of the function of the AEC. And this is where the AEC becomes what Slavoj Žižek calls non-ideology, a case of "ideology appear[ing] as its own opposite."[8] It is this type of insidious agenda that led AEC protestors to employ the slogan "War Is Not a

Figure 3.2 Nearly 300 veterans, military families and peace activist shut down what they called the unethical teenage recruitment at the "Army Experience Center." Seven were arrested for refusing to leave, 2 May 2009. Photo by Paul Kawika Martin ©2009.

Game," because what offends this diverse population of antiwar activists (made up of several different peace/antiwar organizations) is the *way* ideology was manipulated at the AEC (Figure 3.2).

Perhaps a better way to understand what happened there is to think along the lines of counter-insurgency. Nicholas Mirzoeff argues that the post-9/11 military strategy of counter-insurgency (as opposed to the Cold War deterrence strategy) leads to "the production of war as culture."[9]

> In the era of United States global policing, war is counterinsurgency, and the means of counterinsurgency are cultural. War is culture. Globalized capital uses war as its means of acculturating citizens to its regime, requiring both acquiescence to the excesses of power and a willingness to ignore what is palpably obvious. Counterinsurgency has become a digitally mediated version of imperialist techniques to produce legitimacy. Its success in the United States is unquestioned: who

in public life is against counterinsurgency, even if they oppose the war in Iraq or invasions elsewhere? War is culture.[10]

Such a project works to normalize and legitimize what otherwise might seem strange – to the point of integrating the seduction of the military into the space of the shopping mall. "Legitimacy," Mirzoeff argues, "must in the end be literally and metaphorically visible for all to see."[11] In fact, the AEC makes sense precisely because the "war" will never end, and recruits need to be indoctrinated for the future: "The narrative now is that there is no possible way to end the game except by continuing to play, just as the latest platform games invite the player to participate in permanent play rather than exit."[12] For Bea Jauregui, the Army Experience Center is "nothing short of a restructuring of the citizen-soldier relationship" – a place where the overall interaction between civil society and the military is revised.[13] Nina Huntemann and Matthew Thomas Payne argue that "Placing the Army's latest 'state-of-the-art education facility,' which was funded by public money (taxes), inside a private, commercial space fosters an intimately commodified relationship not only between the military and its would-be soldiers but between all civilians."[14] Both analyses point to a very physical connection between private and public, mall and government, store and recruiting center. The greatest irony is that this performance space, which established a major, multimillion-dollar presence in a shopping mall, quietly closed just two years later in July 2010. Protestors hailed the closure as a success and marked the announcement in June with a party in Philadelphia. Critics have indicated that the credit was most likely not due them, and that the closure had more to do with promising recruitment figures in the face of ongoing employment troubles.[15] The line between civilian and soldier, private and public, mall and government that the AEC crossed in a physical way, became intangible – perhaps accomplishing the AEC's mission. War and peace got a little closer.

"War is peace"

The collapse of distinction between "war" and "peace," especially after World War II, has been pointed out by a variety of thinkers and writers, from George Orwell to Noam Chomsky, to Paul Virilio and Arundhati Roy.[16] In the post-9/11 global environment there exists a perception of difference from the world of 10 September, but this is a performed difference backed up only by political theatre and very little factual evidence. For example, despite the fact that the threat of an Al Qaeda attack was well-known before 9/11, George W. Bush spoke on 20 September 2001 of "new and sudden national challenges" faced by the United States and the world.[17] Bush's post-9/11 speech was consumed with language marking the past from the future, from his characterization of the attack as the first on US soil since Pearl Harbor to his "Either you are with us or you are with the terrorists" threat to the rest of the world. In his invocation of an "age of terror," Bush both signaled the beginning of the global war on terror while instructing the American people to "live your lives and hug your children," give money to charity, and keep flying. He talked about terror and fear while predicting normalcy and economic growth. He talked about war *being* peace.

In terms of military strategy, the salient end to the Cold War issued a sense of peace to the world but ushered in years of military involvement in countries such as Iraq, Somalia, Bosnia, Kosovo, and others. It is during this era when the Revolution in Military Affairs (RMA) became a widely discussed and debated topic concerning the move toward a technologically savvy, smaller-scale, cleaner, precise approach to combat, boosted by the "success" of the Persian Gulf War in 1991 and the zero-casualty presence in Kosovo. The promises of the RMA rhetoric helped to lead the United States into Afghanistan just weeks after 9/11 and less than two years later into Iraq. Assumptions of quick victories, as the world knows all too well a decade on, were terribly wrong. A shift occurred in the mid-2000s from shock-and-awe back to counter-insurgency, a strategy – a topic – mainly avoided since the Vietnam War. In 2006, General David Petraeus wrote what was the first Army manual in 20 years and Marine manual in 25 years dedicated to counter-insurgency (COIN).[18] Petraeus's manual has a focus on securing the civilian population with a high soldier-to-civilian ratio and a shift toward political rather than military efforts.

The RMA marked a break from Cold War nuclear deterrence but further complicated future conflict. Paul Virilio argues that the first attack on the World Trade Center in 1993 was a post-Cold War turning point:

> Inaugurated by the collapse of the Berlin Wall and even more by the Gulf War, the end of the age of nuclear deterrence is today confirmed by the civil war in the former Yugoslavia but also by this luckily abortive attempt to bring down the New York tower. [...] After the age of the *balance of terror*, which lasted some forty years, the *age of imbalance* is upon us.[19]

The Cold-War "balance of terror" managed through deterrence ended and "imbalance" began, at least for Virilio, with the first World Trade Center attack. The development of the new "age of imbalance," which is simultaneously categorized as a time of "peace" and "surgical," or what James Der Derian calls "virtuous," war evolved swiftly into a "global war on terror" marked by a business-as-usual attitude usually reserved for "peace." In turn, the re-emergence of counter-insurgency as a foundational strategy has become, as Mirzoeff argues, a move toward "the production of war as culture."[20]

Games finite and infinite

Mirzoeff's analysis relates to James P. Carse's idea of finite and infinite games: "A finite game is played for the purposes of winning, an infinite game for the purpose of continuing to play."[21] Carse calls war the "ultimate finite game," but terms like "perpetual war" and "permanent war" and "eternal war" seem to more accurately describe the twenty-first-century global war on terror. With its unstable enemies and shifting battlefields, the GWOT is an unwinnable, and unending conflict. Counter-insurgency therefore seems to better fit Carse's description of infinite rather than finite games:

> The rules of a finite game are the contractual terms by which the players can agree on who has won. [...] The rules of an infinite game must change during the course of play. [...] The rules of an infinite game are changed to prevent anyone from winning the game and to bring as many persons as possible into the play.[22]

Counter-insurgency is the attempt to "bring as many persons as possible into the play"; it is a "means of acculturating citizens" to globalized capital. Counter-insurgency works in the theatres of war – where "insurgents" can be (theoretically) identified and targeted, a process inevitably tied to the acquiescence of the civilian population. Counter-insurgency also works "at home," where – in the place of mandatory military service – governmental power can anticipate the possible resistance of young civilians to volunteering and insert culture games that serve to indoctrinate players into a military mindset. The "game," then, operates on the level of both video game and war game in flexible contexts, from play to training to combat to therapy in an "infinite" loop.

War as game

The severe discrepancy in the scale of consequence makes the comparison of war and gaming nearly obscene, the analogy either trivializing the one or, conversely, attributing to the other a weight of motive and consequence it cannot bear.[23]

No war has ever been so enabled by the attributes, defined by the language, and played by (and against) the rules of the game than the war in Iraq. As the velocity of strategic movement was force-multiplied by the immediacy of the televisual moment: as the virtuality of high technology warfare was enhanced by the reality of low battlefield casualties; as the military and the media as well as weapon-systems and sign-systems become mutually embedded; as the viewer became the player; war and game melded in real-time on primetime.[24]

These are not bad apples. This is standard practice. You can hear it from the tones of the voices of the pilots that this is in fact another day at the office. These pilots have evidently and gunners have evidently become so corrupted, morally corrupted, by the war that they are looking for excuses to kill. That is why you hear this segment, "Come on, buddy! Just pick up a weapon," when Saeed, one of the Reuters employees, is crawling on the curb. They don't want him for intelligence value to understand the situation. The man is clearly of no threat whatsoever. He's prostate on the ground. Everyone else has been killed. They just want an excuse to kill. And it's some kind of – appears to me to be some kind of video game mentality where they just want to get a high score, get their kill count up. And later on you'll hear them proudly proclaiming how they killed twelve to fifteen people.[25]

War is not a game. Or is it?

It is important to distinguish "war games" from war "as" game – games that simulate war versus war taking on the properties of a game. James Der Derian points out this distinction, attributing "the conflation and confusion of war with game" to the "rapid development and prolifera-tion of war gaming in the United States defense and foreign policies" since the end of the nineteenth century.[26] The relationship between "war" and "play" is therefore complex. Richard Schechner notes that play "is double-edged, ambiguous, moving in several directions simul-taneously. Play is intrinsically part of performing because it embodies the 'as if,' the make-believe."[27] War games, simulation, performance, the "as if," play, and playing are all concepts familiar to the military, an organi-zation which needs to train – to transform – men and women from "civilian" to "soldier" to "warrior." Zach Gill has investigated the mili-tary's move to "perpetual warrior training" through theatre immersion and Robertson Allen has written about the push by the Army to incorporate military video games into soldier's R&R time in order to maximize training.[28] Richard Schechner argues that "War games offer a chance to practice through games to prepare for the real thing. Once you get to the real thing it feels like a game and, ironically, the real thing is called the 'theatre of war' or 'theatre of operations.'"[29] Such confusion, I argue, relates to the concept of "war as culture" that distinguishes post-9/11 US society.

Der Derian notes that as war games became more advanced, war increasingly took on the properties of a game: "the better the simulation, the higher the risk of confusing war as game."[30] For Der Derian, contemporary war is "virtuous war," a "hybridization of warring and gaming" that "projects a technological and ethical superiority in which computer simulation, media dissimulation, global surveillance, and networked warfare combine to deter, discipline, and if need be, destroy the enemy" that is very much related to the post-9/11 era of a foreign policy of "coercion over diplomacy."[31] In such a game, operations can be endlessly rehearsed, as Zach Gill explains in his essay about military performative training strategies:

> The claims to mimetic realism fall short, revealing a system of training aimed at perpetuating rehearsal and postponing any final performance indefinitely by posing combat as a copy of training. Performance becomes a debased mimicry of rehearsal. This performative strategy stabilizes and extends the control of the Army, subsuming the actual in Iraq to the already rehearsed at home.[32]

Perpetual rehearsal therefore mediates the final execution – the "live" performance, with a variety of results. For Gill, the "actual in Iraq" is the "already rehearsed at home." For the drone pilot, the actual in Iraq, Afghanistan, or Pakistan is the same as the rehearsal in that s/he never leaves the virtual cockpit in Nevada. As Jean Baudrillard made clear after the first Gulf War,[33] so also mass media plays a key role for Der Derian in the collapse of war and game. Writing of the 2003 invasion of Iraq, Der Derian argues that journalists "embedded" with troops complemented the former military personnel who "exercised full spectrum dominance on cable and network TV" while the studios of competing networks featured hi-tech simulations of "command and control centers of the military."[34] For the embedded journalist, therefore, the actual becomes a media event, whether in the case of the strategically placed reporters at the start of the Iraq War or the hyperreal tales of Sebastian Junger in

Afghanistan delivered via print and film.[35] The actual is subsequently rehearsed, as I write about below, in digital games that re-enact past – often very recent past in the case of a game like *Kuma\War* – events for a participatory audience.

Perpetual rehearsal before, during, and after the actual. War as game. War as performance. Visitors to the official Army website are greeted with this sort of confusion: High quality audiovisual elements appear with the message: "At the Ready." Under this title: "Get the skills of an Army soldier by immersing yourself in real-life missions." I clicked, and the audio offered that I could "Walk in the boots of an Army soldier. Learn what they learn. See what they see."[36] Before the visitor "walks," however, they are met with an option to login to Facebook to "personalize" the experience. When I visited, I clicked "Don't Allow," and to return to the Main Menu a few times before I figured out how to bypass the Facebook link and simply watch the video, which was one of three instructional videos using recreated scenarios from combat in order to show what different Army occupations involve.

The casual approach to "rehearsal" and conflation of education and training cause problems in combat, of course, where your first "actual" mistake can be your last. They also speak to the perverse representations of the mundane actual in the case of Abu Ghraib. For Jean Baudrillard the images of Abu Ghraib both disrupt and simultaneously exemplify "war as game." The images, he writes, constitute "a parody of violence, a parody of the war itself, pornography becoming the ultimate form of the abjection of war which is unable to be simply war, to be simply about killing, and instead turns itself into a grotesque infantile reality-show, in a desperate simulacrum of power."[37] The nature of the Abu Ghraib images make "facts" and even "journalism" irrelevant:

> Truth but not veracity: it does not help to know whether the images are true or false. From now on and forever we will be uncertain about these images. Only their impact counts in the way in which they are immersed in the war. There is no longer the need for "embedded" journalists because soldiers themselves are immersed in the image – thanks to digital technology, the images are definitively integrated into the war. They don't represent it anymore; they involve neither distance, nor perception, nor judgment. They no longer belong to the order of representation, nor of information in a strict sense.[38]

Baudrillard's analysis reveals the danger that Der Derian warns of: the conflation of war and game. The familiarity we now have with the images of Abu Ghraib, however, really constitutes the tip of an iceberg. Soldiers throughout Iraq and Afghanistan regularly "update their status" – to use a contemporary term of the Facebook age – they, as Baudrillard knew, don't need journalists embedded with them. They can speak to the world themselves and offer their view on their "actual." Videos uploaded by soldiers to liveleak.com, for example, feature personal accounts of the war in Iraq: "This is me in Iraq," one soldier tells the camera in a dimly lit video. Describing the convoy he was on the day of the video, he explains "they are risking their lives every fucking day just to drive for some bullshit" and asks why an in-person meeting, which requires a convoy escort, is needed when a conference would suffice.[39] In another video a soldier describes the children he encounters in Afghanistan as constantly begging. After several minutes of tape during which the viewer gets mainly a taste of the boredom of daily life in Afghanistan (walking, complaining, masturbating), the video ends with footage of the soldier holding the camera shouting out "I'm Rick James, bitch!" to a line of Afghani children, who enthusiastically repeat the statement back to the soldier with bright smiles on their faces.[40]

Performing counter-insurgency within the "game"

> war game – A simulation, by whatever means, of a military operation involving two or more opposing forces using rules, data, and procedures designed to depict an actual or assumed real life situation.[41]

War games of all types have a long history from Georg Leopold Baron von Reisswitz's early nineteenth-century *Kriegsspiel* ("war game") adapted from *Chess*, through the Cold War boom in wargaming marked especially by the popularity of Charles S. Roberts's *Tactics* (1952).[42] In a logical progression, the twentieth century brought advances to the nineteenth-century war game through ever-improving simulations. As the Cold War waned, and the perception that reality was becoming easier to mimic through technology, war games improved.[43] Ian Bogost cites Steve Russell's *Spacewar* (1962), a "space combat simulator that pitted two human opponents against each other in the depths of space" as an example of the "further conflation of influences t[ying] war and games together just as the computer becomes viable (at least for research labs and universities) in the 1960s.[44] In his essay on the "military-entertainment complex," Tim Lenoir provides a history of technological advances since the 1960s including computer graphics and virtual reality, detailing how these innovations developed at first separately in the military and entertainment industries, but became increasingly intertwined over time.[45]

The advances in the commercial video game industry in the 1980s led the US Army's SIMNET (Simulator Networking) program, which began in 1983, to consider alternatives to expensive government contracts. At the time, simulators, which were in use by the military for decades, were large, stand-alone units that cost tens or hundreds of millions of dollars.[46] SIMNET marked a shift away from hardware to "learning first what functions were needed to meet the training objectives" before designing structures that mimicked military aircraft or vehicles.[47] The trend therefore was multifaceted: there was a move to make use of the superior innovations found in the commercial video game industry; but there was also an acknowledgement that the best simulation training would provide not the best replica of the physical environment of military operations but the most accurate representation of the circumstances in order to train for the *mental* capacity to function in the war theatre.

Developing simulators, however, maintained an *overall* focus on cost-effective practice: "No one wants to let a rookie fly anything as dangerous, or as expensive, as an F-17 until the pilot has logged some serious time on a simulator," wrote Kara Platoni in her 1999 article on military investment in and research on video games.[48] Platoni traces the military's turn to the commercial video game industry to 1980, when the Army "ordered a modified version of *Battlezone*, Atari's tank-driving game." Sebastian Deterding notes that *Battlezone* represents a turn from board games to video games.[49] But *Battlezone* "didn't look like the real thing. [...] Amusing, yes, but not an adrenaline-pumping experience."[50] By the 1990s, there was an overt push in the Federal Acquisitions Streamlining Act (1994) to "move away from the historically based DOD reliance on contracting with segments of the US technology and industrial base dedicated to DOD requirements [...] toward the acquisition of commercial items, components, processes, and practices."[51] The costly and bulky simulators – such as the $846 million "Close Combat Tactical Trainer" "composed of various simulators that replicate combat vehicles, tactical vehicles, and weapons systems interacting in real time"[52] – gave way to what the Department of Defense called "COTS (commercial off the shelf)" games that could "be modified for military use for under $200," leading many Silicon Valley game developers to sell their products to the government.[53] Clive Thompson describes this shift:

> The military's simulators, of course, were still elite tools. But they were prohibitively expensive (a single military flight simulator can cost up to $30 million), and they were products of the cold-war era, designed

for combat in which large armies face one another head-on. In the eyes of someone like Neale Cosby, director of the simulation center of the Institute for Defense Analyses, a private group that advises the Pentagon, the old technology was outdated. "We do not have good simulations for combatants who walk to work," he said. "Tanks, Bradley vehicles, that's all cold-war stuff." For the needs of today's lighter, more flexible Army and its urban campaigns, in which soldiers walk door to door, video games that made you stroll through dungeons looking to slay shrieking monsters suddenly seemed relevant.[54]

Thompson and others trace the new era of military simulation from the adaptation of the game *Doom* in 1997[55] through the founding of the Institute for Creative Technologies at the University of Southern California, a project initially funded in 1999 with $45 million from the Army.[56] The opening of the ICT was another overt move by the military toward the private sector, this time with the full recognition of not only the entertainment industry's superior technologies but also the "promise that any technological advances" of the ICT could "also be applied to creating more compelling video games and theme park rides."[57] Indeed, the "soft" nature of private sector technology has gained appeal in the modern military. Lenoir writes:

> [M]ovies, theme park rides, and (increasingly) even video games are driven by stories with plot, feeling, tension, and emotion. To train for real-world military engagements is to train not just on how to use the equipment, but on how to cope with the implementation of strategy in an environment with uncertainties, surprises, and participants with actual fears.[58]

One of the most prominent turns toward the "soft" side is the computer-generated re-creation of the *Battle of 73 Easting*,[59] an event of the first Gulf War. The *Battle of 73 Easting* project is a sort of documentary performance piece created with 150 accounts of the battle. "The goal of the project was to get timeline-based experiences of how individuals felt, thought, and reacted to the dynamic unfolding of the events – their fears and emotions as well as actions – and to render the events as a fully three-dimensional simulated reality that any future cadet could enter and relive."[60] The precision level of *73 Easting*'s documentation was described in the first issue of *Wired* magazine by Bruce Sterling:

> They came up with a fully interactive, network-capable digital replica of the events at 73 Easting, right down to the last TOW missile and

.50-caliber pockmark. Military historians and armchair strategists can now fly over the virtual battlefield in the "stealth vehicle," the so-called "SIMNET flying carpet," viewing the 3-D virtual landscape from any angle during any moment of the battle. They can even change the parameters – give the Iraqis infrared targeting scopes, for instance, which they lacked at the time, and which made them sitting ducks for high-tech American M1s charging out of blowing sand.[61]

From the starting point of the most accurate documentation possible, the re-enactment of the Battle of 73 Easting could do more than just replay the battle; it could serve as a template for a multitude of scenarios for training purposes – a way to make the "as if" become the most plausible in a given set of circumstances. Sterling writes:

> The whole triumphal blitzkrieg can be pondered over repeatedly (gloated over even), in perfect scratch-free digital fidelity. It's the spirit of Southwest Asia in a digital nutshell. In terms of American military morale, it's like a '90s CD remix of some '60s oldie, rescued from warping vinyl and remade closer to the heart's desire.[62]

It could end in many different ways (until they got it right... again?) and became one of the first military simulations to make the most use of audio-visual tools, with "panoramic views on three 50-inch TV screens at the resolution of a very good video game."[63] *73 Easting* was indeed a turning point for military training; the project seemed to capture precisely the blurring Der Derian refers to between war games and war as game. Sterling writes:

> "The Reconstruction of the Battle of 73 Easting" is [...] fast and exhilarating and full of weird beauty. But even its sleek, polygonal, bloodless virtuality is a terrifying thing to witness and to comprehend. It is intense and horrific violence at headlong speed, a savage event of grotesque explosive precision and terrible mechanized impacts. The flesh of real young men was there inside those flaming tank-shaped polygons, and that flesh was burning.
>
> That is what one knows – but it's not what one sees. What one really sees in "73 Easting" is something new and very strange: a complete and utter triumph of chilling, analytic, cybernetic rationality over chaotic, real-life, human desperation.[64]

The study of *73 Easting* and its conceptualization as what Richard Schechner would call "proto-performance,"[65] the material of which so many military performances have since been made, indeed represents a shift from war to virtual war.

Documentary games

73 Easting was an early "documentary game," a genre that "uses real people, places and subjects as its referents."[66] In their critical analysis of the genre, Ian Bogost and Cindy Poremba find that although adapting the term "documentary" – as it is used for film – is tricky when looking at digital games, finding that in general, whereas films can "represent only one instance of the subject [...] digital media offer the possibility of simulating situations difficult to deconstruct or follow visually."[67] Keith Halper, CEO of Kuma Reality Games, describes what his company's documentary games offer gamers as "a highly interactive alternative to CNN."[68] The Kuma website tells gamers: "Stop watching the news and get in the game!"[69] Players can experience a real event not just by watching it on the news, but by *performing* it:

> Kuma is aiming at another level of realism altogether. The capture of the Hussein brothers, for example, is set in the Mosul villa where they were killed, re-created by programmers using satellite photos and declassified military intelligence. Players carry weapons and ammo used by US troops – AT4 antitank weapons and 5.56-mm M4 carbines – and lug them up the same number of stairs those soldiers ascended.[70]

Kuma\War offers "nearly 100" different missions from the war on terror to play online, for free. Apparently the game, at least in 2005, was a "huge hit among Iraq's youth," according to journalist Colin Freeman, who described a scene in a Baghdad café where Iraqis played *Kuma\ War*.[71] Other game companies have attempted to use games to present audiences with an interactive documentary. Many games go to great lengths to achieve realistic scenarios. Game designers for *Medal of Honor* (2010) as well as the military-funded ELECT BiLAT training simulation visited the theatre immersion training camp at Fort Irwin, California where soldiers get a taste of the "sandbox" via theatrical interaction with Iraqi ex-pats who are paid actors with fully developed characters.[72] Atomic Games developed *Six Days in Fallujah* with the input of "dozens of soldiers who were involved in the real-life 2004 battle for the Iraqi city to add realism" to the game.[73] In a fashion similar to the way that documentary theatre is constructed, *Six Days* used evidence – satellite imagery, an accurate timeline of the events, and even the diary of a soldier. Players have "an over-the-shoulder point of view to simulate the look of an embedded journalist."[74] This perspective differs from the "first-person" view of one's gun used in most popular digital "violent" games. The over-the-shoulder view offers a bit of distance from the over-bearing sight of the tip of a gun, a sight that perhaps turns player-human into gun-machine. It also puts the image of the player into the picture, placing a distance between player and action that *shows you who and where you are in the game* in relation to other objects, guns, and "players." The potential offered through this perspective has something to do with maintaining a sense of humanity and identity, reminding play-ers that they are not just guns or machines but people, albeit virtual people – avatars – moving through a virtual environment. To use theatre's metaphors, whereas the "gun" view is naturalistic, the over-the-shoulder view is Brechtian. And yet, the player is the actor – s/he is the agent of the virtual violence of the gun – and therefore detachment becomes something pathological instead of critical. It is as if indeed you are just the journalist looking over the shoulder and not the one possessing the agency to commit the actions you make happen by pressing buttons: an out-of-body experience. Inside this space among player, avatar, and gun exists the uncertainty and instability of anxiety – a sociocultural anxi-ety that speaks to the breakdown between civilian and soldier, real and virtual, agent and event that corresponds to a digital generation who play games within and outside theatres of war.

Six Days caused enough controversy and outcry from anti-war activists and military families that as of this writing there has been no release. And *Six Days* isn't the only game that upsets people. Electronic Arts' lat-est release in its *Medal of Honor* series had a feature allowing players to take on Taliban identities to fight essentially US soldiers. Under pressure the company pulled the option from the game shortly before its release.[75] In these cases, the choice behind the US Army to allow *America's Army* players to only play "good guys" begins to make more sense. However, as many critics of what might be perceived as censorship argue, there are many games – including the hugely successful 1999 version of *Medal of Honor* set during World War II – in which players can take on enemy identities. The question of what makes the public feel more comfortable with enemies in such contexts might be explained by both the distance of time as well as the concrete nature of "the enemy" in WWII.

Although some compare the war documentary games like *Medal of Honor* and *Six Days in Fallujah* to other "serious" or "documentary" games such as *Darfur Is Dying* (Viacom, 2006) or *Ayiti: The Cost of Life* (GameLab,

2006),[76] what is being engaged in differs according to who is the author of essentially violent activity. That is, documentary video games about war, I argue, must be distinguished from other educational videogames. Both types may try to find through gaming a way in which different pasts, presents, and futures can be imagined or brought into being by the performance of the game, but the means of such interaction – violence – sets the war games off from the others.

Key to the documentary game, then, is the opportunity it offers: "Documentaries excel in specific instances, but documentary games deal in *real* virtualities; possibility spaces in which multiple instantiations for real-world activity can exist."[77] While I would argue that although the use by Bogost and Poremba of "documentary" as a lens – something I would encourage – I would go further to acknowledge what documentary theatre and performance can offer in the "moment." If documentary film – and much documentary theatre – can do not much more than present a "reality" or version of "facts" that audiences may approach "with a 'desire to know' and a primary expectation to be informed as well as entertained,"[78] I maintain that *some* documentary theatre and performance, in addition to documentary games like *73 Easting*; *JFK Reloaded* (2004), Traffic; *Kuma\War: The War on Terror* (2005), Kuma Reality Games; *Waco Resurrection* (2003), C-Level; *Medal of Honor* (1999), Electronic Arts; and others, work to create performative spaces in which "documentary" – essentially working in the past – can help to make new presents, and perhaps even futures. The interactive, performative aspect of digital games is emphasized by critics as being the key difference in documentary games versus documentary film. However, these analyses fail to account for the growing genre of documentary theatre and performance, which can also engage participatory audiences in live, 3-D contexts. For example, the "reality theatre" company Rimini Protokoll's *Best Before* allows audience members to interact as anonymous avatars – as performers – with the "experts" on stage to create a new world called *Bestland*. The use of *Virtual Iraq* and *Virtual Afghanistan* to treat PTSD, which I discuss below, similarly exemplifies an attempt to fully exploit the potential of the interactive nature of documentary games. These programs were adapted from the urban warfare digital game *Full Spectrum Warrior* (Pandemic, 2004). Such a connection speaks to a cyclical approach to gaming. The cycle I refer to begins with games like *America's Army*, which indoctrinates youth into military culture through "rehearsal" for the real thing, through games used in actual training (more "rehearsal"), through games not directly associated with the US military (but certainly part of the "military-entertainment complex") played in the popular sector (like *Full Spectrum Warrior*), through the adaptation of such games for the purposes of replaying actual events for therapeutic reasons (*Virtual Iraq* and *Afghanistan*).

America's Army

I will turn therefore to *America's Army* and its place in the "cycle." Although development began in 1999, *America's Army* is part of a growth spurt of the "military-entertainment complex" just before, but especially after 9/11, when some game developers approached the military with an offer to help. *America's Army*, available for download for free via the US Army,[79] is the "Official U.S. Army Game," developed in 1999 after Congress responded to dwindling enlistment numbers by increasing the Army's annual recruitment budget to $2.2 billion.[80] With the help of the Leo Burnett advertising firm, the Army launched an initial campaign in January 2001 with a new slogan, "An Army of One," which replaced "Be All You Can Be."[81] Colonel Casey Wardynski, the project originator and director for *America's Army*, credited a trip to the Best Buy game section with his sons, where he "was just amazed to discover that about 60 percent of the games available involved something that looked like an army." For Wardynski, this was confirmation that there existed "a native demand for entertainment that looks like the Army" and "that's what clinched it."[82] *America's Army* is a first-person shooter game now in its third version.

The game premiered on 4 July 2002. With a "T" for Teen rating, *America's Army* targets a wide market of ages 13-35 around the world. The highly successful brand has continually evolved, adding updates, Xbox versions, and a series of documentary features called "Real Heroes" that insert the narratives of selected soldiers into the game's scenarios and educational tools. The game maintains a strict balance between "serious" game and pure entertainment:

> In the America's Army game, players are bound by Rules of Engagement (ROE) and grow in experience as they navigate challenges in teamwork-based, multiplayer, force versus force operations. In the game, as in the Army, accomplishing missions requires a team effort and adherence to the seven Army Core Values. Through its emphasis on team play, the game demonstrates these values of loyalty, duty, respect, selfless service, honor, integrity and personal courage and makes them integral to success in America's Army.[83]

America's Army is not the only video game used for US military training,[84] but it has become the most ubiquitous crossover with civilian access and is the main interface of the games that make up the Virtual Army Experience and the Army Experience Center. It is marketed as a fun and educational way to learn about the military – in fact it is expressly *not* supposed to be a "training" but an "educational"[85] game – and has been cited as a tool to increase retention. It is an advergame[86] and a product of experiential marketing. It is something that bridges the militarization of popular culture with performance through its participatory nature.[87] The logic goes something like this: by offering *America's Army* to everyone via free download, young people can play this state-of-the-art first-person shooter game as often as they wish. The intent is of course that they will play often – as veteran wargamer James F. Dunnigan explains: "The most important thing for a good wargame is that it be addictive. [...] Once [the game] becomes crack, the soldiers will train without a sergeant kicking them in their butts."[88] The game walks a careful line between realism, which would have to represent the boredom and real violence of warfare, and entertaining fiction, which keeps the game fun enough to keep playing.

The goal of *America's Army* developers is to strike a balance to make the game closely match what the "real" Army experience is like, so that those who join having played the game don't drop out during or after basic training.[89] Anthropologist Robertson Allen relates such use of games to Foucaultian biopower:

> the Army Game Project can be seen as a networked apparatus that attempts to regulate, analyze, and administer the subjectivities of both soldiers and civilians from the interior, bypassing more localized modes of subject formation traditionally centered at specific disciplinary institutions such as prisons, schools, factories, hospitals, or barracks.[90]

America's Army has the express objective of providing educational entertainment to a global audience. Learning about the military is the objective, and understanding what Army personnel do is the goal, and these experiences are represented in the game. Colonel Casey Wardynski, who directed the development and launch of *America's Army*, explains how *America's Army* aims to improve the quality of recruitment:

> The game is involved in creating a better-prepared customer. When a young adult arrived at the Army in the old days, what did he know? Now after they play *America's Army* they know what basic training looks like, what airborne and ranger school is, what occupations are

available. So they arrive at a discussion with a recruiter with information symmetry. If he signs up to be in the Army, odds are he's going
to be happy. If he arrives and there's been asymmetry and he doesn't
know what he's getting into, well the recruiter has gotten a recruit
but the Army may have an unhappy soldier and that's not good. The
game can help level the playing field so that the customer, the kid, is
much better experienced – which is better for the kid, better for the
country, better for the Army in the long run.[91]

But as combat is represented in an attempt to show the player what
"war" is like, the realities of war – injury and death – are de-emphasized.
Daphnée Rentfrow writes: "War is not a game, we are told, and yet games
are designed to produce soldiers ready for war in which death doesn't
happen and blood and gore do not exist."[92] *America's Army* exemplifies
Der Derian's idea of virtuous war, which "cleans up the political discourse
as well as the battlefield" and "promote[s] a vision of bloodless, humanitarian, hygienic wars." In contrast to a traditional concept of war:

> virtuous war has an unsurpassed power to commute death, to keep it
> out of sight, out of mind. Herein lies its most morally dubious dan-
> ger. In simulated preparations and virtual executions of war, there is
> a high risk that one learns how to kill but not to take responsibility
> for it. One experiences "death" but not the tragic consequences of it.
> In virtuous war we now face not just the confusion but the pixilation
> of war and game on the same screen.[93]

America's Army doesn't have the blood, gore, and dismemberment of real
war – because it is virtual, and because it is virtuous – it is about playing
on the "right" side of the war on terror. *America's Army* can be viewed
as a tool of the type of counter-insurgency that Mirzoeff refers to – one
that is irresistible. The game produces a feeling of otherness because
"we" believe that the "war on terror" is a battle against an "other."

Enemies "real" and "unreal"

In *America's Army* we all play the "good guys" – US soldiers. There is no
option to play the "enemy." We, as US soldiers, as ourselves (and global
players also playing US soldiers, playing "other"), fight an amorphous
enemy. By doing so "we," the players, participate in cultural myths –
acquiescing to hegemonic US geopolitical force. It is crucial to unpack
the irony of role-play in *America's Army*. Despite the fact that *America's*

Army represents combat and war, it is a game in which everyone is a "friend," fighting against other "friends" disguised only to the player *as* the "enemy" but revealed in the subjective perspective of every player as "friend." Here the friend-enemy distinction defined by Carl Schmitt as the origin of the concept of the political – "The specific political distinction to which political actions and motives can be reduced is that between friend and enemy" – begins to blur.[94] At first it seems that the game conforms to the friend-enemy model. But the inability to play the enemy invalidates such a claim. The enemy of *America's Army* is unformed, "unreal"[95]; it was designed only to represent the *behavior* of the terrorist, void of ethnic or religious identity. The *America's Army* enemy is created in a context described by Derrida in *The Politics of Friendship*: "[w]here the principal enemy, the "structuring" enemy, seems nowhere to be found, where it ceases to be identifiable and thus reliable."[96] Allen Feldman elaborates on Derrida's description of the enemy in the post-Cold War era, in which:

> The principal enemy is replaced by figures of the enemy, metaphors, doubles, typifications, traces, apparitions, place holders, envoys and specters that operate as mnemotechniques for political identity threatened by the loss of the enemy as a political archive and exteriorized support.[97]

So although there is clearly a "friend" (US soldier) and an "enemy" (terrorist) in *America's Army*, the enemy is no longer identifiable in a traditional way, in part because s/he is really a "friend" behind the scenes – as are indeed many of the United States' "enemies" – but also because s/he is not a "principal" or "structuring" enemy, but a "place holder" of the enemy, an attempt at political correctness – an enemy opposed enough to the "friend" played by Americans, while inoffensive to the "friend" played in Yemen, Iraq, or Indonesia. The game recruits, indoctrinates, and educates while it accomplishes the core, long-term, and overall mission of counterinsurgency: We're all "friends" as we play; we are all playing Army values. *America's Army* and games like it differ from documentary games with their amorphous, unidentified enemies, but both game genres enable an ongoing, unwinnable, anyone-can-be-the-enemy in the war on terror.

Colonel Casey Wardynski explains the reason behind making sure all players are "good guys": "If we let kids play 'bad guys' we couldn't bind them to the Army's rules and values, we would have mayhem like in an entertainment game, and the point would be lost."[98] The reason is virtuous; it is based in values – Army values. The indirect nature of recruitment achieved by *America's Army* is a "coming around" to a way of being and of seeing – read: "Army values" – that is essentially a project of counter-insurgency. David Nieborg writes: "the 'we' and 'us' in *America's Army* is always-already the US Army [...] Thus the terrorist [...] is purposely elided to guarantee that gamers identify only with the right point of view: that of the American soldier."[99] Colonel Casey Wardynski describes the process accurately: "With game technology we can make something very vivid. We can deliver it into pop culture; we can structure it in a way that was designed for teens 13 and above. So now we're not going to get there last, we'll get there about the same time as other ideas for what to do with your life."[100] From the time that a child begins to have "ideas," and through the ongoing rehearsal of *America's Army*, the potential not-recruit, the possible insurgent, or even skeptic – critical thinker? – will forego analysis, abandon agency, for the soldier's creed. Games such as Hezbollah's *Special Force* (2003) and *Special Force 2* (2007) prove just how relative the "enemy" is, and just how "real" it *can* be. Upon the release of the new version, Hussein Haj Hassan told the *Daily Mail*: "It is not only a game, it is an education and culture." His comments begin as if they come from an *America's Army* representative. But he continues, explaining that the game confronts "American and the Western companies" who "created games featuring us as terrorists" that are "widespread on the market." *Special Force 2*, he says, is an "achievement [... in] addition to the tools of resistance and confrontation."[101] The enemy in *Special Force* is clearly the Israeli soldier. Similarly in Afkar Media's *Under Ash* (2001) and *Under Siege* (2005), there is a clear enemy: "occupying forces." The company's website includes an express denunciation of "terrorism": the game, according to the description of *Under Siege*, "does not include any suicide bombing or terrorist simulation."[102] Narratives are based on the "real stories of Palestinian people." In short, while *America's Army* players fight any and all "terrorists" at all times, the "terrorists" – that is, the imagined enemies, the place holders – play "friends" fighting the "occupying forces" that America considers "friends."

"All But War Is Simulation"

The "web of connections between the military and the game industry"[103] and the "military entertainment complex"[104] were certainly predicted by Bruce Sterling's first article in *Wired*. The extent to which these networks have led a larger phenomenon of play and gaming that fuses recruiting and training, play and war, however, cannot be overestimated. What is most telling in the Sterling exposé are his 1993 predictions: he writes of

Figure 3.3 "All but war is simulation," former logo for the US Army Program Executive Office for Simulation, Training, and Instrumentation.

the military-industrial complex seeking its own simulation industry; of the "Distributed Simulation Internet" that didn't yet exist; of a desire on the part of the US military to reach out to the entertainment industry; for war to become simulated; and for war to be fought remotely, over the "Internet." Sterling's insights were telling, and many were not predictions but revelations about how the first Gulf War was fought; that is, with drone fighters and surgical attacks aided by computer graphics. But still he could, in 1993, only point to what has really happened. That is, what Sterling calls the "Distributed Simulation Internet" is now not merely a networked space for military to train – instead, it is a networked site of performance within which "war" and "play" occur simultaneously. The former logo for the US military's Program Executive Office for Simulation, Training, and Instrumentation (PEO STRI) captures perfectly the problem of conflating war and game. It reads: "All But War Is Simulation" (see Figure 3.3). Gamers all over the world play *America's Army* (Figures 3.4 and 3.5) at any given time, while drone pilots remotely operate deadly weapons thousands of miles from their consoles. The difference between gamers in the 1990s and gamers now, between drone pilots in the first Gulf War and drone pilots in twenty-first-century

Figure 3.4 This alley screen shot from *America's Army 3* shows the realistic lighting and shadows. Photo courtesy of US Army.

Figure 3.5 Soldiers in *America's Army: True Soldiers* attack an enemy encampment in the fictional country of Ganzia. The player controls the weapon in the foreground. Before using a weapon in combat, players must meet Army training standards. Photo courtesy of US Army.

Nevada, is the even further blurring between "war" and "peace" and the development of the equation "war is culture" ushered in by the "war on terror." It is the difference between the heightened, CNN display of mission control in Florida commanding the invasion of Iraq in 1992 and the statement by former US member of Congress James Walsh in praise of federal funding for new Reaper drones to be housed at Hancock Field in upstate New York: "The pilots could be literally fighting a war in Iraq and at the end of their shift go home and be playing with their kids in Camillus,"[105] There is a new normal, and virtual space in the post-9/11 era has redefined what it means to "perform." The sites of performance in cyberspace have become places to play, to perform the culture of US military might and to enact its power. But the sites of performance in the Army Game Project, it must be noted, are not *only* in cyberspace.

There is a history of live performance that exists alongside the history of military simulation and technological development. Kara Platoni cites the performance in March 1999 called "Operation Urban Warrior" in Oakland, California during which an imaginary country called "Orange" invaded a country called "Green" and 6000 "real" troops were called to participate: "The purpose of Urban Warrior was to test the Armed Forces' newest technologies – everything from tracking devices to water purifiers."[106] The project's stated "Mission Goals" read like a drill for 2005 New Orleans that never materialized: "Using a sea-based, Navy-Marine Corps team, provide humanitarian and disaster relief assistance to a large, metropolitan city, including food, water, shelter and medicine."[107] The rest of the "Mission Goals" sound *very* war-on-terror:

> Successfully conduct an amphibious landing, helicopter assault and mass casualty drill in response to an incident involving chemical or biological weapons, and in coordination with civilian police and fire departments. Conduct a mid-intensity combat operation in an urban environment against a backdrop of civil unrest, and restore order.[108]

Over the next few years, and once the "real" war on terror premiered, live performances continued with the launch of *America's Army* (originally released in July 2002) at the May 2003 Electronic Entertainment Expo, or E3 Expo.

> Chopping through a clear blue California sky, a cluster of Black Hawk helicopters swept over downtown, then hovered above the glass-curtained main complex of the Los Angeles Convention Center as pedestrians glanced upward in surprise. US Special Forces, clad

in green camouflage and clutching machine guns descended from the copters onto the building's roof, rappelled down the wall to its ground, then stormed the center's entrance. Traffic halted on Pico Boulevard as some civilians rubbernecked in disbelief, while others cautiously fled – no doubt wondering whether the troops were here to tackle an anthrax scare, dirty bomb, sleeper cell, or some other impending threat to Western Culture by Those Who Hate Us.[109]

The spectacle – a marketing performance for *America's Army* – took place just two weeks after George W. Bush's "Mission Accomplished" performance on an aircraft carrier off the coast of nearby San Diego. The initial "storming" of the LA Convention Center was followed up by subsequent events in 2005, when parachutists landed in a parking lot and a nearby parking lot was converted into a platform for "real" Special Forces to stage a "grab mission" featured in the game.[110] These and other performances place emphasis on what happens in the game and what happens in reality by featuring weapons, uniforms, and equipment that the military uses in actual operations and represents in the game. With the 2007 launch of the Virtual Army Experience (VAE), the Army Game Project stepped up its efforts by expressly combining "new media, community outreach, and the 'soft sell.'"[111] Appearing mainly at air shows, the VAE "provides participants with a virtual test drive of the United States Army."[112] Within the 9750 square-foot[113] structure, visitors can spend a half-hour watching videos about "actual soldiers who embody the training, occupations, and abilities that make the US Army the world's premier land force."[114] After a briefing, participants then "enter the mission simulator area where they cross into enemy territory and execute an operation."[115] The operations are carried out on HMMWV and UH-60 Black Hawk helicopter simulators poised in front of large display screens with a mission adapted from the *America's Army* software. Nina Huntemann and Thomas Matthew Payne describe a VAE air show appearance: "The desert camouflage beige 5200-pound[116] inflatable dome protecting this audacious display of digital technology from the elements announces to the soggy queue of mostly boys and men that they are waiting to enter the Virtual Army Experience."[117] The VAE is both a traveling Army Experience Center and a massive mobile arcade customized to bring the videogames, simulators, and recruitment information *to* target audiences. The result has been successful: Huntemann and Payne describe the experience as "nothing less than riveting – an adrenaline rush impossible to duplicate on the console system in your living room."[118] Others, including the advertising industry, agree: the VAE has won awards like the 2009 Jay Chiat Award for Brand Experience & Innovative Design; and a Silver Effie (2009) for Brand Experience.

Playing the game

It is helpful to consider play theory in order to begin unpacking – or perhaps slow down – the cycle of play, rehearsal, training, and therapy associated with military gaming. Training and practice are considered "functions" of play in animals and humans, identified by ethologists such as Caroline Loizos. Play can serve: "1. As schooling or practice for the young"; "2. As an escape from or alternative to stress"; "3. As a source of vital information about the environment"; and "4. As an exercise for muscles involved in agonistic and reproductive behavior."[119] Loizos argues that these functions are "neither sufficient nor necessary" but that play adapts behaviors out of non-play contexts, leading to "exaggerated and uneconomical" movements.[120] In his review of play theory, Richard Schechner notes that ethologists differ from Gregory Bateson's approach to play, which emphasizes the "play frame": "[T]he statement 'This is play,'" Bateson argues, "looks something like this: 'These actions in which we now engage do not denote what those actions for which they stand would denote.'"[121] Hence the "contradiction between ethological theory, which indicates play is practice and training, and Batesonian theory, which asserts play is a way around violence, a way to express aggression without doing harm."[122] According to Bateson, "such playing does good by clearly outlining the play frame and keeping the performance inside it."[123] Schechner explains that this contradiction is at the heart of debates around violent video games.

The arguments against the Army Game Project (AGP) wouldn't agree with Bateson. For them, the AGP is simply a way to start early; to have "girls" and "boys" begin their transformations "before" basic training. The agenda of the Army's "educational" programs, in fact, go beyond early preparation for basic training to encompass a replacement for conscription by engaging with the saturation of the virtual in youth culture, in order to indoctrinate youths so that enlistment becomes a "natural" step in their progression to adulthood. An institution such as the Army Game Project merely extends what the military has already done for decades – that is, engage in simulation, role-play, and virtual environments in order to prepare soldiers for war. The extension comes in the stretch into civilian life over time (age) and space (the mall). Play functions as training for the training for the real thing (and the simulator in the mall is simulating the simulator).

Military digital games exhibit multiple functions in different contexts that strongly relate to the two play theory poles of play as training and play as catharsis. For example, much of the motivation behind using video games and virtual reality in military training is to increase experiential learning so that mistakes that lead to injury and death do not happen in the field: Veteran military educators Jeffrey Lesser and James Sterrett write: "Since soldiers first mistakes in combat may well be their last, military education faces the challenge of moving learning from the battlefield into the classroom."[124] However, "all but war is simulation": Marines interviewed in 2005 in Camp Fallujah told the AP's Nick Wadhams that the games they voraciously play on the base could not "prepare them for combat in any significant way" (see Figure 3.6) As many veterans will explain, any virtual set of circumstances cannot reproduce the fog of war – although games like ELECT BiLAT and other projects at the ICT are aggressively trying to do so. In reality, soldiers find it difficult to distinguish insurgents from civilians, and in reality, people do not demonstrate the same behavior as they do in "play," when, as Elaine Scarry writes, "the person at play, protected by the separability of himself from his own activity, does not put himself at risk."[125] Sgt Jeffery Mickel told Nick Wadhams: "When bullets are zooming by you, there's nothing like it. [...] Some guys get scared and take cover, other guys go right ahead and take care of the threat."[126] It is military training and

Figure 3.6　Screen shot from *Six Days in Fallujah* for Xbox360, http://xbox360.ign.com/dor/objects/14336300/six-days-in-fallujah/images/six-days-in-fallujah-20090406021437261.html?page=mediaimgviewer, uploaded 6 April 2006.

rehearsal that attempts to take this fight-or-flight instinct out of behavior and replace it just with "fight" – or, perhaps, "perform."

While soldiers use – successfully or otherwise – games to prepare for combat, Nina Huntemann interviewed gamers who play *Kuma\War*, *Metal Gear Solid*, *SOCOM*, *Splinter Cell*, and *Rainbow Six* to find out why they play. She concludes that to a certain extent the reasons people play has to do with catharsis and realism: "Playing the game again and again, purchasing sequels with new, frightful scenarios of terrorist attacks and exciting, yet comforting counter-terrorist measures," she writes, can work to dispel fear in the context of the war on terror. "In this way, military-themed video games provide emotional management tools for real-world fears about terrorism." However, she notes that the games "in no way delude players into a false sense of long-term security."[127] So although players of *Kuma\War* "perceive the battles to be realistic enough to quell anxiety about the state of peace or war in Iraq,"[128] this relief is temporary: "The Global War on Terror continues [...] Thus, continued cathartic activity is required: Playing the game again and again."[129] Huntemann echoes Mirzeoff's claim of there being "no possible way to end the game except by continuing to play." And continuing to play is what some soldiers are now doing. Realism and catharsis are part of a deliberate attempt in the context of *Virtual Iraq* and *Afghanistan* to return veterans to "frightful scenarios" in order to exorcise them from the emotional field.

Virtual Iraq

As so many soldiers know too well, the thing about the real thing is its realness. Once out of the game, and into the real material of explosions, blood, guts, and fear, one in five veterans of the Iraq and Afghanistan wars experience post-traumatic stress disorder (PTSD) characterized by flashbacks and nightmares, among other symptoms, that last more than one month.[130] Anticipating that such a phenomenon would follow the conflicts in Afghanistan and Iraq, clinical psychologist Skip Rizzo applied for funding to develop virtual reality for "exposure therapy," often used to treat people with phobias, in which patients engage fears in order to overcome them. Initially denied funding "because the war [in Iraq] started well enough that few people expected to see a lot of stress-related disorders," the USC researcher was later given $4 million "over three years to study how virtual reality can be used to treat PTSD."[131]

Inspired by the program *Virtual Vietnam*, software used since 1997 to treat Vietnam veterans with successful results,[132] Rizzo and his colleagues at the USC Institute for Creative Technologies (ICT) adapted the video game *Full Spectrum Warrior* (*FSW*) to create *Virtual Iraq* (*VI*). "The treatment environment" of *VI* "is based on a creative approach to recycling and adding to the virtual assets that were initially built for the combat tactical simulation and commercially available" *FSW*. Originally developed for use in military training, the virtuosity achieved in *FSW* – a realism intended to prepare soldiers for war and make civilians feel like they are "really" in combat – provided clinicians with the raw material to *return* veterans suffering from PTSD to traumatic events.[133]

Virtual Iraq consists of several environments, including a Middle-Eastern city and a desert. Patients can experience *VI* from different perspectives such as walking along a street or sitting inside a vehicle. The program works on almost all of the senses, including "the aroma of roasted lamb" within a 3-D virtual setting. In an attempt to make the experience as believable and effective as possible, researchers responded to soldier's feedback and now offer a choice of either a joystick *or* a replica M-16 gun to carry "on patrol."[134]

The "key element" of the software is what the creators call a "wizard of oz" interface that "provides the clinician with the capacity to monitor the patient's behavior and to customize the therapy experience to their individual needs by placing them in VR scenario locations that resemble the setting in which the traumatic events initially occurred."[135] "Wizards" – those Richard Schechner calls "professional watchers"[136] – can also control "triggers" that "foster the anxiety modulation needed for therapeutic habituation."[137] The imposition of triggers in a virtual reality context makes *VI* potentially more effective than traditional exposure therapy, which requires that a patient *imagine* traumatic moments despite the fact that "avoidance of cues and reminders of the trauma" is key to a PTSD diagnosis.[138]

> In fact, research on this aspect of PTSD treatment suggests that the inability to emotionally engage (*in imagination*) is a predictor for negative treatment outcomes. [...] VRET offers a way to circumvent the natural avoidance tendency by directly delivering multi-sensory and context-relevant cues that evoke the trauma without demanding that the patient actively try to access his/her experience through effortful memory retrieval. Within a VR environment, the hidden world of the patient's imagination is not exclusively relied upon and VRET may also offer an appealing, non-traditional treatment approach that is perceived with less stigma by "digital generation" service members and veterans who may be reluctant to seek out what they perceive as traditional talk therapies.[139]

In an environment where triggers are delivered to patients in an interactive, performative context, several factors meet, fuse, diffuse, or conflict. Members of the "digital generation" who have grown up playing videogames for pleasure or training are more accustomed to virtual, rather than conventional oral communication ("talk therapy"). These veterans experienced war in a video game *before* experiencing the "real thing," causing reality to always be compared to the virtual (life imitating art), and their status in such a wedge between the virtual and the real is so secured that their only way out of it is through the virtual.

To make some sense of this virtual hyperreality, I return to Gregory Bateson. In *Steps to an Ecology of the Mind*, he describes the "metaphor that is meant," referring to the collapse between symbol and represented object, using "the flag which men will die to save" as an example. I like his example in the context of a discussion of military digital games, because, after all, it is the flag that *America's Army* asks us to "play" for. He continues with a discussion of play that might offer a way back in to an understanding of playing, performing, and reality.[140]

That which would be denoted by the bite – blood, gore, death – is similarly not pointed to in games like *America's Army*. Bateson touches on the power of performativity – the power of the "as if" that *Virtual Iraq* seeks: when the spear comes through the 3D screen, there is no questioning of reality. Consider this feedback from a General after testing the ICT virtual reality equipment: "It feels very real [...] This is the kind of simulation that makes you sweat." The General, therefore "experience[d] the simulation at the emotional and corporeal level" due to "the acuity of the visual and aural interface [which] generated physical responses."[141] In Dan Leonard's analysis, "[t]he sweat of conflict and speed of action during a first-person shooter game are exactly what the ICT researchers hope to achieve in their training sessions."[142]

The problem is: what happens when the bullet goes past your head? Or is this even a problem?

ELECT BiLAT: first-person thinker

More recent work at the ICT works both on the tools needed for counterinsurgency as well as the elimination of the fog of war. *ELECT BiLAT* is one of the more recent (2008) projects at the ICT that "presents an ambitious training agenda for mastering the official procedures for conducting complex bilateral negotiations with Iraqi power brokers." This simulation is a counter-insurgency tool that uses virtual reality to achieve acquiescence or at the very least smooth relations. But the program doesn't just teach trainees how to negotiate; it teaches US military personnel how to negotiate to *get what we want*. Dan Leopard describes a troubleshooting session he sat in on for SASO-ST ("Stability and Support Operations Simulation and Training") at the ICT. The scenario described by Leopard is simple: a commander must inform a field doctor that his clinic must be moved because US forces will be bombing the area soon. The program doesn't really allow for the doctor to win, or for the clinic to stay where it is, or for the US military to change its mission in order to avoid the clinic. And yet the "character" of the doctor is programmed to resist the instructions – hence the lesson in counter-insurgency: the doctor must be brought around; he must not fight against the will of the US military.

> While Dr. Perez can barter and negotiate with the Captain, power ultimately resides with the user. If Dr. Perez fails to comply and move his hospital, with or without the help of the US Army, his location will be bombed in the days to come. [... T]he implication is that Dr. Perez is idealistic and manipulative, wanting to leverage the situation to maximize the benefit to his hospital, and is therefore reluctant to simply comply with the Captain's entreaties to move.[143]

Another mission involves investigating why a local market, built by US forces, is not being used.[144] Students of the program are learning negotiation skills *while* they are essentially researching the social environment they are in. For example, the "student must gather information on the social relationships among the characters in the scenario."[145] The program operates at a distant, and perhaps dangerous, end of the human spectrum; how can a computer replicate the intricacies of face-to-face human interaction, especially in potentially confrontational settings? Leopard's descriptions indicate that it is not easy, that the program has lots of bugs, and that there is no doubt that the best talents brought in by the ICT are faced with a nearly impossible task that they are taking in stride. Project Director Julia Kim describes soldiers in training who go through the program as not quite sure what they are learning and why, but that once they return they report that the program taught them how to deal with the real-life situations they encountered.[146]

"Virtual Torture"

If *ELECT BiLAT* points to the absurdity of an attempt to represent, replicate, and perform such human interaction as intercultural negotiation in a computer program, then Mark Sample's essay on digital games involving interrogation exposes a similarly bizarre project. In "Virtual Torture," Sample describes several digital games, including *Tom Clancy's Splinter Cell* (200), *24: The Game* (2006), and *The Sims* (2000) that involve interrogation and/or torture. *Splinter Cell*, Sample explains, sets up a scenario in which the player – the character Sam Fisher, who is, of course, a veteran interrogator – needs to obtain one or more key codes that will open a door. In order to get these codes, "Fisher" apprehends a guard. The game informs the player whether or not the guard has "useful information" – a code – indicating whether the player should proceed with an interrogation. The game trains the player in interrogation methods with an obvious payoff. Sample argues that "There is a proximity, then, between the site of torture and the site of information efficacy, where the intel is put to use. Such proximity reinforces the notion that not only does torture work well, it works well *now*."[147] Interrogation in *Splinter Cell* is therefore a straightforward, logical, rational, *natural* thing to do. In the game *24*, like the television show it adapts, interrogation and torture appear often and in a similarly "natural" and justifiable way. Players again learn "how" to interrogate and are able to monitor their "progress" in getting the information torture needs in order to be justified. Sample argues that "the way torture-interrogation is modeled in-game and acted out by the player relies on a wishful logic that mirrors official rationales for torture."[148] With a "stress graph," players can track progress. Sample describes the "Cooperation Zone" within which a player obviously wants to get and stay. Here *24: The Game* sounds much like *ELECT BiLAT*, which features comparable monitors that communicate to the user how well the negotiation is going. The intricacies and subtleties of human communication are reduced in both cases to visible, measurable results on a computer screen, the presence of which seems to defy the reality of the minutiae of face-to-face interaction. In stark contrast, Sample also describes a scenario designed by *Sims* player and blogger "Evergrey," who locked two avatars in a "cell-like 'Box'" without light, food, or services. The Evergrey experiment in inaction seems to offer a much more precise monitoring of the effects of torture. Left to rot in the cell, Mr. and Mrs. Victim slowly deteriorate, as observed via a "mood panel" that "distills joy, displeasure, and misery onto eight colorful bar graphs." But Evergrey doesn't want or need any information from the Victims. Instead, this blogger's experiment offers more in the way of information about the dehumanization of the torturer as the victim breaks down under his/her control.

Conclusion

Splinter Cell, *24: The Game*, and *The Sims* all depict torture in a virtual environment. They represent something else, and they offer the opportunity to exist in play, in performance. They are part of the military-industrial-entertainment complex I have described in this chapter. From the Army Experience Center, through military training programs, through drones bombing with the click of a mouse, to re-creating the urban warfare environment for the veteran suffering from PTSD, games and play, rehearsal and performance are the means to no end. They are part of a cycle that constitutes the counter-insurgency culture we live in. In the next chapter I begin with "virtual torture" to consider another cycle: this one dealing in representation and reality, fiction and truth, art and life-war, with a particular focus on "torture."

4

Torture Simulated and Real

Scenes from the Coney Island *Waterboarding Thrill Ride*

Smack in the middle of the Coney Island Arcade (Figure 4.1), Spongebob lies face up on a table. His nemesis, Squidward, stands over him, wearing a mean face and holding a watering can – ready to pour. In a speech bubble Spongebob exclaims, "IT DONT GITMO BETTER." Welcome to the *Waterboarding Thrill Ride* (Figure 4.2).

But Spongebob is only the teaser. He's painted on a wall of a "jail cell" housing the *Thrill Ride*. Riders need to climb three steps to peer through a small opening protected by rusty bars to see what's inside. What they find is not that exciting: a small, dark room with a dirty sink and two mannequins, one in an orange jumpsuit and one in a black hooded sweatshirt. If they follow the directions placed on the outside wall and insert a dollar into a slot, riders will get the full effect: the mannequins start to move; music starts to play (music inspired by the tunes played in detainee cells and during interrogations at Guantánamo Bay[1]); lights come on; the back wall is lit to reveal the message "Don't Worry It's Only a Dream"; and for 15 seconds, the two mannequins reveal their true nature – animatrons. The orange-clad "detainee" convulses as the black-sweatshirted interrogator pours water over the detainee's cloth-covered face (Figure 4.3).

This is waterboarding, folks. Made available to all: "It's about time," says Steve Powers, who designed the 2008 installation for the public art presenter Creative Time, "that this uniquely American ritual of intense water horror, a practice long reserved for New England witches and Al-Qaida brass, was made available to the people."[2] Step right up.

On the day I visited, I spent a good amount of time standing across the street trying to get a decent photo of the storefront. At first, I had to wait

Figure 4.1 A view from across the street of Steve Powers's *Waterboarding Thrill Ride*, which occupied a former photo booth on 12th Street in Coney Island, 2008. Photo by David B. Smith.

Figure 4.2 Behind this painted storefront, animatrons "perform" waterboarding when a dollar is inserted into a slot. The *Waterboarding Thrill Ride* by Steve Powers, Coney Island, 2008. Photo by David B. Smith.

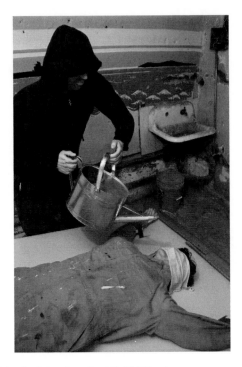

Figure 4.3   Inside the *Waterboarding Thrill Ride* viewers see one animatron pour water over the face of another. The *Waterboarding Thrill Ride* by Steve Powers, Coney Island, 2008. Photo by David B. Smith.

for a few artsy-types to move on. They loitered in front of Spongebob for some minutes (I finally found a good side-angle), conversing about art, Creative Time (the curating body for the piece), commissions, "so interesting," and such talk. By the time I got rid of them and had the "ride" to myself, I was met by two British tourists, male, cameras in tow. They, unlike the previous guests but much like most of the people I saw at the *Ride*, happened upon the project: passersby. Powers later told me that any 15 minutes around the former photo booth yields a sampling of locals and tourists, New Yorkers and internationals, progressing through their very own waterboarding education. The Brits had a sense right away that this was art and it had a point. They faithfully inserted a dollar ("most people only put in one" Powers said) and stuck their heads through the cell bars to witness torture. A quarter of a minute later, they stepped off the small concrete platform looking a bit worse for wear.

Soon a group of teenage girls disrupted the Brits' pensive state with their loud exclamations of laughter and high-pitched yelps (the first at

Figure 4.4   Visitors look through prison bars to see what's inside. The *Waterboarding Thrill Ride* by Steve Powers, Coney Island, 2008. Photo by David B. Smith.

the sight of Spongebob, the second at the word "Waterboard" – that's my guess, anyway, confirmed by Powers's experience at the site). They dared each other to go up the steps – one started to read the informational diagram Powers had created and posted next to the barred window (Figure 4.4). Words like "ew!" and "Oh my god!" were flung into the air. I know, I thought, how *could* that guy do that to that other guy – I mean, animatron. I imagined a conversation I didn't feel like having with the young women – a conversation about torture, about object performance, about Coney Island. But they quickly recovered from their horror at seeing an object being tortured, and moved on down West 12th Street, laughing and squealing. I imagined what else I might say to them: Wait! Don't go! Don't you know that we are living in an annually renewed State of Emergency?[3] Don't you know that terror is all around us, and we are better off waterboarding the bastards in Guantánamo than dying in a Manhattan explosion? Don't you know that torture doesn't work?

Real fiction, fake reality

The contemporary debate about the US government's use of torture has shifted from an express attempt to justify it, through a stated acknowledgement that it constituted torture, to a quiet denial that, evidence suggests, evolved into subsequent cases. As the US public moved from the shame of torture's realities released by the 2004 Abu Ghraib scandal to a feeling that the country, under Obama, is a kinder, gentler nation (a feeling also based in 'truthiness'), the issue of what to do about the past remained. At an April 2009 press conference, President Obama said: "Waterboarding violates our ideals and our values. I do believe that it is torture."[4] His statement was a relief to those concerned about how the new administration would deal with the issue, but over time became cheapened by the Obama Administration's unwillingness to deal with the legacy of the Bush Administration. By 2010, with a broken promise to close the prison at Guantánamo Bay and a soldier, PFC Bradley Manning, in solitary confinement for allegedly leaking military documents to the website Wikileaks, Obama's performed improvement on George W. Bush grew more insincere.

How torture came to be justified and implemented relates directly to the context in which the so-called war on terror was constructed. How was performance used by government and mass media to produce emotional affect? In what ways did such manipulation provide for an environment in which the justification of torture proceeded without incident? Why does the ticking-bomb scenario so successfully rationalize torture? As Diana Taylor points out, "The scenario hides its own theatricality – it passes as urgent, always for the first time, now! – while its power stems from its iterability."[5] Iterability, in this case, allows for the ongoing affective response of fear. How such fear or terror operates on a real level however, combines in troubling ways with fiction, from the reality that waterboarding doesn't *simulate* but *replicates* drowning, to the belief that Jack Bauer's tough-guy torture techniques in the television series *24* "work."

"Lookin' for Jack Bauer"

The website "Wikiality: The Truthiness Encyclopedia," a wiki inspired by comedian Stephen Colbert and his mock news show *The Colbert Report*, includes the following description of the television character Jack Bauer from *24*:

> Some people think Bauer is a TV character, played by Kiefer Sutherland, but that's not true, Jack Bauer is in fact a real person. Bauer had so much awesomeness that all of his lesser qualities didn't fit and therefore had to be put in a second body, and that was how Kiefer Sutherland was made.[6]

Not only does Jack Bauer precede Kiefer Sutherland, he is also indispensable:

> Jack Bauer has been the single greatest asset to the United States in the War on Terror and has made the most significant impact on national security by protecting our nation from future terrorist action.[7]

Stephen Colbert and his wiki fans, however, aren't the only ones proclaiming Jack's existence in the real world. Consider, for example, the following exchange from the 15 May 2007 Republican presidential candidate debate in South Carolina,[8] highlighting the terror attack scenario presented to the candidates by Fox News moderator Brit Hume:

Mr Hume: The questions in this round will be premised on a fictional, but we think plausible scenario involving terrorism and the response to it. Here is the premise: Three shopping centers near major US cities have been hit by suicide bombers. Hundreds are dead, thousands injured. A fourth attack has been averted when the attackers were captured off the Florida coast and taken to Guantanamo Bay, where they are being questioned. US intelligence believes that another larger attack is planned and could come at any time.[9]

Among the responses to Hume's question about how far each candidate would go to get information from the "attackers" was that of Tom Tancredo of Colorado:

Rep. Tancredo: Well, let me just say that it's almost unbelievable to listen to this in a way. We're talking about – we're talking about it in such a theoretical fashion. You say that – that nuclear devices have gone off in the United States, more are planned, and we're wondering about whether waterboarding would be a – a bad thing to do? I'm looking for "Jack Bauer" at that time, let me tell you. (Laughter, applause.)[10]

Tancredo's hyperbole is but one example of politicians and pundits invoking the holy name of Jack Bauer to get out of a jam. In such cases the line between Jack Bauer as 'fictional' and politics as 'real' doesn't seem so distinct. Jon Stewart had a fitting response to Tancredo on his *Daily Show*: "Oh my god – I just figured out the problem with the Republican party: The country *they* want to run is *fictional!*"

Instead of exemplifying theatre's "make-believe," such performances practice what Richard Schechner calls "make-belief," in which "there is an intentional blurring of the boundary between what is fictionalized, constructed, made to order and what might be actually real."[11] There exists a double blur in the contemporary sociopolitical moment, both in the United States and globally. On the one hand, television and other popular mainstream entertainments traditionally accepted as 'not real' – as *representation* of reality, as 'fiction' – have been either designed to be perceived as 'non-fiction' (e.g., reality television) or have been crafted as hyperreal, with such attention *to* reality that they are accepted as a (superior) substitute for 'reality.' On the other hand, what has traditionally been taken for 'reality' – news programs, political campaigns, and so on – have increasingly tended toward the constructed, the fictional. As Kipling Buis points out in his winning contribution to *Vanity Fair*'s 2007 essay contest, which asked "young Americans" to "define our national reality": "Personally, I don't find junk television and video games [that] harmful. Few Americans mistake them for reality. Quite a few Americans mistake our 'serious' news programs for reality, however, so this is where our denial of reality reaches outlandish heights."[12] There is of course much evidence that such trends are older than the early twenty-first century. However, such confusion between 'reality' and 'fiction' has been deployed in devastating ways since the terrorist attacks of 11 September 2001. There has been a move full-circle to a position in which theatre and performance scholars of the twenty-first century, and not (only) historians and journalists, have particular relevance.

To unpack this phenomenon I turn to John Bell's "Performance Studies in an Age of Terror," in which the puppet and object performance scholar explains: "The concept of performance [...] can help us understand and respond to [...] the conscious manipulation of the threat of terror by the United States government both at home and abroad in highly professional propaganda campaigns." It is through such fear-producing tactics that society accepts "the onset of a global war without end on the part of our 'world's largest army.' In performance, we have "concepts, means of analysis, and methods of action which can help us figure out where we are and what we ought to do."[13] Janelle Reinelt similarly argues for the relevance of theatre and performance scholars, arguing that "the tools of our trade can be useful in the broader arenas of public discourse when the highly theatricalized nature of contemporary existence is examined through methodologies developed by our field."[14] Through juxtaposition of the fiction in the popular real-time television series *24* with the resulting reality – based on *24's* fictional template – of military actions, including forms of torture used in interrogations, the difference between "reality" and "fiction" begins to blur, and trying to decide which is Baudrillard's Disneyland becomes difficult. I agree with Janelle Reinelt

> that the present historical moment is in fact specifically and techni-cally theatrical and performative [...] It is not only a conception of theatre as the unreal or merely artificial that is useful for understand-ing contemporary public life, but on the contrary, theatre's capacity for creating a new real, making manifest the real, embodying the real within the realm of images and sensations as well as the realm of discursivity.[15]

I am interested in exploring the tension between the performativity of the "present historical moment" and the potential for performance to disrupt that moment with a "new real."

Blurring fiction and reality in popular entertainment: *24*

> *The torture scenes in* 24 *are obviously based on real incidents such as those inflicted by prison guards and interrogators at Abu Ghraib prison in Iraq, or carried out by foreign government operatives against prisoners "rendered" by the US to other countries. Incidents and allegations of such torture are now found regularly in the pages of US newspapers.*
>
> (blogger Debra Watson[16])

The 'mistaken reality' of *24* operates on several levels. Not only have satirists and politicians alike given Jack Bauer the status of a real per-son, but more problematically, his actions apparently became templates for interrogation performances in the field. According to Lieutenant Colonel Diane Beaver (staff judge advocate), Jack Bauer "'gave people lots of ideas'" during brainstorming sessions at Guantánamo Bay in the Fall of 2002.[17] Philippe Sands, who interviewed Beaver, has also pointed out the "fascinating" timing of the show and events at Guantánamo: "The abusive interrogations started in November 2002, just three weeks after the start of the second series of *24*." It seems, Sands claims, "that there was a direct connection between that program and the creating of an environment in which individuals felt it was permissible to push the envelope."[18] "'We saw it on cable,' Beaver recalled. 'People had already seen the first series. It was hugely popular.' Jack Bauer had many friends at Guantánamo, Beaver added."[19] In the developing history of the war on terror and torture scandals of Bagram, Guantánamo Bay, Abu Ghraib, and so-called black sites around the world, evidence such as Beaver's description of "brainstorming sessions" held to develop interrogation techniques and the "hugely popular" status of *24* remains severely disturbing as they are inherently tied to "make believe" – to improvisation and theatre.

That "reality" was troubled by Jack's tricks became apparent in November 2006, when US military and human rights activists met with *24*'s producers to ask that they reconsider the extensive representation of torture on the program. Soldiers in Iraq and Afghanistan, they explained, were imitating methods seen on the show in their own interrogations. Anthony Kubiak, in his study of theatre and terror, warns of such a troubling case of life imitating art: "This collapse of difference between theatre's terror and the 'theatres of terrorism' describes an important crisis of representation in performance that threatens to subsume and neutralize all possible resistance to state or cultural coercion in performance."[20] Where Kubiak focuses specifically on "theatre" and "terrorism," I suggest thinking more broadly in terms of "popular entertainment" and the "performance of torture." Diana Taylor explains the problems inherent in the connection between fiction and reality in this political moment: "Popular entertainment – television programs, films, and games – places 'us' as co-participants in the drama, asking 'us' to imagine when 'we' too would cross that limit. When did I become swept into this 'we' that debates torture as a legitimate topic and practices it in 'our' name?"[21] Taylor speaks to the particularity of the post-9/11 war on terror psychological "we": in this social grouping the "ordinary" citizen is interpellated to condone what previously was considered – in a past formally governed by the Geneva Conventions – unacceptable. But in the war on terror, "we" participate both in fiction and reality – on TV and in the field.

How did the special mixing of mainstream fictional television and the ideology of the war on terror occur? A 2006 study by the Parents' Television Council documents an increase in primetime scenes involving torture beginning in 2000, but rising sharply after 2001. This trend becomes infinitely more interesting, however, when considered in the context of another Hollywood meeting: The so-called Beverly Hills Summit. On 11 November 2001, Karl Rove, at the time Senior Advisor to the

President, met with dozens of the industry elite at the Beverly Peninsula Hotel with the objective to garner support in Hollywood for the war on terror. Rove outlined seven issues, including:

> that the war is against terrorism, not Islam; that Americans must be called to national service; that Americans should support the troops; that this is a global war that needs a global response; that this is a war against evil; that American children have to be reassured; and that instead of propaganda, the war effort needs a narrative that should be told.[22]

Although certainly not the *only* program to adhere to Rove's suggestions, *24* has become one of the most well-known for touting the "war on terror" line. Interestingly, however, the series was already in development with Fox at the time of the Beverly Hills Summit and its first episode aired the same month. The show is popular and successful, winning Emmy and Golden Globe awards[23] and boasting consistently improved ratings and an average viewership of 11.5 million. Episodes play in dozens of countries around the world: *24*, it seems, responded with enthusiasm to Rove's call for a Hollywood conducive to the White House.

The infamous premise of *24* is real-time: each episode unfolds over one hour of one day. Keeping episodes consecutive proved so important to the show's producers that the 2007 writers' strike caused a one-year delay for the entire seventh season. The show's trademark image is a digital clock ticking away the seconds. The main character, Jack Bauer, is a counter-terrorism expert[24] who, in each "day," or each season of the series, must basically save "America" from various incarnations of threats, from nuclear and biochemical weapons to Muslim extremists and assassins. Plots are unnecessarily complicated, offering a myriad of outcomes and possible plot tangents. The editing style feeds the frantic tone by using split-screen scenes where more than one thread of the plot appears simultaneously. The entire concept of the show enables a constant ticking time bomb scenario. "[C]ommercial breaks," writes Slavoj Žižek,

> contribute to the sense of urgency: the breaks are part of the one-hour temporal continuity. Say the on-screen clock reads "7:46" before the break, we return to the series with the clock saying "7:51" – indicating the real length of the break, as if a live transmission has been interrupted.[25]

While I would argue that the commercial breaks conveniently allow for non-essential business such as driving from one place to another, showers, and meals, Žižek argues that this

> sense of urgency has an ethical dimension [leading to] a kind of suspension of ordinary moral concerns. [...] The CTU agents, as well as their terrorist opponents, live and act in a shadowy space not covered by the law, doing things that "simply have to be done" to save our societies from the threat of terrorism.[26]

Time and time again, what "simply has to be done" or "whatever it takes," translates to torture: Jack and other characters on the show inflict physical and psychological pain on "perceived" enemies – using perception that is so ambiguous that at times Jack has tortured friends and even family members – often garnering unrealistic results of reliable intelligence.

24 and the representation of torture

> *There are more healthcare [workers in the world] involved in the design and the instrumentation of torture than there are involved in providing healing for the survivors. And it is, in many [instances], because healthcare people get engaged and confused by the same ticking timebomb theories that fuel* 24 *and other fantasy programs, which [...] unfortunately seem to be the basis of learning for many of our policymakers. It's fantasy-driven, and it causes people to do stupid things.*
> *(Douglas Johnson in an interview with Amy Goodman[27])*

In the fall of 2006, however, "real life" paid a visit to *24*'s fictional set. Organized by David Danzig of Human Rights First (HRF) as part of the organization's Primetime Torture project and attended by Fox executives, *24* staff, and the US military, the November meeting served to alert *24*'s creative team about a real danger emerging from the representation of torture on the program: US soldiers mimicking the methods used by *24* characters on detainees in the field. According to the Parents Television Council, *24* has aired the highest number of scenes involving torture on primetime television over its six seasons.[28] In her *New Yorker* article exposing the gathering, Jane Mayer describes how an Army general was mistaken for a *24* character:

> US Army Brigadier General Patrick Finnegan, the dean of the United States Military Academy at West Point [...] accompanied by three of

the most experienced military and FBI interrogators in the country, arrived on the set as the crew was filming. At first, Finnegan – wearing an immaculate Army uniform, his chest covered in ribbons and medals – aroused confusion: he was taken for an actor and was asked by someone what time his "call" was.[29]

The "real" general apparently disrupted the process of creating the hyper-real spectacle of counter-terrorism. "A hyperreal," according to Jean Baudrillard, "henceforth sheltered from the imaginary, and from any distinction between the real and the imaginary, leaving room only for the orbital recurrence of models and the simulated generation of differ-ence."[30] The "confusion" caused by the general makes him no longer as real as his mimetic counterparts, who in turn have provided scripts for soldiers to perform on real bodies. "It is by putting an arbitrary stop to this revolving causality," Baudrillard asserts, "that a principle of politi-cal reality can be saved."[31] At least in theory the general's visit should have provided such an arbitrary stop. His trip to the *24* studio – life meeting with art – was intended to communicate the military's concern about television's impact on methods used in the field and to stop the extensive and unrealistic torture scenes on the program.

As part of their research on primetime's real-life effects, Human Rights First reported on their website that "interviews with former interroga-tors and retired military leaders," have revealed that "the portrayal of torture in popular culture is having an undeniable impact on how interrogations are conducted in the field."[32] As news of the November meeting spread after the publication of Mayer's article in February of 2007, mainstream outlets including CNN covered the story, if briefly. CNN anchor and *Situation Room* host Wolf Blitzer invited terrorism ana-lyst and former Special Operations Intelligence Officer Ken Robinson to talk about the influence of popular programs such as *24* on military per-sonnel. Robinson explained: "The United States military is concerned about it because they've started receiving evidence that soldiers in the field have been impacted by it downrange in Iraq, utilizing techniques which they've seen on *24* and then taking them into an environment into the interrogation booth."[33] Also invited were Fox producers and the Department of Defense. Although *24* writer/producer David Fury appeared, saying "[o]ne would think that their [military personnel] training would be far more extensive in the real world and that they understand that this is a heightened reality," the Department of Defense did not, but issued a statement sounding quite like Fury: "Our policy is to treat detainees humanely. Our men and women who handle detainee operations are professionals and they understand the difference between a TV show and reality."[34] However, what evidence continues to reveal, and what former interrogators continue to reiterate is that they indeed *lacked* sufficient training.

The issue of insufficient preparation for the field relates directly to, among other government actions, the executive memorandum signed by President George W. Bush on 7 February 2002. The memo, supported by Assistant Attorney General Jay S. Bybee's memo to Attorney General Alberto Gonzalez on the same day, makes the argument that "the war against terrorism ushers in a new paradigm," in which "none of the provisions of Geneva apply to our conflict with Al Qaeda in Afghanistan or elsewhere throughout the world because, among other reasons, Al Qaeda is not a High Contracting Party to Geneva," although they "would apply to the conflict with the Taliban." Detainees, however, would not be covered: "common Article 3 of Geneva does not apply to either Al Qaeda or Taliban detainees."[35] The memo goes on to deny Al Qaeda or Taliban detainees prisoner of war status, and instead labels them "unlawful combatants" who, in a seemingly ironic twist given the above text, are to be treated "humanely and, to the extent appropriate and consistent with military necessity, in a manner consistent with the principles of Geneva."[36] This and the other infamous "torture memos" developed an amorphous set of "definitions" of what can and cannot be performed upon the bodies of detainees in prisons. Journalist Tim Golden describes the chaotic environment: "You had these young soldiers, [with] very little training, just as the rules were changing, and they weren't told what the new rules were."[37] Soldiers' mimicry of television relates directly to the blank slate, back stage, dark side mentality of the so-called global war on terror. This ambiguity speaks to the prisoner abuse that occurred. In the context of such confusion and disorganization it seems more than plausible that military personnel would have turned to fiction to find templates for reality.

Alex Gibney's documentary *Taxi to the Dark Side* (2007) includes interviews with former interrogators from Bagram Air Force Base and Abu Ghraib who, without formal instruction in interrogation methods – let alone ethics – had to question detainees under enormous pressure for intelligence results. Private Damien Corsetti, who was charged with dereliction of duty, maltreatment, assault, wrongful use of hashish, and performing an indecent act with another person, after serving at Bagram Air Base, was acquitted of all charges in 2006. When he deployed to Afghanistan in the summer of 2002, he was 22. Although he was not an interrogator, he was tasked with questioning detainees. His "[t]raining consisted of one five-hour course."[38] Corsetti explains in *Taxi to the Dark Side*: "My interrogation training consisted of – basically they taught us some approaches, you know, how to get people to talk. And then, here, go. Go watch these guys interrogate, which were the people that we were replacing, for about five, six hours before I did my first interrogation."[39] With such a lack of education there can be little doubt, given the pressure amateur interrogators were under – "Soldiers are dying," Corsetti says he was told, "Get the information" – that these men and women turned to their own imaginations, and to images circulated in popular media. They were presented with the fundamental justification for torture: the ticking time bomb.

Former military interrogator Tony Lagouranis, who also attended the November 2006 meeting at Fox's *24* studio, claims that soldiers pass around DVDs of *24* and other programs.[40] He has further described his own experience of how television has impacted detainee interrogations:

Rapport-building was being used among the [...] more experienced interrogators. [...] But then I got out and worked with other units ... and they weren't as interested in rapport-building. That took too much time, they felt, and it wasn't how they wanted to see themselves as interrogators. They wanted to be like Hollywood interrogators, you know.[41]

[W]hen we were interrogating in Iraq in 2004, we were being told that Geneva Conventions didn't comply. So we didn't have training that informed us what to do anymore, because we were taught according to Geneva Conventions. So people were getting ideas from television. And among the things that I saw people doing that they got from television was water-boarding, mock execution, using mock torture. They wanted to hook up one of our translators to an electric generator and pretend that they were torturing him and allow prisoners to see that so that they thought that they would experience the same thing.[42]

Lagouranis has become an outspoken advocate against the use of improper interrogation techniques and prisoner abuse as well as a somewhat controversial figure since his many appearances on news programs and the publication of his *New York Times* op-ed piece "Tortured Logic" (2006) and book, *Fear Up Harsh: An Army Interrogator's Dark Journey Through Iraq* (2007). He holds an in-between status as an interrogator who claims to have used questionable techniques such as using dogs as threats to detainees; however, he has not been charged with any crime. His claims to have witnessed inappropriate techniques and torture have elicited responses from members of the military wishing to discredit his testimony.[43]

Despite such controversy, Lagouranis has maintained his credibility and has collaborated with David Danzig's Primetime Torture project. One of the key findings of the organization's research is a shift that has occurred in the style of television representation of torture, seen in mainstream shows such as *Alias*, *Lost*, and *Law and Order*. According to Danzig: "it used to be the bad guys who tortured [...] and torture never worked [...] now it's people like Jack Bauer [...] So the message that 18-, 19-, 20-year-old soldiers in Iraq and Afghanistan get is that good guys use this stuff and it works."[44] Instead of associating torture with what the "bad guys" do, reminiscent of pre-9/11 popular films from *The Battle of Algiers* (1966) to *Marathon Man* (1976) and *Midnight Express* (1978), to *Indiana Jones and the Temple of Doom* (1984) and *Death and the Maiden* (1994), torture becomes *justified* in *24*. Another former interrogator and one who, as I discuss below, now trains those looking for "authentic military experiences," Mike Ritz, similarly argues that *24* portrays unrealistic scenarios: "Much like other cop interrogation scenes the American public has witnessed for years," Ritz explains, *24* "relies on cookie-cutter, torture-like interrogations that would seldom work in the real world due to the unreliability of the reactions it provokes in the source and because torturing further complicates the interrogator's ability to 'read' the truth."[45] Ritz's comments acknowledge the problem with representing anything as complicated as torture in popular culture. The simplification or reduction required for a television program or film of an issue like interrogating a terror suspect amounts to a kind of negligence of the popular media, exemplified in the *24* scenes. The show's creators misused scenarios to create unrealistic performances taken for plausible. The conditions needed for such plausibility emerged in the culture of fear maintained by the war on terror; that is, when a society collectively believes the terrorists are anywhere, everywhere, and anyone who will commit mass murder on a moment's notice – a belief supported by the spectacular events on 11 September 2001 – they will also perhaps too easily believe that figures like Jack Bauer need to get tough quick and do the necessary to save populations from mass murder. The military personnel who visited the *24* set, however, knew quite well that "interrogation" is far more complex than any such "scenario."

Although Fox executives found the November 2006 meeting useful, and despite the fact that soldiers have found *24* useful on occasion, one of the most surprising discoveries of the encounter for David Danzig was the revelation that after six seasons, the creators of *24* had never consulted in any thorough or formal manner with military personnel.[46] Other television programs are famous for their "expert" consultations, from *CSI* to *NCIS*. The Primetime Torture project responded to this news by creating a short "training" video for junior soldiers featuring scenes from *24* and other television programs alongside interviews with military educators and former interrogators who distinguish between acceptable and unacceptable practices.[47] It is interesting to note that despite good intentions, HRF falls back on the circulation of popular mainstream entertainment in order to de-program soldiers, who, recalling David Fury and the Department of Defense, should already know better. Baudrillard's cycle continues.

The ticking time bomb

A close look at a particular season of *24* – Day Four, first aired in 2005 – had the most per-episode torture scenes of the show's first six seasons.[48] Day Four concerns a terrorist plot to cause nuclear reactors around the United States to melt down, threatening to kill hundreds of thousands if not millions of people. In order to uncover the core mission of the plot, however, the Los Angeles branch of the Counter-Terrorism Unit or CTU, a fictional wing of the CIA[49] charged with investigating domestic terrorism threats, undergoes constant twists and turns – incessant overstimulation with impossible situations hourly. Such a plotline, through the production of multiple imminent threats, creates a relentless ticking time-bomb scenario. Although the ticking time bomb has been exposed as a "million-to-one scenario" and "so exceptional it is all but mythical," it "has been firmly lodged in the public debate as likely and common."[50] An example of the ticking time bomb occurs early in season four when Jack Bauer breaks into an interrogation room, shoots a suspect in the leg, and demands answers. Writhing in pain, the suspect confesses that the target of the moment is the Secretary of Defense – *success*.

Ticking time bombs are dramatic, even melodramatic, and the formula is reproduced in a variety of creative ways, applying to each of the threats posed on each hour of the series. Each scene of *24* can be analyzed on several levels, and contradictions abound. These characteristics make the pace and plot even more frantic. Anyone can be an enemy, from the stereotypical "Arab" to your co-worker. Fathers doubt sons, wives doubt husbands. At any time, a CTU analyst can break the wrong rule and get sent to "holding." Mistrust makes it hard to distinguish between "good guys" and "bad guys." Jack Bauer can break the rules (at one point in season four he "quits" his job so that he can torture without "consequences"). Jack Bauer contradicts what common sense knows to be the case: that the ticking time bomb is not a common event, and that torture doesn't work. And yet he is confronted with the ticking time bomb over and over again. He – and *24* – break all the rules, and keep everything in check, terrorizing and delighting fans.

The post-9/11 versions of the ticking time bomb repeatedly performed in *24* find support in the fantastic war-on-terror scenarios in contemporary US politics, from Senator Hillary Clinton's "3a.m." commercial, aired during the 2008 presidential primary campaign, to the late Tim Russert's fictional quandary presented to Democratic candidates at the September 2007 debate held in New Hampshire:

> Imagine the following scenario. We get lucky. We get the number three guy in Al Qaeda. We know there's a big bomb going off in America in three days, and we know this guy knows where it is. Don't we have the right and responsibility to beat it out of him? You could set up a law where the president could make a finding or could guarantee a pardon.[51]

The answers to the question are not as interesting as Russert's *24*-like twist: he subsequently revealed that he was actually citing someone else's scenario: former President Bill Clinton. In a later interview on *Meet the Press*, Bill Clinton remarked:

> You know, there's a one in a million chance that you might be alone somewhere, and you're Jack Bauer on "24." That's the Jack Bauer example, right? It happens every season with Jack Bauer, but to – in the real world it doesn't happen very much. If you have a policy which legitimizes this, it's a slippery slope and you get in the kind of trouble we've been in here with Abu Ghraib, with Guantanamo, with lots of other examples.[52]

Jack Bauer isn't *real*; he's *realer than real*. Torture, it follows, is just a scenario. What falls out of the conversation in such an unending cycle of hypotheticals is the actual effectiveness of torture. Ben Saul reminds us:

> Debating the effectiveness of torture immediately concedes that torture may be morally permissible if it works. Nonetheless, since arguments for its effectiveness continue to be loudly voiced, it is necessary to combat such arguments, even if it means getting our hands dirty

in the process. Experienced interrogators know that torture produces misinformation rather than information, since victims of torture will confess to anything to make it stop. This could jeopardize rather than protect public safety, as investigators waste precious time chasing up false leads. Torture fell into disuse historically because it didn't work.[53]

How exactly torture *doesn't* work is complicated in itself: consider for example the case of the Algerian nationalist group, the FLN, which, during the Algerian war for independence, trained their members to withhold information and withstand torture for only 24 hours, during which time the information would be made useless by the FLN and after which time the detainee was free to give the French whatever they asked for. Despite the justifications of torture in "real life" propagated by Alan Dershowitz, John Parry, and others,[54] a sounder argument comes from Harvard constitutional law professor Charles Fried: "torture is horrible, immoral, and causes the total meltdown of our human inhibitions and about how we treat each other."[55] More troubling is the difference – so eroded in *24* – between the representation of torture and actual torture. In her study of Argentina's Dirty War and representations of spectacle, violence, and torture, Diana Taylor argues that such depictions operate in danger of replicating the very trauma they wish to expose.[56] The debate *about* torture functions through the hypothetical, through the scenario, and therefore always remains distanced from consequences on real bodies and minds.

In his essay "Torture Makes the Man," political science scholar Darius Rejali analyzes how torture operates, focusing on masculinity and strength as particular qualities of the nature of the torturer, arguing that:

> [V]iolence, and torture in particular, requires and generates a kind of manly strength. Briefly put, this is the view that only a real man knows what needs to be done and doing torture is the evidence that one is a real man.[57]

Citing interviews with interrogators alongside torture narratives in literature, Rejali contrasts "the theme of manliness"[58] with weakness. In the case of *24*'s season four such "weakness" is represented by an indecisive vice-president who must step up to the plate when the president's plane is shot down. Jack Bauer, on the other hand, embodies manly strength and sacrifice, making the tough decision to torture his girlfriend's estranged husband in order to obtain supposedly vital information that can prevent catastrophe. "Kiefer Sutherland seems to have a level of success with torture of which most torturers can only dream," Rejali writes.[59] Jack is not just a man; he's immortal; inhuman – or, as Stephen Colbert claims, "Jack Bauer is the epitome of awesome" (Wikiality). The play of power, morality, and masculinity that surrounds Jack Bauer is just that. *24's mise-en-scène* is phantasmagoria: constant manifestations of identities that simultaneously reinforce and subvert a stereotype. What remains consistent is the "real" figure for fans to "believe" in: the uber-patriot Jack Bauer.

Lurking in the background of the show is "the [...] worry that we have become sissies and our enemies know it."[60] Rejali refuses any validity of the ticking time bomb, explaining that its useful value is inextricably tied to a masculine anxiety:

> [T]he story of the ticking timebomb [...] fills one with reassurance. Only real men will have the courage to torture. Ultimately the ticking timebomb is not simply a scenario that furnishes a justification for torture. If that was the case, it would have disappeared long ago since such cases are so uncommon. [... T]his thought experiment is not so much a description of a likely real scenario, but a rite of manhood, a moral test of character. That is why many soldiers, lawyers, and professors – usually all men – are drawn to it. Only real men will say "yes" to the question "will you torture in this case?", affirming it with their life.[61]

Although Rejali insists that it is "usually men" who "are drawn" to the ticking time bomb and the necessity (and fantastic success) of torture, his argument relies on a normative construction of masculinity. There is a play with power and masculinity throughout *24*, manifested in binary relationships and with both sexes, including the ever-airborne president, the weak and underground-bunker vice-president; the out-of-shape and cowardly Edgar (an analyst) who is jealous of the butch analyst Chloe as they both type furiously at their computer stations; the hypermasculine Jack Bauer and the 'soft' husband of Bauer's girlfriend Audrey; and so on. Slavoj Žižek calls Jack Bauer "homo sacer," referring to Giorgio Agamben's idea of those who can be killed but not sacrificed; those whose lives are no longer subject to the law.[62]

In the end, *24* is a simulacrum; it is not *about* the "war on terror," it *is* the war on terror (and the "real" war on terror, after Baudrillard, "does not take place"[63]). It makes the war on terror, narrates it, defines it, explains it, and justifies it. The ticking bomb is a scenario, after all, and, as Diana Taylor writes, "Scenarios are hypothetical; rather than offer evidence or reproducible findings they reveal deep social imaginaries, fears, and desires."[64] More insidious is Taylor's observation that "[t]he scenario hides its own theatricality – it passes as urgent, always for the first time, now! – while its power stems from its iterability."[65] The repetition of ticking bombs on *24* contributes to the complicity – both subtle and overt – of its audience in the justification of torture in the field. The appearance in season five – albeit a cameo – by anti-torture advocate Senator John McCain produced more than a bit of a contradiction. But that is *24's* appeal – crossing political, age, and cultural lines – making everyone happy, everyone "safe."

As if the evidence that interrogators 'train' by watching *24* isn't bizarre enough, a July 2008 *Slate* article – with more than a touch of irony – attributes the entire US torture policy in the war on terror to Jack Bauer:

> The most influential legal thinker in the development of modern American interrogation policy is not a behavioral psychologist, international lawyer, or counterinsurgency expert. Reading both Jane Mayer's stunning *The Dark Side* [2008] and Philippe Sands' *The Torture Team* [2008], I quickly realized that the prime mover of American interrogation doctrine is none other than the star of Fox television's *24*: Jack Bauer.
>
> This fictional counterterrorism agent – a man never at a loss for something to do with an electrode – has his fingerprints all over US interrogation policy. As Sands and Mayer tell it, the lawyers designing interrogation techniques cited Bauer more frequently than the Constitution.[66]

There seems to be nothing left that can't be explained by Jack Bauer's greatness. Greatness, in turn, is defined by Jack Bauer. Even the real-life Jack Bauer, Jack Idema, could never live up to the character. Idema, who served nearly three years in jail in Afghanistan for imprisoning and supposedly torturing detainees on behalf of Afghan and US officials, is known more as a fraud and imposter than any sort of "hero."[67] An astonishing endorsement for Jack Bauer came in the summer of 2006 in the form of a right-wing reaction by politicians, intellectuals, and pundits to widening criticism of *24* in 2006. In an uncanny case of "make-belief," the conservative Washington think-tank The Heritage Foundation hosted a panel discussion on *24* in June 2006 entitled: "24 and America's Image in Fighting Terrorism: Fact, Fiction, or Does it Matter?" The panel, moderated by Rush Limbaugh, included Heritage Foundation fellows, *24* cast members, and Fox producers. In his introduction to special guest

Homeland Security Secretary Michael Chertoff, Heritage Foundation Executive Vice-President Phil Truluck posed a question "sent in" by an audience member: "Would it be considered unethical to clone Jack Bauer?" to which Secretary Chertoff jokingly responded, "We're doing it already," garnering a response in the audience of "laughter [and] light applause."[68] Chertoff went on to tell the audience that the most realistic aspects of *24* were the stressful moments of decision-making but ultimate perseverance: "American history shows that we cannot be defeated in a fight unless we lose our nerve or we lose our will."[69] He added, however, that in 'real life' nothing gets done in 24 hours (lest we start to think the war on terror might come to an end).

As the conversation ensued, panel members revealed that "real" terrorism analysts envy the resources of CTU, citing how efficiently computers work and how advanced their technology is. Panel member James Jay Carafano, Senior Research Fellow at the Heritage Foundation, told participating *24* cast members: "I talked to some of the guys that worked at the National Counterterrorism Center [...] and they all love the show, and they're all terribly envious because all of your technology works so well. I mean, it's all instant."[70] On *24*, satellites respond immediately; they can penetrate concrete walls and even the ground. Perhaps there is comfort in the show – in knowing that *someone* out there is taking care of the "threat."

This is precisely where an "arbitrary stop" to Baudrillard's endless cycle of simulacra must occur – this is where theatre's make-believe really does need to be separated from reality. This is how to avoid Kubiak's collapse of difference "between theatre's terror and the 'theatres of terrorism,'" which presents "an important crisis of representation in performance that threatens to subsume and neutralize all possible resistance to state or cultural coercion in performance." It is the theatre expert, the performance scholar, who can uniquely recognize when *reality is theatre* in an important, if desperate attempt to articulate the difference between the two. How else can a "new real" be found but in the moment of theatre – in the playfulness of acknowledging that *here* is performance and *there* is an audience. In that moment of defamiliarization, perhaps "a principle of political reality can be saved." The idea that there may be hope in interruption – an idea inherent in Brechtian defamiliarization – provides a needed separation in the context of unending cycles of simulation. In a different context, interruption is the source of something much more sinister. Interruption in fact defines a form of torture that is in itself a performance – a simulation – waterboarding.

"Mock Death": waterboarding, performance, exception

You may have read by now the official lie about this treatment [water-boarding], which is that it "simulates" the feeling of drowning. This is not the case. You feel that you are drowning because you are drowning – or, rather, being drowned, albeit slowly and under controlled conditions and at the mercy (or otherwise) of those who are applying the pressure. The "board" is the instrument, not the method.

(Christopher Hitchens, "Believe Me, It's Torture"[71])

"I was a big supporter of waterboarding."

(Dick Cheney, 14 February 2010[72])

In the current US "state of exception" executive power has wielded unprecedented force to curtail rights and, essentially, limit democracy. One of the most important post-9/11 government actions is the 13 November 2001 "Detention, Treatment, and Trial of Certain Non-Citizens in the War Against Terrorism" military order, through which the White House cast a wide net "to protect the United States and its citizens," justifying the detention of non-citizen individuals who have "engaged in, aided or abetted, or conspired to commit, acts of international terrorism, or acts in preparation therefore," among other qualifications. Key to the document is Bush's claim "that it is not practicable to apply in military commissions under this order the principles of law and the rules of evidence generally recognized in the trial of criminal cases in the United States district courts." Instead, "individuals subject to this order," will only "be tried for violations of the laws of war and other applicable laws by military tribunals," such as the prosecution of Salim Ahmed Hamdan, Osama bin Laden's former chauffeur, completed in August 2008. The November 2001 order set the stage for the rounding up and transporting around the world of those who have become known as "enemy combatants," a term used in the US in the past, but specially applied since 9/11 to those suspected of having Al Qaeda or Taliban connections. These measures exemplify how, as José Muñoz describes, "the state stages the state of exception to naturalize and justify unchecked and abusive manifestations of power amid a general scene of savage social asymmetry."[73] Within this state, in which supreme executive power is "naturalized," detainees – as the media has made spectacularly known since the release of the Abu Ghraib photos – have not, as the November 2001 order assures, been "treated humanely," but instead, on numerous occasions, been subjected to torture, or "enhanced interrogation techniques," including a variety of methods from sensory deprivation, forced nudity, and electrocution to the technique known as "water torture," "the water cure," "the waterfall," "the barrel," *el submarino* (or the wet submarine), dunking, forced ingestion,[74] and, of course, "waterboarding."[75]

Although used as a form of torture for centuries, from the Spanish Inquisition to the US invasion of the Philippines at the turn of the twentieth century, to World War II and Vietnam, waterboarding has resurfaced as a contested subject in the US "war on terror" rhetoric. Further, the technique has inspired a sort of fascination among military personnel, journalists, politicians, and even artists. Waterboarding, or the process during which an interrogator or torturer pours water directly onto the covered (usually by cloth) face of a detainee, is justified and facilitated by both the actual and imagined state-of-emergency since the 11th of September 2001. The people – the bodies – subjected to waterboarding are the "bare life": "those whose suffering," as Jill Lane writes, "and sometimes death – articulates the juridical, social, or political boundaries of the state itself."[76]

The November 2001 military order, according to Agamben, "radically erases any legal status of the individual, thus producing a legally unnamable and unclassifiable being."[77] Detainees therefore become *homo sacer*. "Neither prisoners not persons accused, but simply 'detainees,' they are the object of a pure de facto rule, of a detention that is indefinite not only in the temporal sense but in its very nature as well, since it is entirely removed from the law and from judicial oversight."[78] Agamben credits Judith Butler's analysis in *Precarious Life*, in which she shows that "in the detainee at Guantánamo, bare life reaches its maximum indeterminacy."[79] The detainees – "those who are held in waiting, those for whom waiting may well be without end,"[80] are in-between; they are "living dead," or, as Slavoj Žižek described Khalid Shaikh Mohammed, "creature[s] legally dead while biologically still alive."[81] "The very body of *homo sacer* is," as Agamben writes, "in its capacity to be killed but not sacrificed, a living pledge to his subjection to a power of death."[82]

In its capacity to bring a life to the brink of death and back in a very short period of time, waterboarding provides what seems, ironically, an appropriate action upon the *homo sacer*: it creates a physical manifestation of the "living dead," forcing the detainee to exist, quite literally, if momentarily, in-between life and death. Waterboarding produces a body that is in-between legitimacy and exception. It is, therefore, an action that performs the in-between-ness that characterizes the *homo sacer* – it creates the in-between state; it manifests an example of in-between-ness.

Described by some as "simulated drowning,"[83] waterboarding's recent notoriety hinges precisely on its collapse between what is "real" and what is "simulated." Like Baudrillard's simulated illness, the performance of waterboarding "produces 'true' symptoms,'"[84] which will always ultimately lead to actual death. As described by Malcolm Nance, who "personally led, witnessed and supervised waterboarding of hundreds of people" at the US Navy's SERE (Survival, Evasion, Resistance Escape) school in San Diego, during waterboarding "the lungs are actually filling with water"; rather than any kind of simulation, the technique involves "slow-motion suffocation with enough time to contemplate the inevitability of blackout and expiration. When done right, it is controlled death."[85]

Waterboarding: the worst form of torture, and our favorite

And this is why Alfred McCoy cites waterboarding as the "worst form of torture": because it accesses a "primal fear of death by drowning," a fear so great that it causes death sooner than it would naturally come.[86] McCoy argues that it is the most cruel form of torture. Such a practice, it follows, becomes the most rehearsed (the favorite) of the torture techniques – in one's head, in society, in politics, and in art. Performers and audiences alike gravitate toward waterboarding. Amnesty International created a scene of waterboarding for a 2008 advertisement (Sweney, 2008: n.p.); a British reality show had contestants undergo the process because "pain is great to watch."[87] The "mock death" produced by waterboarding has driven some to simulate the process in order to debunk the idea that it is a simulation.

Since 2004 the idea of waterboarding has consumed the popular imagination around the world with an especially ambivalent existence in the United States. The images and emotions associated with waterboarding – pouring water over a hooded face – quickly became repulsive reminders on a global scale of a clear example of torture. But in the United States, the revelation that CIA interrogators had performed "waterboarding," among other techniques, on detainees, coincided with a sudden reluctance of journalists to characterize such actions as torture. A 2010 Harvard study researched how newspapers described the practice over decades and found that despite the fact that for most of the twentieth century, "there was consensus within the print media that waterboarding was torture," there was an abrupt change in 2004 "despite the fact that the editors themselves seem to have still been convinced that waterboarding was torture, often labeling it as such in their editorials."[88] Waterboarding therefore made a fantastic entrance into the popular imagination: it was a known phenomenon that was perceived as something new – because it had been given a new name. It was Demi Moore's training in *GI Jane* (1997) and an innocent detainee's nightmare in *Rendition* (2007). In his etymological investigation of the word, William Safire asked political science professor Darius Rejali what he thought of the old trick with a new name. Rejali answered:

"There is a special vocabulary for torture. When people use tortures that are old, they rename them and alter them a wee bit. They invent slightly new words to mask the similarities. This creates an inside club, especially important in work where secrecy matters. Waterboarding is clearly a jailhouse joke. It refers to surfboarding" – a word found as early as 1929 – "they are attaching somebody to a board and helping them surf. Torturers create names that are funny to them."[89]

Waterboarding is therefore performative on several levels. The practice exists somewhere between a simulation of drowning – a "not the real thing" – and "controlled death" – a term grounded in reality. Indeed, the justifications for using waterboarding teeter between the idea that it is not a harmful technique since it only "simulates" drowning, and yet those who have experienced it call it something beyond a reference to drowning and more like actually drowning. The fascination waterboarding has inspired in the twenty-first century has led to more simulation and representation, from the waterboarding simulations of former interrogator Mike Ritz to the work of theatre and performance artists who have incorporated the technique into their work.[90] I would like to consider several incidents of waterboarding in order to interrogate the apparent viability of the technique as a subject for the media[91] and to analyze what if any potential the performance of the practice might hold for disrupting what José Muñoz describes as the "political moment we currently live in, where the state mobilizes political theatre in lieu of truth and often against obvious and open dishonesty."[92] First, I will address the recent admission by the US government that certain detainees have been subjected to waterboarding; I will then turn to several examples of "simulated" waterboarding in very different contexts. These include cases in which waterboarding "is" performance as well as examples of waterboarding "as" performance.

My analysis of waterboarding and performance begins not with an original event since the technique has been in use for centuries, but with what feels somewhat like a starting point in the context of the war on terror. I consider: (1) the 2004 admission by the US government that detainees Khalid Sheikh Mohammed, Abu Zubaydah, Abd al-Rahim al-Nashiri, and Ibn al Shaykh al-Libi[93] were subjected to waterboarding in 2002 and 2003 (KSM et al.); (2) the SERE (Survival, Evasion, Resistance, Escape) US Navy training school in San Diego where waterboarding is simulated for training purposes; (3) the case of Dan Levin, formerly acting assistant attorney general, who underwent waterboarding in a controlled environment on a military base outside of Washington, DC in 2004 because he "became so concerned about the controversial interrogation technique of waterboarding that he decided to experience it firsthand"[94]; (4) the protest carried out by Iranian-American activist Maboud Ebrahimzadeh during which fellow activists poured water over his plastic- and cloth-covered face as he lay with his head angled below his feet; (5) the experiment by Christopher Hitchens, in which he too underwent waterboarding under controlled conditions, documented in *Vanity Fair* magazine and extensively on its website[95]; and (6) Installation artist Steve Powers's *Waterboarding Thrill Ride*, in which a "former photo booth" in Coney Island was "redesigned to look like a jail cell"[96] in which viewers could insert a dollar to activate "an animatronic diorama depicting a prisoner being waterboarded," behind an outside wall displaying a graffiti-style mural of Spongebob Squarepants being waterboarded while exclaiming, "It don't GITMO better!" Each of these actions, experiments, simulations, and the like, reveal how the use of the visual and sensory realms in performance disengage textual rhetoric about definitions and justifications of "torture." The firmly lodged and terrifying image of the "water torture" doesn't *risk* replication of its own terror, it performs it without a doubt in simulation.

(1) KSM et al.

the individual is bound securely to an inclined bench [...] The individual's feet are generally elevated. A cloth is placed over the forehead and eyes. Water is then applied to the cloth in a controlled manner. As this is done, the cloth is lowered until it covers both the nose and mouth. Once the cloth is saturated and completely covers the mouth and nose, the air flow is slightly restricted for 20 to 40 seconds due to the presence of the cloth. This causes an increase in carbon dioxide level in the individual's blood. This increase in the carbon dioxide level stimulates increased effort to breathe. This effort plus the cloth produces the perception of "suffocation and incipient panic," i.e., the perception of drowning. The individual does not breathe water into his lungs. During those 20 to 40 seconds, water is continuously applied from a height of [12 to 24] inches. After this period, the cloth is lifted, and the individual is allowed to breathe unimpeded for three or four full breaths. The sensation of drowning is immediately relieved by the removal of the cloth. The procedure may then be repeated. The water is usually applied from a canteen cup or small watering can with a spout. [... T]his procedure triggers an automatic physiological sensation of drowning that the individual cannot control even though he may be aware that he is in fact not drowning. [I]t is likely that this procedure would not last more than 20 minutes in any one application.[97]

On 5 February 2008, CIA Director Michael Hayden testified before the Senate Intelligence Committee that waterboarding had been used on three detainees: Khalid Sheikh Mohammed (who apparently was waterboarded 183 times), Abu Zubaydah (83 times), and Abd al-Rahim al-Nashiri (at least twice), in 2002 and 2003.[98] First reported on in 2004,[99] this acknowledgment confirmed what many suspected, and was justified, Hayden explained, by "the belief that additional catastrophic attacks against the homeland were imminent."[100] Hayden's remarks support the ticking-bomb mentality used to justify torture for decades but heavily relied upon in the post-9/11 era.

The ticking bomb is a fiction deployed to legitimate the state of exception's wielding of power over the *homo sacer*. I return to Diana Taylor's point that instead of appearing with its own theatricality, the scenario "passes as urgent, always for the first time, now!" and its performance wields power.[101] Using the fiction of the scenario is precisely how Attorney General nominee Michael Mukasey dodged the question of whether waterboarding should always be considered torture and always be considered illegal. In a letter to the Senate Judiciary Committee after his confirmation hearing, Mukasey wrote:

hypotheticals are different from real life, and in any legal opinion the actual facts and circumstances are critical. [... L]egal questions must be answered based solely on the actual facts, circumstances, and legal standards presented. A legal opinion based on hypothetical facts and circumstances [...] has scant practical effect or value.[102]

For Mukasey, what waterboarding *is*, and whether it is justified must always depend on "hard facts," while the CIA has argued that the government's use of the technique was indeed justified by the "*belief* that additional catastrophic attacks against the homeland were imminent."

The case *for* torture, *for* waterboarding, *relies* on the *hypothetical*, on the *scenario*, as proponents of torture such as Alan Dershowitz and John Parry have demonstrated.[103] The CIA was allowed to use waterboarding in cases where other techniques were not working, there was "credible intelligence that a terrorist attack is imminent," and "substantial and credible indicators the subject has actionable intelligence that can prevent, disrupt or delay this attack" were present.[104]

(2) SERE training

It will disappoint *24* fans to know that not only does Jack Bauer *not* use the one torture method that has so effectively captured the US imagination in recent years, but also that his methods, dreamed up in Fox Television's offices, have not been the *only* ones used on unlawful combatants in Afghanistan, Iraq, Guantánamo Bay, and various "black sites" around the world. Instead, much of the post-9/11 torture program has engaged in a different kind of mimicry: the use of SERE school techniques. During SERE training, military operatives are exposed to various techniques with the objective that by undergoing such torture, they will be prepared in case they are captured by an enemy.[105] Although the development of these techniques was intended for *training* US military and not for *use* on US enemies, the scripts provided by SERE helped to fill the post-9/11 void. So the simulation of torture in a controlled environment was subsequently simulated in the field. On yet another level, representations such as Demi Moore's SERE training in *GI Jane* and, more recently, Coco Fusco's performance *A Room of One's Own* and related documentary *Operation Atropos*, among others (see Figure 4.5), differ only by a matter of degree in the performance of simulation. The most infamous technique in the current torture debate, waterboarding, further complicates things because it is defined as a "simulation" of drowning.

As one of the torture techniques that some Navy trainees are subjected to at the SERE school, waterboarding, Christopher Hitchens writes, has been, "[u]ntil recently [...] something Americans did to other Americans." Its very inability to be simulated without consequences is precisely why the military uses the process to prepare soldiers. Apparently, however, such simulations have, in the post-9/11 state of exception, been redeployed as scripts to be followed. In an interview with author Philippe Sands, Lieutenant Colonel Diane Beaver revealed that during brainstorming sessions at Guantánamo Bay intended to develop interrogation techniques, "Ideas came from all over. Some derived from personal training experiences, including [...] SERE."[106] Military imitates life imitates military.

Figure 4.5   A Room of One's Own: Women and Power in the New America, perform-ance by Coco Fusco, 2006–2008. Photo by Eduardo Aparicio.

The investigation of just how the Department of Justice issued legal memos allowing for the use of waterboarding has revealed that in fact the performance of waterboarding in the "field" on "enemy combatants" was quite different from the practice in the context of SERE training. It was not a technique included on every syllabus, but one demonstrated on a very limited number of students, and one that had been discontinued by all programs except for the Navy's SERE training regime "because of its dramatic effect on the students who were subjects."[107] Government reports have made clear that the training methods intended to teach military personnel how to "evade, resist, and escape" do not amount to the same phenomenon practiced in terrorist suspect interrogations. Even students who understood that they were undergoing a simulated exercise of simulated drowning were traumatized enough by the expe-rience that the SERE program limited and/or stopped its use. For the practice to be employed in the context of a detainee who does *not* know whether or to what extent the experience is controlled clearly consti-tutes torture. So it is important to recognize the mistaken similarity of waterboarding in the context of SERE versus the field interrogation – that is, a performance based on a training technique – while distin-guishing the cruelty of waterboarding in the field. The difference is both mental and physical; a detainee would *not* have any sense that an interrogator did *not* clearly intend for the "feeling" of drowning to lead to death, as well as the "tougher" exercise of waterboarding in the context of actual interrogation covering both the nose and mouth of the victim as opposed to the SERE practice of blocking just the nose.

(3) The politician

The Kafkaesque nature of the waterboarding debate is only augmented by the simulation of the practice for political or artistic ends. Put simply, the question of "whether" waterboarding is torture has been answered time and time again by first-hand experience. The first example of such a performance involves Dan Levin, formerly acting assistant attorney general, who underwent waterboarding in a controlled environment on a military base outside of Washington, DC in 2004. While working on the Justice Department's policy on torture, Levin, according to ABC News, "became so concerned about the controversial interrogation technique of waterboarding that he decided to experience it firsthand," and traveled to a "military base near Washington [where he] underwent the procedure."[108] After the experience, Levin "concluded waterboarding could be illegal torture unless performed in a highly limited way and with close supervision." He further "believed the Bush Administration had failed to offer clear guidelines for its use."[109] Levin did not, in the end, declare without exception that the practice is always unjustifiable, always illegal, and always torture. However, his qualifications around the practice and attempt to place limits on the context of its use coincided with his firing from the Justice Department after Attorney General Alberto Gonzales took office.

(4) The protester

In contrast to Levin's private performance and subsequent refusal to even comment specifically on the experience are several examples of highly visible "simulations" of waterboarding. The first, ironically, was staged outside Levin's former place of employment: the Justice Department. On 5 November 2007, just days before the confirmation of Attorney General Michael Mukasey, Iranian-American activist Maboud Ebrahimzadeh allowed fellow protestors to act out a scene of interrogation and, upon Ebrahimzadeh's staged resistance, pour water over his plastic- and cloth-covered face as he lay with his head angled below his feet. Later, Ebrahimzadeh told reporters: "This is easily the most terrifying experience I've ever had, ever felt, and although it's a controlled environment when water goes into your lungs and you want to scream and you can't, cause you know as soon as you do, you are going to choke."[110] The contrast in the performance between the pre-torture interrogation during which a female protestor yells at Ebrahimzadeh, demanding "give me the names," in a poorly acted, hokey style, and the *actual* distress inflicted on Ebrahimzadeh while water is poured over his covered face is astonishing – despite the fact that he was partially protected by plastic. In this performance theatre's make-believe falls short of political efficacy, leaving only the action of waterboarding – with its real-life effects on a particular body – to enact political protest in front of a government building.

Other antiwar protests have included waterboarding "demonstrations," such as an event on the UCLA campus organized by World Can't Wait.[111] This event employed more theatre than other demonstrations by fastening a plastic mask on the cloth cover held over the victim's face. The mask appears more effective at protecting the protestor-victim than Ebrahimzadeh's plastic cover. Spectators therefore *thought* they were watching a real demonstration of waterboarding, but protestors quickly inform the audience that what they saw was *not* real, and that in fact if the man lying on the ground had been waterboarded he would most likely be unconscious. The effect of using theatre to make the audience *believe* that what they witnessed was theatrical – that is, the prelude of protestor-actors yelling at the victim with demands for "information" led *not* to the performance of waterboarding, but only theatrical representation of the technique. The protestor leading the demonstration asks the audience whether they think waterboarding is torture, and the audience replies "yes!" loudly, making clear that real waterboarding wasn't necessary for them to "believe." Steven Lane, a protestor from Montgomery Peace action, has used a similar cloth-mask in waterboarding demonstrations, including one "for" California senator Diane Feinstein as she walked from her limousine to the CNN studio. Feinstein had recently said she would be voting for Mukasey. On her way to the door, protestors cut Feinstein off, "at the same time revealing Steve Lane being held to a board with a gallon of water being poured in his face. Feinstein put on her best plastic smile and hurried on."[112] In an ironic twist, the same protestor, Steven Lane, was forbidden by the National Park Service from demonstrating waterboarding in 2009. A permit issued by the Department of the Interior for the 25 June 2009 anti-torture event specifically stated that a "Waterboarding exhibit will not be allowed for safety reasons."[113] By citing "safety reasons" the government makes clear that there is a problem with the practice.

(5) The journalist

In some ways the experiment by Christopher Hitchens, documented in *Vanity Fair* magazine and extensively on its website, is similar to Maboud

Ebrahimzadeh's experience. However, instead of directly performing 'protest' in the service of a particular result, Hitchens had motivations more in line with Daniel Levin. As a way of "[e]xploring this narrow but deep distinction" between waterboarding as "something that Americans were being trained to *resist*, not to *inflict*," the journalist signed a waiver and traveled to North Carolina to experience first-hand what all the fuss was about.[114] "I have to be opaque about exactly where I was," he writes, pointing out the safety nets he nevertheless had in place: "I knew I could stop the process at any time."[115] Even so, the waiver stated that safety measures "may fail and even if they work properly they may not prevent Hitchens from experiencing serious injury or death," a fact that made Hitchens particularly nervous. He didn't last long – literally seconds – as opposed to Khalid Sheikh Mohammed, whom Hitchens claims might have lasted up to two minutes (a story "not confirmed").[116] Hitchens, like Ebrahimzadeh, quickly discarded the "simulated drowning" idea: you are "being drowned, albeit slowly and under controlled conditions and at the mercy (or otherwise) of those who are applying the pressure." He concludes: "The 'board' is the instrument, *not* the method. You are not being boarded. You are being watered."[117]

There are many other examples of waterboarding performances – a web search produces queues of examples. Shorts include the conservative talk-show host Mancow Muller's showy demonstration, which begins a bubbly "let's go" pre-waterboard attitude that turns into an eerie stillness when the water is poured over his face, finally ending with his admission that clearly the technique is torture and that he "wouldn't have done it if he knew." There are examples from the world of performance art and buddies just trying it out. Titles of videos include "Voluntary Waterboarding" and "Idiot Gets Waterboarded." Despite many of these videos having a *Jackass*-like feel, they usually end with a stunned "victim" who never asks for another go.

(6) "It Don't Gitmo Better"

One unique 'artistic' representation of waterboarding is Steve Powers's Coney Island installation the *Waterboarding Thrill Ride* with which this chapter opened. Set in the Coney Island arcade, the "former photo booth" has been "redesigned to look like a jail cell."[118] From the sidewalk, the storefront has a graffiti-style mural of Spongebob Squarepants being waterboarded while exclaiming, "It don't GITMO better!" Viewers can insert a dollar to activate "an animatronic diorama depicting a prisoner being waterboarded." The piece intends to use the context of the side-show and dark humor to make a larger sociopolitical point about the troubling debate over the practice. As part of the larger *Democracy in America* project produced by Creative Time, Powers organized a private performance with volunteers – himself and some lawyers – who each underwent waterboarding in controlled conditions at an "undisclosed location in Coney Island" on August 15, 2008. The documentation of the closed performance was subsequently displayed at the Park Avenue Armory in New York City. In preparation for the event, Steve Powers said: "Now actual waterboard riders will reveal, in their own words, exactly what a taste of death by water feels like"[119] – playing with the tension between "rider" as spectator and "rider" as participant (in Creative Time 2008: 2). He explained to me that there will be only a little visual documentation of the event: "There are so many examples [of water-boarding] on Youtube that there's little point in showing another one" (2008). Powers is happy to allow his public "example" to remain, where, for a dollar, you don't have to be waterboarded to participate, to be complicit, or to get the point.

Powers explained to me later how surprised he was to realize, after believing that the subject of waterboarding would seem old hat by the time the installation opened, that so many locals had no idea what waterboarding was before coming across the *Ride* – and that the piece therefore had an unexpected educational aspect.

Powers, however, seems OK with the education he's offering some spectators. It's in tune with his overall objectives: "The point of the project was to investigate what waterboarding was about" (Powers interview, 2008). Using dark humor within the context of the sideshow, the *Waterboarding Thrill Ride* strives to make a larger sociopolitical point and open up the troubling debate over the practice using "the inherent spectacle of Coney Island" (Creative Time, "Steve Powers' *The Waterboarding Thrill Ride*," 1). In my 2008 interview, Powers explained the corresponding spectacle of waterboarding: "It's primal, it's using this essential thing – water, this really basic need – in a violent way. Water becomes weap-onized." Water participates in a spectacle of pain: in-between an active body and an incapacitated body, water performs. Presented as part of the larger *Democracy in America* project curated by Creative Time, the *Thrill Ride* embodies the Kafkaesque fascination the United States has with the "water torture."

As installed, the *Waterboarding Thrill Ride* isn't about a simulation of waterboarding. It's about the spectator becoming a participant. As she rises to peer through the prison bars, she must decide: put in a dollar or not? Powers says of the payment: "the dollar creates a contract; a conscious decision to see what this is about. It's an important part of

Coney Island" (2008 interview). Once the money is in, the jarring music (I heard the Sesame Street theme song) reminds the spectator that she's no longer part of an audience, but a participant in the spectacle; she made the animatrons move; she, in a certain way, poured the water. The dollar, and the "ride," exemplified for me the state we live in. Always complicit in a very indirect way.

Interrogation training

Mike Ritz used to be an interrogator. But more recently he has used what he knows to teach others. His Team Delta has two training camps, in Pennsylvania and Georgia, where groups – "corporations, associations, and other groups" – can pay to have an "authentic military experience."[120] Programs range from War Games ("paintball with an edge") to POW Resistance, which teaches "'R' segment of the SERE school"[121]. Team Delta has produced documentaries featuring the simulations they create, including *We Can Make You Talk* for the History Channel (2003), and *Torture: Guantanamo Guidebook* for the United Kingdom's Channel 4 (2005).[122] The artist Steve Powers hired Mike Ritz to waterboard him. In preparation for her performance exploring the subject of female interrogators in the US military, performance artist Coco Fusco gathered a team to participate in a training session with Team Delta. Using the footage shot during the several days with Team Delta, Fusco produced the documentary film *Operation Atropos*. In a subsequent interview with Ritz, Fusco admits to an early revelation: "lesson number one for those in the group who secretly believed that interrogators are sadists by nature was that only highly trained professionals can actually do the job well."[123] Ritz is himself an outspoken critic of the US military's misuse of interrogation as an information-gathering operation, regularly condemning the use of torture or enhanced interrogation techniques and arguing that the best interrogations use rapport-building techniques.[124]

In her interview with Ritz, Fusco emphasizes the role of theatre in interrogation and torture: "The tortured individual is made to believe that things may happen through illusions created by the combined effects of stress and suggestion."[125] Ritz in turn confirms what Fusco suggests:

Not all interrogators are actors, but *good* interrogators are good actors. Interrogators must assume characters that specific prisoners will most likely relate to, fear, confide in, etc. Through proper assessment of the prisoner, the interrogator determines what "type" of person he/she needs to become in order to motivate the prisoner to cooperate. Interrogators are authorized to lie about who they are (what position they have within the camp/prison) and what rank they possess. We're known to use accents to convince a prisoner that we're not from the US. [...] The vast majority of good interrogators have a background in dramatic performance before attending interrogation school.[126]

Acting, for Ritz, is a skill "equally as important as other interrogation skills like questioning, map reading, maintaining a timeline, detecting deception, etc.," and the type of acting required for interrogation is "completely improvisational."[127] The "dramatic performance for an audience of one" is structured around a basic "roadmap" of phases that the interrogator must go through, but is free to *ad lib* around to adapt to the circumstances. Team Delta training replicates the type of military training used at the SERE School and other sites where theatre is key to moving a soldier from novice to expert, from stumbling through – and perhaps vulnerable to grasping for tactics from inappropriate places like *24* – to a warrior mindset in which the right reaction comes naturally: "Teaching soldiers when they're in a stressful 'fight or flight' situation allows the instructor to insert the lesson directly into the soldier's head (bypassing conscious thought) so that, should the soldier find himself in a similar situation in the future, he will instinctively react in the appropriate manner."[128] This is precisely the objective in the military training Zach Gill analyzes in his essay "Rehearsing the War Away"[129] as well as the theatre immersion training that Scott Magelssen writes about in "Rehearsing the Warrior Ethos."[130] It is the type of experiential training that many skills entail – that is, training that attempts to create an *expert*, someone who experiences the "flow" described by Csikszentmihalyi[131] in which one loses oneself to the activity (the actor in the role, living in the moment; the pilot in the air, making quick life-saving decisions; etc.). It is a type of cognitive training that takes time; the importance of decision-making in military training is in part the reason for the growth of the use of video games that I discuss in Chapter 3. It is training that is completely reliant on performance, on theatre, on rehearsal, that attempts to mold the mind through repetition (and "revision"?) to ensure the right decision at the right moment, whether that moment yields the right information or pulls (or doesn't pull) the trigger.

Conclusion

Each of these actions, experiments, simulations, and so on, reveal how the use of the visual and sensory realms in performance disengage textual rhetoric about definitions and justifications of "torture." The firmly lodged and terrifying image of the "water torture" doesn't *risk* replication of its own terror, it performs it without a doubt in simulation. The only difference is how far those inflicting – those "controlling" the drowning – will go before stopping. Just as Henri Alleg, the journalist waterboarded in 1957 by the French during the Algerian war, lived to describe his "impression of drowning, and a terrible agony, that of death itself, [taking] possession of [him],"[132] those detainees who have been subjected by the US government to being "watered" provide further examples of "bare life reach[ing] its maximum indeterminacy." That the three known detainees subjected to waterboarding have survived the process indicates the extent to which the control of this "mock death" relies on keeping its victims *homo sacer*, living dead.

So where are we (whoever "we" are)? After the silly television show, after the complete distortion of military training intended to keep soldiers from succumbing to torture, after Jack Bauer (can there be anything after Jack Bauer?), after our unending complicity, what is there? The "dark side" has brought us through the gloves coming off, to a chaotic prosecution of an amorphous, massive, improvisatory "war," during which not knowing how to deal with the created enemy led to a complete breakdown of a democracy's ethical and moral foundation. If there is no investigation, prosecution, unpacking, understanding of how performance has been used to perpetuate and propagate a never-ending "war on terror," then what will there be? A sobering reminder that there might still be a difference between fiction and reality can be found in the testimony of detainees gathered by the International Committee of the Red Cross and submitted to the CIA in 2007.[133] In this report Abu Zubaydah, Khalid Sheikh Mohammed, and Abd al-Rahim al-Nashiri describe being waterboarded. Zubaydah:

> I was put on what looked like a hospital bed, and strapped down very tightly with belts. A black cloth was then placed over my face and the interrogators used a mineral water bottle to pour water on the cloth so that I could not breathe. After a few minutes the cloth was removed and the bed was rotated into an upright position. The pressure of the straps on my wounds caused severe pain. I vomited. The bed was then again lowered to a horizontal position and the same torture carried out

with the black cloth over my face and water poured on from a bottle. On this occasion my head was in a more backward, downwards position and the water was poured on for a longer time. I struggled without success to breathe. I thought I was going to die. I lost control of my urine. Since then I still lose control of my urine when under stress.[134]

Counter-intelligence relies on theatre to succeed. As Mike Ritz explains, the best interrogator – the best counter-intelligence agent, the best spy – is the best actor. That's because interrogation and torture relies on theatre to be successful: the prisoner must believe that the interrogator is going to do what s/he says s/he will do. The *point* is the 'as if.' And as film and television like *24* and films like *Rendition* (2007) and *Unthinkable* (2010) demonstrate, it is Hollywood that goes a step further because it *can*; because it already operates within the 'as if.' Jack Bauer shoots the guy in the leg; Samuel L. Jackson as a veteran interrogator kills the wife of the terrorist in order to make him believe that his children are next. Counter-intelligence and counter-insurgency are about bringing the other around, and they both rely on theatre to make that happen, for better or worse – but it's important to maintain a sense of reality and fiction in the process.

5
Obamania

What if Barack Obama really is what his supporters believe him to be, what his critics fear him to be, and what those in-between hope he could be?

What if he really is a good guy?

What if he deserved the Nobel Prize?

What if he arrived in the White House and realized, as he feared, that he would *not* be able to make the "changes" that are necessary, due to political-corporate pressure?

What if he decided to go deep throat?

What if Obama is the Wikileaks source? What if his posturing that Bradley Manning deserves to be in prison – Obama told a reporter "He broke the law" in April 2011 – is just a cover-up?[1]

Now *that's* hope.

Same method, different president

This chapter, like the first, considers the way in which the same tool used by Bush – performance – offered change, hope, and belief in the rapid rise of Barack Obama to the US presidency. My analysis is critical in its investigation of Obama's first term, asking whether Obama's post-election performances amounted to political difference from George W. Bush or a perpetuation of the status quo. Specifically, I examine the distinction between behaviors and actions against what qualifies as "just" performance – that which remains ephemeral. I ask what, if any, such performances can be said to constitute or even influence political, economic, and/or social change. These questions are difficult, as anyone who analyzes the performance of politics knows. How can the cultivation of political capital not have real value? How can countless promises not amount to *any*thing? What is at stake in promising a lot, reaching for the sky, and accomplishing comparatively little? What role does performance play in these endeavors?

"Whatever It Takes": pure theatre

I begin with a return to my subtitle "Whatever It Takes." Meant to operate as a forceful performative that would coerce real and imagined detractors in the post-9/11 global community to submission, the phrase has been exposed as the most theatrical of lines from the Bush years. Its power, in the Bush context, relates only to abuse upon governmental bodies and human bodies. As a phrase meant to point to US perseverance, it has little significance for the Bush Administration. In light of the pinnacle moment of Obama's first term – the assassination of Osama bin Laden – the clause takes on new meaning. Uttered repeatedly in the wake of 9/11 and through two of the longest wars in US history, "whatever it takes" became a short combination of empty words representative of irresponsible foreign policy. In May 2011, when Obama ordered Navy Seals into Pakistan to kill or capture bin Laden, a high-risk project that overcame more than one obstacle to "succeed," the phrase "whatever it takes" suddenly became meaningful and symbolic of Obama's chutzpah. "Whatever it takes" is a clause *satisfied* by Obama, not Bush. The act also perfectly captures the double-sided nature of Obama: his persona of an intelligent politician with a conscience versus his willingness to "do what it takes" to succeed.

Bush too had a double-sided nature (what politician doesn't?). Bush promoted himself as a Texas rancher who was concerned with everyday people. But Bush was, as Vicente Fox called him, a "windshield cowboy" who repeatedly supported legislation that benefited the rich, not average Americans. Bush and his Vice-President, Dick Cheney, assured the world that justice would come to "the terrorists" even if the United States had to "work the Dark side." "Whatever it takes," in the months after 9/11, became a cue for improvisation. Karen Greenberg's study of Guantánamo details how military leadership broke down as the White House, the intelligence community, and military brass failed to communicate. The gathering of terrorist suspects in Afghanistan was in itself "improvised internment"; their subsequent removal to Guantánamo was similarly poorly planned and expressly relied on the practical improvisatory techniques that the military personnel are trained to handle.[2] The global war on terror, in other words, was an improvised mess from the start while being performed as swift retribution, a narrative supported by the ticking clock of *24* throughout its premiere in the autumn of 2001. The work of housing detainees and getting to the bottom of real terrorist threats against the United States via interrogation became pure drama. Based on the "results" of the drama – that is, faulty intelligence invalidated by intelligence officials – Bush gave reasons in public to justify an invasion of Iraq. Although the "reasons" turned out to be fictional, the "double" nature of these performances didn't matter – the damage has been done in Iraq. Furthermore, after leaving office, Bush stood by much of what happened during his presidency.

But for the figure of Obama, there has always been more at stake in his performances. To describe Obama of having a "double nature" hints to a postcolonial analysis that I don't necessarily intend to engage, one that cites Homi Bhabha's colonial mimicry and insinuates Obama's brown body as some kind of imposter to the white-male office of the US presidency. I reject this type of critique because although there is no doubt that the performance of Obama's presence as a person of color carries baggage, his perceived race is only one aspect of his otherness. His persona simultaneously engages an elitist identity through his education, law degree, and experience as a law professor at a top law school while incorporating a history of a middle-class upbring-ing, a mother who struggled, and a student loan paid off just a few years before he entered the White House. So yes, race no doubt plays a huge role in the public performances of Barack Obama; but his poli-tics exceed race. The Obama Administration makes unique use of the "screen" in part due to Obama's own characterization of such a filter. In his book *The Audacity of Hope*, Obama, in his famously self-reflexive style, comments:

> I reject a politics that is based solely on racial identity, gender iden-tity, sexual orientation, or victimhood generally. [...] Undoubtedly, some of these views will get me in trouble. I am new enough on the national political scene that I serve as a blank screen on which people of vastly different political stripes project their own views.

Obama goes on to address the dilemma of all major politicians:

> As such, I am bound to disappoint some, if not all, of them. Which per-haps indicates a second, more intimate theme to this book – namely, how I, or anybody in public office, can avoid the pitfalls of fame, the hunger to please, the fear of loss, and thereby retain that kernel of

truth, that singular voice within each of us that reminds us of our deepest commitments.[3]

Written in 2006, Obama's description of his own blank slate offered an openness that eventually enabled a remarkably successful presidential campaign. His body, he indicates, was a screen onto which supporters could see themselves and politics could carry out real and imagined change. Nicholas Mirzoeff points out the significance of Obama's "screen" for race in the United States:

> Obama has often said that he is a screen onto which people project what they want to see. While that has long been true for African Americans, such projections have often been those of fear and prejudice, a justification of the wages of whiteness. In Obama's case, a realignment appears to have taken place. Given his indeterminate background, not quite African, not quite American (in the 'heartland' view of that descriptor), Obama offered people an alternative to the now low-paying wages of whiteness in his assertion of an inclusive and progressive nation state. In the long litany of those he sought to bring together under the banner of "no red states, no blue states, only the United States," Obama presented himself as the surrogate of the long deferred American dream. Precisely because, as a person of African descent, Obama generates echoes of the long surrogation of slavery in the US, this performance of self as substitute worked (Roach, 1996). Obama never articulated the strategy and never directly spoke to the historic change that he embodied because everyone could see it.[4]

Obama performs a transparency with his body that "everyone can see" that extends to his proclaimed commitment to clarity in his administration. On its contact page, the Obama White House website reads: "President Obama is committed to creating the most open and accessible administration in American history."[5] This attempt at openness is just one of the overt shifts the Obama Administration performs. There is a stated attempt at transparency in opposition to the Bush Administration's notorious closed-door policy and infrequent press conferences. However, the Obama Administration has not held a significantly higher number of press conferences than his predecessor. The measure of success when it comes to these sorts of political performances can be found to some extent in approval ratings, where above all *perception is reality*. Bush was spiking in approval ratings around 9/11, but his trajectory was a downward one. In his first term, Obama's ratings suffered but remained relatively stable, and generally higher than much of Bush's two terms. The difference between Bush and Obama, to a great extent, is a matter of degree, and a degree of perception.

The test

Just as the Bush Administration, as Jon McKenzie describes, put the world to the test – to "perform or else" – when Bush warned every nation "you are either with us or against us," Obama was faced with a similar "test" in one corner of the Arab Spring. The challenge came not from a widely publicized platform of mainstream mass media but from the marginalized perspective of the daughter of a human rights activist in Bahrain who had been taken into custody by Bahraini authorities. The activist, Abdulhadi al-Khawaja, had been arrested and beaten along with several other family members. Unable to get information about his status or well-being, his daughter Zainab began a hunger strike in April 2011 in protest. In a phone interview, journalist Amy Goodman asked Zainab about her demands:

Amy Goodman: You have written a letter to President Obama. Bahrain is extremely close to the United States. It is the home to the US Navy's Fifth Fleet. What is your message to the President of the United States?

Zainab Al Khawaja: My message to Obama is basically that he has to choose. He has to choose if his administration is really with human rights, democracy, and freedom, as he claimed, and with change towards democracy, or is he more concerned about supporting his friends who are dictators in the Middle East?[6]

Zainab Al Khawaja's challenge to Obama has more to do with a test of the substance of his Administration than a worthy bet. Al Khawaja's is not the first attempt to take Obama to task; many liberal critics from philosopher Slavoj Žižek to MSNBC pundit Rachel Maddow to filmmaker Michael Moore have publicly accused Obama's policies of going nowhere near where his political capital would let him go. At the beginning of his presidency, Obama famously denounced waterboarding as torture and promised to shut down the military prison at Guantánamo Bay, but reports of prisoner abuse continued to surface and the Caribbean naval base still housed detainees. The feel-good rhetoric performed throughout his campaign with the key words "hope," "change," and "yes we can" brought him through to an impressive victory, a hugely popular inauguration in spite of its timing just months after the 2008 global economic meltdown, and a surprising honor of the 2009 Nobel Peace Prize.

Bush used performance, to some extent, in the manner of the word's etymological root – that is, in the manner of *parfournir*, the Old French word meaning "to furnish forth," "to complete," "to carry out thoroughly." The performances given by Bush and his supporters, including his cabinet members, television pundits, and some journalists functioned to use the "screen" described by Dougal Phillips to complete several missions, from curbing civil rights through the Patriot Act, to selling the Iraq War, to deflecting attention away from the harmful economic implications of a continued pursuit of unregulated free-market capitalism. Not all of Bush's performances "furnished" the desired consequences, as his large "Mission Accomplished" spectacle proved.

Obama also used performance to furnish forth victory. His campaign became a perfect synthesis of charisma, branding, social networking, and positivity. A brilliant marketing achievement, the 2008 Obama campaign overcame obstacles and reached out to a wide demographic set with simple messages and small, but numerous donations. The television and radio host Tavis Smiley traces Obama's move from a relative "nobody" – Smiley cites Barack Obama's unsuccessful attempt to attend the 2000 Democratic National Convention – to the forty-fourth US president in less than a decade. Smiley calls Obama's rise "an example of failing your way up"[7] The 2008 Obama campaign was nothing but a failure, despite some of the things Obama had going against him, from the sound and feeling of a first name like "Obama," to the more concrete problems in the context of post-9/11 United States with the middle name "Hussein," to his mixed race, Kenyan father, years spent abroad, time in a Muslim school in Jakarta, Indonesia, association with the controversial preacher Jeremiah Wright. But he kept succeeding; his popularity was viral, as exemplified in Obama Girl's videos and the exponential copying and adaptation of the unsanctioned "portrait" of him created by artist Shepard Fairey. Above all, the extent to which positive thinking seemed to "furnish forth" Obama from junior US Senator to Leader of the Free World seems the most relevant, because Obama's positivity is synonymous with his everyday demeanor – his effortless and subtle charisma that puts forth an articulate yet seemingly "nice," and laid-back politician. Obama went viral because potential supporters became actual supporters, and then voters. They voted for him because they could relate to him; his cool confidence offered something for so many.

Just say yes

Because of the huge role played by positivity in Obama's campaign and presidency it is important to take a closer look at the phenomenon of positive thinking and its role in US culture. In her 2009 book *Smile or Die: How Positive Thinking Fooled America and the World*,[8] Barbara Ehrenreich unpacks the relentless 'yes' mentality in US society, finding the insidious affirmative in politics, healthcare, economics, and religion. Ehrenreich's anger over the abuse of thinking positively helps theorize how the positive is performed in contemporary culture, from George W. Bush's unwavering and arguably irrational resolve, through the mass delusion caused by a 'yes-mentality' in mortgage lending, to the 'hope' offered by Barack Obama's candidacy. Obamania – that overwhelming feeling of hope and unyielding support instilled specifically by the charismatic prowess of Barack Obama's public speeches – creates "emotional performatives" in which to *say* something is to *feel* something is to *do* something.

Freedom isn't free

Political analysts have consistently cited US President Jimmy Carter's 1979 'malaise' speech as not only a turning point in US politics, but also an obvious example that Americans don't want negativity. With Ronald Reagan's cool, confident persona, the public found a performer to believe in, even if his words misrepresented his actions. If Jimmy Carter employed a strategic *negativity* in an attempt to adequately and accurately respond to a public frustrated with economic recession, an energy crisis, high gas prices, and long pump lines, offering perhaps a realistic but uncomfortable emotional state, then Reagan used *positivity* to appeal to the public's emotional investment in the future. With performances such as his 'morning in America' campaign ad, Reagan remained cool, calm, composed and above all, positive:

> It's morning again in America. Today more men and women will go to work than ever before in our country's history. With interest rates at about half the record highs of 1980, nearly 2,000 families today will buy new homes, more than at any time in the past four years. This afternoon 6,500 young men and women will be married, and with inflation at less than half of what it was just four years ago, they can look forward with confidence to the future. It's morning again in

America, and under the leadership of President Reagan, our country is prouder and stronger and better. Why would we ever want to return to where we were less than four short years ago?

Reagan's immensely successful advertisement, leading to his re-election in 1984, is part of the long-term response to Carter's speech in US right-wing rhetoric. Bush senior rode on Reagan's coat-tails and Bill Clinton remained a feel-good centrist. The last three decades, therefore, has seen a particular use of positive thinking in the political sphere, and specifically positive thinking without much substance.

It is of course with the election of George W. Bush that the United States got a new dose of positive resolve, first seen in Bush's 'regular guy' attitude during his campaign (seen most vividly in Alexandra Pelosi's documentary *Journeys with George*) and later refined in the aftermath of 9/11, when positivity was deployed for political ends. Now that nearly a decade has passed since the events, it may seem difficult to remember the surge of pro-American sentiment that circulated the world in the days following the terrorist attacks of 11 September 2001. There were flags on houses, stickers on cars, pins on lapels. There was, in the face of grief and sorrow related for some directly to the loss of friends or family and for others indirectly to the loss of fellow human beings, a quiet but growing positive energy. Even the spurt in military recruitment after 9/11 could be attributed both to an angry vengeance and a positive desire to contribute to a cause of defending one's country. In his essay "Welcome to the Desert of the Real," Slavoj Žižek summarizes well the ultimately dark nature of such positivity; 9/11, Žižek writes, ushered in a reality previously imagined in movies: "Therein resides the rationale of the often-mentioned association of the attacks with the Hollywood disaster movies: the unthinkable which happened was the object of fantasy, so that, in a way, America *got what it fantasized about*, and this was the greatest surprise." His description of America *getting* that which it *wanted* as displayed in the *fantasy* of Hollywood movies is an essentially *positive* characterization. Žižek similarly describes the bubbling American pride and goodwill after 9/11 with cynicism:

> When, in the aftermath of September 11, the Americans *en masse* rediscovered their American pride, displaying flags and singing together in public, one should emphasize more than ever that there is nothing "innocent" in this rediscovery of the American innocence, in getting rid of the sense of historical guilt or irony which prevented many of them to fully assume being American. What this gesture

amounted to was to "objectively" assume the burden of all that being "American" stood for in the past – an exemplary case of ideological interpellation, of fully assuming one's symbolic mandate, which enters the stage after the perplexity caused by some historical trauma. In the traumatic aftermath of September 11, when the old security seemed momentarily shattered, what more "natural" gesture than to take refuge in the innocence of firm ideological identification?[9]

Key to Žižek's analysis here is his discussion of the response of 9/11 – the surge of nationalism and obsession with identity – as a naturalizing force. What is interesting about his talk of "natural" is its relationship to "positive." By describing a fallback onto ideology as a "natural" move connects such behavior to positivity. If it is natural, it is a given, and as a given, it is original and "good." That which is natural is positive. These ideas were performed in songs, benefit concerts,[10] and memorials.[11] There were volunteers at Ground Zero and new recruits in Basic Training. President George W. Bush used a solemn, but resolved, confident, and hopeful tone when he responded to the attacks on 20 September 2001: "Americans are asking 'Why do they hate us?' They hate what they see right here in this chamber: a democratically elected government. Their leaders are self-appointed. They hate our freedoms: our freedom of religion, our freedom of speech, our freedom to vote and assemble and disagree with each other." Bush's characterization of Al Qaeda's motivations referred to a positive description of "America" and "Americans." He spoke of the "great achievement of our time": "the advance of human freedom." He contrasted the light of freedom with the darkness of terrorism, speaking toward the future:

> Our nation, this generation, will lift the dark threat of violence from our people and our future. We will rally the world to this cause by our efforts, by our courage. We will not tire, we will not falter and we will not fail.[12]

Bush's political team transformed the crisis of 9/11 into a positive opportunity. In Naomi Klein's nomenclature the *shock* of 9/11 created the environment for making corporate profits – for the neocolonial project of the deletion of meaning, a creation of void, and a positive addition to that newly "empty" space.[13] But in terms of positive thinking, 9/11 opened a space for Americans to feel American; for men and women to volunteer to fight for their country; for regular people to be OK with having rights taken away in the Patriot Act. It was all OK because we were freedom-loving Americans.

Bush's rhetoric reflects not just *not the truth* but also what Slavoj Žižek calls non-ideology, a case of "ideology appear[ing] as its own opposite."[14]

> We should always bear in mind that, within our ideological space, the reference to one's Nation is the supreme form of ideology in the guise of anti- or non-ideology (in short, of ideology *tout court* [just plain]): "let's leave aside our petty political and ideological struggles, it's the fate of our nation which is at stake now.[15]

And instead of 9/11 being the downer that it could have been, forcing government to interpret such violent acts as a wake-up call to the way globalized capital affects people, political spin masters helped launch a never-ending conflict with the "other." With a fierce and optimistic attitude, Bush launched the "war on terror," explaining that it would begin "with al Qaeda, but it [...] will not end until every terrorist group of global reach has been found, stopped and defeated."[16] Applause. A few weeks later, Bush announced the military campaign in Afghanistan, called "Operation Enduring Freedom," with similar resolve and positivity:

> To all the men and women in our military, every sailor, every soldier, every airman, every Coast Guardsman, every Marine, I say this: Your mission is defined. The objectives are clear. Your goal is just. You have my full confidence, and you will have every tool you need to carry out your duty. [...] The battle is now joined on many fronts. We will not waver, we will not tire, we will not falter, and we will not fail. Peace and freedom will prevail.[17]

The end of the beginning: "Mission Accomplished"

There are myriad examples of Bush offering kind and positive words in an attempt to make the untrue true. But one of the more troubling and confusing of these performances is Bush's visit to the aircraft carrier USS Abraham Lincoln on 1 May 2003 off the California coast. Landing on the ship's runway in a Navy S-3B Viking, Bush got out in a jumpsuit, but changed into a business suit and made his way to a podium in front of a huge banner stating: "Mission Accomplished," and proceeded to tell the military crowd:

> The war on terror is not over, yet it is not endless. We do not know the day of final victory, but we have seen the turning of the tide. No act of the terrorists will change our purpose, or weaken our resolve, or alter their fate. Their cause is lost. Free nations will press on to victory.[18]

Although both mainstream and alternative media have discussed at length this now infamous moment in the Iraq debacle, focusing on aspects like Bush's safe location off California when he appeared to be landing in a war zone, the value of this performance piece lies in its pure nerve.

What is interesting here is not just the staged nature of Bush's announcement, but its ultimate optimism. There was a sense of "if you land on it it will be over" with a strong element of Stephen Colbert's "truthiness," that is, "truth that comes from the gut, not books," or, as the American Dialect Society defines it, "the quality of preferring concepts or facts one wishes to be true, rather than concepts or facts known to be true."[19] The website "Wikiality," itself a response to Colbert's invented word, and a place where "entries [...] are judged on their truthiness; if it feels right it's probably truthy"[20] frames the Mission Accomplished event with appropriate feeling:

> **Mission Accomplished** is the essence of truthiness. You saw it there, in red, white, and blue, over the shoulder of our beloved President as he declared victory in Iraq. From that day forward, Iraq was free.[21]

Although not sponsored by the *Colbert Report*'s network, Comedy Central, or authored by Colbert or his team, Wikiality captures the essence of Colbert's idea that "On Wikipedia, we can create a reality that we can all agree on – the reality we just agreed on" and "the revolution will not be verified."[22] Just as Wikipedia can change, since, according to Colbert, "all we need to do is convince a majority of people that some factoid is true," even Bush eventually shifted gears from the aircraft carrier speech. Asked during an interview with CNN days after the November 2008 election whether there were any "moments" he regretted, Bush replied:

Bush: I regret saying some things I shouldn't have said. [...] Like "dead or alive," or "bring 'em on." And, by the way, my wife reminded me as President of the United States, you better be careful what you say. I was trying to convey a message. I could have conveyed it more artfully. Being on this ship [he was being interviewed in the USS Intrepid] reminds me of when I went to the USS Abraham Lincoln and they had a sign that said "Mission Accomplished." I regret that sign was there. It was a sign aimed at the sailors on the ship, but it conveyed a broader knowledge. To some it said, well, Bush thinks the war in Iraq is over, when I didn't think that. But nonetheless, it conveyed the wrong message. So, there are things I've regretted.[23]

Although the "Mission Accomplished" performance may have regret-
fully "conveyed the wrong message," at the time, as Bush told CNN, it
"conveyed a broader knowledge" – the "right" message, and certainly
a "truthy" and above all "positive" message. Bush might agree with
Colbert's sentiment: "I'm no fan of reality."[24]

Bush wants you to own a home

After 9/11 reality lacked a correspondence with many things, including
freedom. Bush told us the "terrorists" hated us because we were "free,"
and several bumper stickers (and Team America) told us that "freedom
isn't free." Americans apparently were "free," unlike "terrorists," and
being "free" meant being "American" and being American meant being
in pursuit of the American Dream. In the wake of the dotcom boom and
bust, the monetary value of the ephemeral became uncertain and the
roof over one's head – one's "freedom" – became more valuable than
ever. It wasn't long before the free-market deregulation that had begun
decades earlier started to really set in motion the housing bubble, led in
part by a smiling president.

George W. Bush made several speeches regarding homeownership in
2002 while the "American Dream Fund" was being developed and later
launched:

> I do believe in the American Dream. I believe there is such a thing as
> the American Dream. And I believe those of us who have been given
> positions of responsibility must do everything we can to spotlight
> the dream and to make sure the dream shines in all neighborhoods,
> all throughout our country. Owning a home is a part of that dream,
> it just is. Right here in America if you own your own home, you're
> realizing the American Dream.[25]

> You see, we want everybody in America to own their own home.
> That's what we want. This is – an ownership society is a compassion-
> ate society.
>
> More and more people own their homes in America today. Two-
> thirds of all Americans own their homes, yet we have a problem
> here in America because few than half of the Hispanics and half the
> African Americans own the home. That's a homeownership gap. It's
> a – it's a gap that we've got to work together to close for the good
> of our country, for the sake of a more hopeful future. We've got to
> work to knock down the barriers that have created a homeowner-
> ship gap.

I set an ambitious goal. It's one that I believe we can achieve. It's a clear goal, that by the end of this decade we'll increase the number of minority homeowners by at least 5.5 million families.
(Applause.)

Some may think that's a stretch. I don't think it is. I think it is realistic. I know we're going to have to work together to achieve it. But when we do our communities will be stronger and so will our economy. Achieving the goal is going to require some good policies out of Washington. And it's going to require a strong commitment from those of you involved in the housing industry.[26]

The problem, we now know (and knew then), is that Bush's proposal was just one of the many really bad ideas leading up to the current global economic crisis. But his performance offered hope – he spoke with a permanent smile; surrounded himself with smiling new homeowners; and told his audience: "You see, we want everybody in American to own their own home. That's what we want." With such a strong appeal to the hearts of the crowd, Bush's homeownership campaign became a perfect example of an emotional performative. Audiences believed his "make-belief," and Bush's emotional performative indeed contributed to a rise in homeownership by the early 2000s and a record number of foreclosures by the end of the decade.

Banker ticking bombs

Nowhere is the play between positive thinking and concrete results more evident than in the deployment of the positive in the financial industry over the past several decades. From economist Milton Friedman's ultimate and unwavering belief in the free market to the most flawed mortgage bundling, the financial industry and lobby seemed to have succumbed totally, and only, to optimism. In the face of red flags, financial experts not only kept hoping for the best, they continued to report the best-case scenario. Both David Hare's theatrical unpacking of the meltdown and Barbara Ehrenreich's journalistic deconstruction of the same events pay particular attention to the ways in which bankers and regulators perceived negativity. For the middle-level trader or banker, negativity was a dealbreaker. For the overpaid executive, negativity didn't exist.

In his play *The Power of Yes: A Dramatist Seeks to Understand the Financial Crisis*, David Hare devises his own version of documentary theatre by fusing a narrative with research and interviews. He quotes

Ronald Cohen, a "private equity pioneer," who claims, "I knew the crisis would come. It was just a question of when. But when I left my job, I didn't want to be the kind of man who predicts doom for everyone who follows him. So I said nothing."[27] Hare goes on to cite Deborah Solomon's *New York Times Magazine* interview with economist Myron Scholes:

Solomon: In retrospect, is it fair to say that the idea that banks could manage risk was a total illusion?
Scholes: What you're saying is negative. Life is positive too. Every side of a coin has another side.[28]

Ehrenreich's investigation, however, continually points out the *lack* of another side to the turn-of-the-twenty-first-century financial system. She cites an interview with "Banking expert Steve Eisman" who explains that

the finance industry had "built assumption on top of assumption" – such as that housing prices would never fall – and that "no one saw any reason to question those assumptions." There was a good reason to remain silent about the enveloping madness, he told [Ehrenreich]: "Anybody who voiced negativity was thrown out."[29]

In part the failure for bad news to reach the top can be blamed on the top. For executives who make millions of dollars a year (like in the double digits), having what they want "was already [their] reality," and therefore they believed they could have the markets the way they wanted – Ehrenreich writes: "It's almost impossible to trace the attitudes of failed titans to particular ideologues of positive thinking – the coaches and motivators who advise, for example, that one purge 'negative people' from the ranks."[30] Use of such guides is secretive, Ehrenreich explains, but common. Nevertheless, the lifestyles of extremely rich executives lead to "extreme isolation – what crisis management consultant Eric Dezenhall calls "'bubble-itis.' Subordinates suffer from 'the galloping desire to bring good news' rather than honest reports."[31] Unable to accept no for an answer, and empowered with the fate of every underling, top-tier executives only understood the power of yes: "If you're worth $500 million," hedge fund manager Steve Eisman asks, "how could you be wrong about anything? To think something is to make it happen. You're God."[32]

Obamania

As Bush headed for re-election in 2004, a bump in the right-wing road came in the form of Senate candidate Barack Obama's keynote address at the Democratic National Convention in July 2004. In front of the Boston audience, Obama preached the "audacity of hope":

> Hope in the face of difficulty, hope in the face of uncertainty, the audacity of hope: In the end, that is God's greatest gift to us, the bedrock of this nation, a belief in things not seen, a belief that there are better days ahead.

> [...]

> America, tonight, if you feel the same energy that I do, if you feel the same urgency that I do, if you feel the same passion that I do, if you feel the same hopefulness that I do, if we do what we must do, then I have no doubt that all across the country, from Florida to Oregon, from Washington to Maine, the people will rise up in November, and John Kerry will be sworn in as president. And John Edwards will be sworn in as vice-president. And this country will reclaim its promise. And out of this long political darkness a brighter day will come.[33]

As Bush's ratings plummeted in his second term, Barack Obama's use of the slogans "Hope" and "Yes We Can" during the 2008 presidential campaign seemed to really offer something to believe in. In contrast to negative, anti-Bush sentiment, Obama fever offered a contagious optimism. In fact, one might argue that the only *real* change observed since George W. Bush left office has been the shift on the center-left from negativity to positivity – so enthusiastically *against* Bush and so positively *for* Barack Obama. His historic election and inauguration ushered in the "hope" needed in the wake of the September 2008 market crash. The announcement by the Nobel Prize committee in 2009 awarding Obama the Peace Prize, however, seemed to best capture the consolidation of hope and the idea of Barack Obama: "Only very rarely," according to the Nobel Prize Press Release:

> has a person to the same extent as Obama captured the world's attention and given its people hope for a better future. His diplomacy is founded in the concept that those who are to lead the world must do so on the basis of values and attitudes that are shared by the majority of the world's population.[34]

In his award speech, the Chairman of the Norwegian Nobel Committee, Thorbjørn Jagland, clearly acknowledged the intangible nature of Obama's accomplishments, and, apparently, even Obama was surprised to win:

> President Obama said he did not feel that he deserved to be in the company of so many transformative figures that have been honoured by this prize, and whose courageous pursuit of peace has inspired the world. But he added that he also knew that the Nobel Prize had not just been used to honor specific achievements, but also to give momentum to a set of causes. The Prize could thus represent "a call to action."[35]

The Nobel Committee's decision therefore relied on future events, constituting an emotional performative and a practice – a performance – of positive thinking, or a *positive performative*.

I have found it helpful to look at Obama's homepage next to that of prosperity preacher Joel Osteen, whose Houston-based Lakewood Church reaches a weekly live congregation in the tens of thousands and television audience of millions.[36] The similarities remind me of the performativity of positive thinking – and here, by performativity I mean the play between fiction and reality – that which enables the practice of positive thinking to have concrete results. Osteen and his wife, Victoria, employ a Christianity that fuses religion and positive thinking. With minimal use of Christian imagery and a forceful positivity, their sermons, public appearances, books, and blogs all point to the same message: that God is a figure that will give you what you want if only you want it enough. Love, life, happiness: these are just some of the key words in Joel Osteen's "prosperity preaching." Joel Osteen Ministries "is committed to helping people from all walks of life experience the unconditional love and unending hope found only in a personal relationship with Jesus Christ." The "About" page of the Osteen website features a panoramic image taken from behind Joel who stands in front of his thousands-strong congregation, with a quote below his feet that reads: "Now, more than ever, people need hope." Osteen and Obama both offer supporters the all-encompassing promise of "hope."

Barack the badass

After winning one of the most important elections in US history that featured unprecedented marketing and political strategies that redefined campaigns forever, Barack Obama enjoyed huge popularity.

His spectacular and hugely popular inauguration extended for days and included appearances by superstars, prominent politicians, actors, and other celebrities; Washington, DC was in lockdown for a week; millions traveled far distances just to participate; and Obama delivered his typical confidence in an inspiring speech. Once reality set in, President Obama struggled through his closely watched first 100 days, during which he had to reckon with the disastrous effects of an economic meltdown he was not entirely responsible for. In his first few months, he must have thought about what he wrote in the *Audacity of Hope*: how he, "or anybody in public office, can avoid the pitfalls of fame, the hunger to please, the fear of loss, and thereby retain that kernel of truth, that singular voice within each of us that reminds us of our deepest com- mitments." As his promises began to remain unfulfilled and his record started to look like that of a politician for whom most of his ardent sup- porters might not even vote, Barack Obama's political identity was at risk. He increased military efforts in Afghanistan; ordered drone strikes in Pakistan that caused relatively high civilian casualties; and compro- mised over and over again on economic and healthcare decisions. His appearances toward the end of 2010 and into 2011 began to carry more resolve; he appeared at the memorial service for victims of the January 2011 Arizona shooting spree that left several dead and US Representative Gabrielle Giffords gravely wounded. He followed up only days later with a calm optimism in his 2011 State of the Union speech.

But as the Arab Spring ensued, beginning in Tunisia in December 2010 and spreading to one Middle Eastern nation after the next, Obama's responses would define the rest of his first term. The region witnessed unprecedented unrest with the "success" of the Egyptian revolution, the subsequent war in Libya, and brutal suppression in Bahrain, Syria, and other surrounding countries. Then there was the embarrassment of a CIA contractor accused in Pakistan of murder. Ray Davis was freed in March 2011, but the events left tension in the Pakistan-United States relationship. Then Obama had to face a seemingly absurd campaign demanding that he prove that he was really born in the United States, leading to his release of his Hawaiian birth certificate in April. All the while, deliberations around Obama's single most risky and decisive act were taking place.

On the night of 1 May 2011 – exactly eight years after Bush's "Mission Accomplished" appearance – President Barack Obama made a late appear- ance on national television announcing the Osama bin Laden had been killed by US forces in Pakistan. His statement launched a massive set of responses. In the days that followed, an explosion of narratives, critiques,

and praises erupted. Questions abound: How did bin Laden go unde-
tected for apparently several years in a villa in Pakistan? Was he armed
when Navy Seals charged the building? Did he resist and how? The
assassination, carried out on a moonless night by four helicopters, was
saturated in drama: the mission itself took place in the shadow of
previously botched special forces operations, including US President
Jimmy Carter's failed attempt to rescue the 52 American diplomats and
military personnel held hostage by Iranian Islamists in 1980, and the
"Black Hawk Down" incident in Somalia in 1993 during which two
Black Hawk helicopters were shot down. Obama ordered a Navy Seal
team on a mission to enter Pakistan by helicopter with the objective to
kill or capture Osama bin Laden. The research on the compound bin
Laden was apparently holed up in had been ongoing since August 2010,
involving a trace on one of bin Laden's couriers. The Seals stormed the
villa, shot Osama bin Laden in the face, removed his body, and gave
him a "Muslim burial at sea." The media began talking about photos of
his body and videos of his burial being released; the White House later
announced they would not be made public. The mission implicated
Pakistan's possible role in hiding bin Laden while usurping the country's
sovereignty. Some cynics argued that bin Laden was long dead and the
Navy Seal mission was staged. Others emphasized the bold undertaking,
citing the rehearsals conducted by the elite Team 6 to prepare for the
covert operation. The torture debate found new ammunition, with the
Republican House Representative Steve King tweeting on 2 May 2011:
"Wonder what President Obama thinks of water boarding now?"

Such an accusation – that Bush and his Administration was right to torture detainees, because it led to actionable intelligence – pointed to the
key perceived difference between Obama and Bush. Yet Obama, it could
not be denied, performed well, and took credit for getting something
done, and these were facts that no spin could easily manipulate. Obama
visited Ground Zero later that week, had lunch with New York firefight-
ers, and met with former New York Mayor Rudy Giuliani. George W.
Bush remained conspicuously absent. Michael Moore, critical of Obama
for not allowing Osama bin Laden to be tried for his crimes, remained
equally critical of Bush for not being able to catch bin Laden after over
seven years. Throughout the week, despite a solid characterization of
the event as *not* entirely due to Obama's prowess, and despite the ridiculous sight of crowds chanting "USA" at Ground Zero in praise of the
death of bin Laden, there was an unmistakable, irreversible sea change:
Obama *took care of business*. His approval rating shot up. ABC News
reported that "Fifty-six percent of Americans now say they approve

of Obama's performance in office overall [...] nine percentage points higher than an ABC News/Washington Post poll found last month, and the highest rating for Obama since 2009."[37] The comedian and talk-show host Bill Maher captured the shift in attitude toward Obama that could be felt in spite of anything Fox News could possible muster, saying on 6 May 2011 that "Barack Obama is one efficient, steely-nerved, multitasking, black ninja gangsta president."[38]

In complete opposition to his Nobel Prize, which was firmly based in the absence of real action, crediting the feeling Obama instilled in the global public as good for peace, the assassination of Osama bin Laden was all *action*: a violent, vengeful event. The image of Obama surrounded by his national security team frames him as a humble leader, sitting in the foreground, *thinking* as he is watching the events of one of the most risky operations undertaken by the US military (see Figure 5.1). Knowing how much could have gone wrong – and indeed, in the drama a lot *did* go wrong, including the loss of one helicopter rumored to be a modified Black Hawk with new, still-secret stealth technology – and knowing the final order came from Obama, the public could have confidence in their leader.

For Michael Eric Dyson, Obama's act reflected a desire to no longer be "other": "The reality is that [President Obama] was being questioned as an un-American ... then, he has to prove he's an American by killing the Muslim. And by going to the extreme, he proves that he's the most American when he's most violent."[39] The double nature of Obama that *allowed* him to engage in a hugely successful political campaign – his "blank screen" – ends up after his inauguration as a growing case *against* him. Shortly after announcing his 2012 re-election campaign, on the tail of Republican candidates holding their first debate, Obama released his Hawaiian birth certificate. Proving with this evidence that he was, after all, "American," born on US soil and therefore qualified to be president, Obama both silenced critics while giving in to what some perceived to be a silly demand. The assassination of Osama bin Laden was certainly not the first violent and bold move by President Obama. He had already approved extensive drone strikes against Al Qaeda and Taliban operatives in Pakistan since 2009, but the attacks have also killed and injured hundreds of civilians. Weeks before the bin Laden operation Obama sent drones into Libya as well. In the wake of bin Laden's death, Obama's violent nerve took on more bold acts. On 5 May 2011, Obama ordered a drone strike in Yemen targeting a US citizen and Muslim cleric, Anwar al-Awlaki. Al-Awlaki, whom the United States has not charged, was not killed, but two other Al Qaeda members

Figure 5.1 President Barack Obama and Vice-President Joe Biden, along with members of the national security team, receive an update on the mission against Osama bin Laden in the Situation Room of the White House, 1 May 2011. Seated, from left, are Brigadier General Marshall B. "Brad" Webb, Assistant Commanding General, Joint Special Operations Command; Deputy National Security Advisor Denis McDonough; Secretary of State Hillary Rodham Clinton; and Secretary of Defense Robert Gates. Standing, from left, are: Admiral Mike Mullen, Chairman of the Joint Chiefs of Staff; National Security Advisor Tom Donilon; Chief of Staff Bill Daley; Tony Binken, National Security Advisor to the Vice President; Audrey Tomason Director for Counterterrorism; John Brennan, Assistant to the President for Homeland Security and Counterterrorism; and Director of National Intelligence James Clapper. Please note: a classified document seen in this photograph has been obscured. Official White House photo by Pete Souza.

were.[40] Such a move would only be legal if the Administration could prove that al-Awlaki posed an imminent threat. These brazen moves – Obama's choice to take out Public Enemy Number One as soon as he got a chance and to order an aggressive strike against a US citizen on foreign soil – performs a certain kind of Americanism that plays well, especially around campaign time.

Notes

Preface

1. Jon McKenzie, *Perform or Else* (London: Routledge, 2001).
2. Quoted in "Watch: Full Video of WikiLeaks' Julian Assange & Philosopher Slavoj Žižek With Amy Goodman," *Democracy Now*, 5 July 2011, http://www.democracynow.org/blog/2011/7/5/watch_full_video_of_wikileaks_julian_assange_philosopher_slavoj_iek_with_amy_goodman, accessed 26 July 2011.
3. See Paul Steinhauser, "Obama's Record-Breaking Campaign Haul," *CNN*, 13 July 2011, http://politicalticker.blogs.cnn.com/2011/07/13/obama-and-dnc-raise-more-than-86-million/, accessed 26 July 2011.
4. Slavoj Žižek, *First as Tragedy, Then as Farce* (London: Verso, 2009), 39.
5. See Alec Liu and Jeremy A. Kaplan, "Arkansas May Be Man-Made, Experts Warn," 1 March 2011, *FoxNews.com*, http://www.foxnews.com/scitech/2011/03/01/fracking-earthquakes-arkansas-man-experts-warn/, accessed 26 July 2011.
6. See "About Hydrolic Fracturing," *Chesapeake Energy*, http://www.hydraulic-fracturing.com/Pages/information.aspx, accessed 26 July 2011.
7. See "Episode 221, Quotes," *Real Time with Bill Maher*, 22 July 2011, http://www.hbo.com/real-time-with-bill-maher/index.html#/real-time-with-bill-maher/episodes/0/221-episode/synopsis/quotes.html, accessed 26 July 2011.
8. See "Pushing Crisis: GOP Cries Wolf on Debt Ceiling in Order to Impose Radical Pro-Rich Agenda," *Democracy Now*, 22 July 2011, http://www.democracynow.org/2011/7/22/pushing_crisis_gop_cries_wolf_on, accessed 26 July 2011.
9. See "Colbert Report: John Lithgow Performs Gingrich Press Release," *ColbertNation.com*, 19 May 2011, http://www.colbertnation.com/the-colbert-report-videos/387033/may-19-2011/john-lithgow-performs-gingrich-press-release, accessed 26 July 2011. For background on the press release, see Michael Calderone, "NBC's David Gregory Defends Medicare Question As Newt Gingrich Spokesman Blasts Media 'Minions,'" *Huffington Post*, 18 May 2011, http://www.huffingtonpost.com/2011/05/18/nbcs-david-gregory-defend_n_863660.html, accessed 26 July 2011.

Chapter 1   Bushismo

1. George W. Bush, "President Urges Readiness and Patience: Remarks by the President, Secretary of State Colin Powell and Attorney General John Ashcroft, Camp David, Thurmont, Maryland," Office of the Press Secretary, 15 September 2001, http://georgewbush-whitehouse.archives.gov/news/releases/2001/09/20010915-4.html, accessed 5 May 2011.
2. Henry Giroux, *Hearts of Darkness: Torturing Children in the War on Terror Paradigm 2010*, excerpted in "Torturing Democracy," *Truthout*, http://www.truth-out.org/torturing-democracy67570, accessed 5 May 2011.

3. Bush made the doctor comment at a September 2004 rally in Poplar Bluff, Missouri and the "fool" saying at a 17 September rally in Nashville. Both are quoted in "Top Ten Bushisms," *Time* online, http://www.time.com/time/specials/packages/article/0,28804,1870938_1870943_1870953,00.html#ixzz1CAgBbD3x, accessed 26 January 2011.

4. See Richard Schechner, *Performance Studies: An Introduction*, 2nd edn (London: Routledge, 2006), 35.

5. Tim Raphael, "The Body Electric: GE, TV, and the Reagan Brand," *The Drama Review* 53.2 (2009): 113–38, here 136. See also his book *The President Electric: Ronald Reagan and the Politics of Performance* (Ann Arbor: University of Michigan Press, 2009).

6. Diana Taylor, "Editorial Remarks: The New Radical Performance Artists: Staging Democracy in the Americas," *e-misférica* 1.1 (Fall 2004), http://hemispheric institute.org/journal/1_1/editorial_eng.html, accessed 26 January 2011.

7. Ibid. (emphasis added).

8. Schechner, *Performance Studies*, 216–17. For more on fascism and theatre, see Günter Berghaus, ed., *Fascism and Theatre: Comparative Studies on the Aesthetics and Politics of Performance in Europe 1925–1945* (Oxford: Berghahn Books, 1996).

9. Antonin Artaud, *Theatre of Cruelty* (New York: Grove Press, 1958), 85.

10. Richard Schechner, "9/11 as Avant-Garde Art?", *PMLA* 124.5 (2009), 1820–9, here 1821.

11. Ibid.

12. For an analysis of Lee's rhetoric, see Grant C. Cos, "Dissent and the Rhetoric of Reflection: Barbara Lee's September 14, 2001, Speech," *Rhetor: Revue de la Société canadienne pour l'étude de la rhétorique* 2 (2007, www.cssr-scer.ca/rhetor), accessed 4 May 2011.

13. *Daily Mirror* front page, 4 November 2004.

14. Unnamed reporter quoted in Bush, "President Urges Readiness and Patience."

15. Bush, "President Urges Readiness and Patience" (emphasis added).

16. Ibid.

17. "Bush: Bin Laden 'Wanted Dead or Alive,' CNN, 17 September 2001, http://articles.cnn.com/2001-09-17/us/bush.powell.terrorism_1_bin-qaeda-terrorist-attacks?_s=PM:US, accessed 8 May 2011.

18. See Alex Spillius, "George Bush the Texan Is 'Scared of Horses,'" *Daily Telegraph* 21 September 2007, http://www.telegraph.co.uk/news/worldnews/1563773/George-Bush-the-Texan-is-scared-of-horses.html, accessed 8 May 2011.

19. "Transcript of President Bush's Address," CNN online, 21 September 2001, http://articles.cnn.com/2001-09-20/us/gen.bush.transcript_1_joint-session-national-anthem-citizens?_s=PM:US, accessed 2 February 2011 (emphasis added).

20. Ibid.

21. Ibid.

22. Ibid.

23. Ibid.

24. Ibid. (emphasis added).

25. Jon McKenzie, "Democracy's Performance," *TDR: The Drama Review* 47.2 (T178), Summer 2003: 117–28, here 120.

26. Ibid., 120.

27. Giroux, *Hearts of Darkness*.
28. Stuart Croft, *Culture, Crisis and America's War on Terror* (Cambridge: Cambridge University Press, 2006).
29. Dougal Phillips, "The Self-Torment of the White House Screen: Language, Lyotard and Looking Back at the War on Terror," *Colloquy* 13 (2007): 5–19, here 7.
30. See, for example, Jane Mayer's *The Dark Side: The Inside Story on How the War on Terror Turned into a War on American Ideals* (New York: Random House, 2008); and Mark Danner, *The Secret Way to War: The Downing Street Memo and the Iraq War's Buried History* (New York: New York Review of Books, 2006).
31. White House Press Release, "President Bush, Colombia President Uribe Discuss Terrorism," 25 September 2002, http://www.whitehouse.gov/news/releases/2002/09/print/20020925-1.html, accessed 14 August 2007.
32. Ed Pilkington, "Colin Powell demands answers over Curveball's WMD lies," *Guardian*, 16 February 2011, http://www.guardian.co.uk/world/2011/feb/16/colin-powell-cia-curveball, accessed 5 May 2011.
33. Dougal Phillips, "The Self-Torment of the White House Screen: Language, Lyotard and Looking Back at the War on Terror," *Colloquy* 13 (2007): 5–19, here 7.
34. Ibid., 12.
35. Naomi Klein, "The Year of the Fake," *The Nation*, 9 January 2004, http://www.naomiklein.org/articles/2004/01/year-fake, accessed 5 May 2011.
36. Ibid.
37. Nicholas Mirzoeff, *Watching Babylon: The War in Iraq and Global Visual Culture* (London: Routledge, 2005), 13.
38. "Michael Moore on His Life, His Films and His Activism," *Democracy Now*, 6 September 2010, http://www.democracynow.org/2010/9/6/michael_moore_on_his_life_his, accessed 31 January 2011.
39. Ibid.
40. Ibid.
41. "What Really Happened to Pat Tillman?" *60 Minutes*, CBS, 4 May 2008, http://www.cbsnews.com/stories/2008/05/01/60minutes/main4061656.shtml, accessed 5 May 2011.
42. Phillips, "The Self-Torment of the White House Screen," 17.
43. Mark Danner, "Frozen Scandal," *New York Review of Books*, 4 December 2008, http://www.nybooks.com/articles/archives/2008/dec/04/frozen-scandal/#fn1-649488691, accessed 5 May 2011.
44. Ibid.
45. Giroux, *Hearts of Darkness*.
46. *Southland*, Season 1, Episode 1, NBC, aired 2009.
47. Vice-President Dick Cheney speaking to *Meet the Press*'s Tim Russert on 16 September 2001.
48. Mayer, *The Dark Side*, 9–10.
49. Ibid., 33.
50. Ibid., 37.
51. See "Bin Laden's Fatwa," PBS NewsHour online, http://www.pbs.org/newshour/terrorism/international/fatwa_1996.html, accessed 26 January 2011.
52. Mayer, *The Dark Side*, 34.
53. Ibid., 31; Bob Woodward, *Bush at War* (New York: Simon & Schuster, 2002), 41.

54. Slavoj Žižek, *Welcome to the Desert of the Real* (London: Verso, 2002). Žižek's essay was written on 15 September 2001.
55. Michael Rolince, head of International Terrorism Ops section of FBI, quoted in Mayer, *The Dark Side*, 34.
56. Naomi Klein, *The Shock Doctrine: The Rise of Disaster Capitalism* (New York: Metropolitan Books, 2008).
57. See ibid.
58. See "Letter from the President on the Continuation of the National Emergency with Respect to Certain Terrorist Attacks," 10 September 2010, http://www.whitehouse.gov/the-press-office/2010/09/10/letter-president-continuation-national-emergency-with-respect-certain-te, accessed 26 January 2011.
59. Giorgio Agamben, *State of Exception* (Chicago: University of Chicago Press, [2003] 2005).
60. Giorgio Agamben, *Homo Sacer: Sovereign Power and Bare Life* (Stanford, CA: Stanford University Press, [1995] 1998).
61. Alfred McCoy, quoted in "Historian Alfred McCoy: Obama Reluctance on Bush Prosecution Affirms Culture of Impunity," *Democracy Now*, 1 May 2009, http://www.democracynow.org/2009/5/1/torture_expert_alfred_mccoy_obama_reluctance, accessed 20 July 2009.
62. See, for example, Alfred McCoy, *A Question of Torture: CIA Interrogation from the Cold War to the War on Terror* (New York: Metropolitan Books, 2006).
63. Schechner, "9/11 as Avant-Garde Art?," 1822.
64. Carol Martin, "Bodies of Evidence," *The Drama Review* 50.3 (2006): 11.
65. Ibid., 13.
66. See Janelle Reinelt's review in *Theatre Journal* 57.2 (May 2005): 303–6.
67. See Karen Greenberg, *The Least Worst Place: Guantánamo's First 100 Days* (New York: Oxford University Press, 2009).
68. X-Ray closed in 2002 when Camp Delta opened.
69. See, for example, http://www.globalsecurity.org/military/facility/images/guantanamo-bay_x-ray020111n696_0963y.jpg, accessed 2 July 2009.
70. Martin, "Bodies of Evidence," 11.
71. Ibid.
72. Stephen Colbert, "The Word: Wikiality," *The Colbert Report*, 31 July 2006.
73. George W. Bush, *Decision Points* (New York: Crown Publishing, 2010), 325–6.
74. Dick Cheney, interview with Jonathan Karl, "Transcript: Cheney Defends Hard Line Tactics," ABC News, 16 December 2008, http://abcnews.go.com/Politics/story?id=6464697&page=1, accessed 5 May 2011.

Chapter 2 Protest Visible and Invisible

1. Jacques Rancière, "Ten Theses on Politics," in *Dissensus: On Politics and Aesthetics*, ed. and trans. Steven Corcoran (London: Continuum, 2010), 37.
2. See "History of Shannon Airport," Shannon Airport website, http://www.shannonairport.com/gns/about-us/media-centre/history-of-shannon-airport.aspx, accessed 12 April 2011.
3. Trevor Paglen, *Blank Spots on the Map: The Dark Geography of the Pentagon's Secret World* (New York: Dutton, 2009), 4.
4. Ibid., 35.

5. Ibid., 4.
6. Ibid., 4 (emphasis original).
7. Ibid., 16.
8. Diana Taylor, *The Archive and the Repertoire* (Durham, NC: Duke University Press, 2003), 275.
9. Rancière, "Ten Theses on Politics," 36.
10. Paglen, *Blank Spots on the Map*, 36.
11. Rancière, "Ten Theses on Politics," 37.
12. Ibid., 38.
13. Bill Moyers, "Takin' It to the Streets – A Bill Moyers Essay," *Bill Moyers Journal*, 2 November 2007, http://www.pbs.org/moyers/journal/11022007/profile3.html, accessed 13 April 2011.
14. Diana Taylor, *Disappearing Acts* (Durham, NC: Duke University Press, 1997), 122–4, quoted in Diana Taylor, "Double-Blind: The Torture Case," *Critical Inquiry* 33 (Summer): 710-33, 717.
15. I talk more about the November 2001 order in Chapter 4.
16. Taylor, *The Archive and the Repertoire*, 19.
17. Democracy Now, "Thousands Take to the Streets in San Francisco and Washington, D.C. to Call for Peace and Justice," 1 October 2001, http://www.democracynow.org/2001/10/1/thousands_take_to_the_streets_in, accessed 13 April 2011.
18. Media Matters, "For Major Papers, 9–12 March – But Not Iraq War Protest – Warranted Front-Page Coverage," 15 September 2009, http://mediamatters.org/research/200909150037, accessed 13 April 2011.
19. Don Mitchell and Lynn A. Staeheli, "Permitting Protest: Parsing the Fine Geography of Dissent in America," *International Journal of Urban and Regional Research* 29.4 (December 2005): 796–813, here 796.
20. United for Peace and Justice, "History," http://unitedforpeace.org/about/history/, accessed 13 April 2011.
21. See "Cities jammed in worldwide protest of war in Iraq," CNN, 15 February 2003, http://articles.cnn.com/2003-02-15/us/sprj.irq.protests.main_1_anti-war-rallies-anti-war-movement-police-use-pepper-spray?_s=PM:US, accessed 13 April 2011.
22. Noam Chomsky, interview with Amy Goodman, *Democracy Now*, 15 March 2010, http://www.democracynow.org/2010/3/15/noam_chomsky_on_obamas_foreign_policy, accessed 22 March 2010.
23. Sidney Tarrow, Preface, *The World Says No to War: Demonstrations Against the War on Iraq* (Minneapolis, MN: University of Minnesota Press, 2010), viii.
24. Media Matters, "Fox Promotion of Tea Parties Follows Years of Attacking Progressive Demonstrators," 17 April 2009, http://mediamatters.org/research/200904170036, accessed 13 April 2011.
25. Rancière, "Ten Theses on Politics," 37.
26. Ibid.
27. Mitchell and Staeheli, "Permitting Protest in America," 809. The authors cite D. Schemo, "Mideast Turmoil: Demonstrations: Thousands Hold Rally in Capital to Back Israel," *New York Times*, 16 April 2002, A18.
28. Mitchell and Staeheli, citing P. Dvorak, "Like Protestors, Chief Hit the Streets of D.C.: Being Close to the Action Was Key," *Washington Post*, 24 April 2002, B1.
29. Mitchell and Staeheli, "Permitting Protest in America," 810.

30. Rimini Protokoll, "Helgard Haug," Rimini Protokoll website, http://www. rimini-protokoll.de/artist_frontend.php?artist_id=3, accessed 11 June 2007.

31. Patrice Blaser, "I Try to Speak About Reality," Interview with Helgard Haug, Stefan Kaegi, and Daniel Wetzel. Vienna, 2004, http://www.rimini-protokoll. de/misc_frontend.php?misc_id=29, accessed 3 June 2007.

32. Peter Boenisch, "Other People Live: Rimini Protokoll and Their Theatre of Experts," *Contemporary Theatre Review* 18.1 (2008): 107–13, here 110–11.

33. In 2005, Rimini Protokoll created an unusual adaptation of Friedrich Schiller's *Wallenstein*, in which, although "mirror[ing] exactly the dramaturgical line of the original play, following its plot, entrances and exits, not a single line of it was spoken" (Boenisch, "Other People Live". Instead, performers used their own autobiographies to advance the plot.

34. Curators Multitude e.V. and Unfriendly Takeover designed the *Dictionary of War* with the intention to "create key concepts that either play a significant role in current discussions of war, have so far been neglected, or have yet to be created." Multitude e.V. and Unfriendly Takeover, "A to Z: The Precarious Alphabet of War," *Dictionary of War*, http://dictionaryofwar.org/en-dict/node/ 644, accessed 27 September 2007. During two-day events in five cities, Frankfurt, Munich, Graz, Berlin, and Novi Sad, Serbia, "scientists, artists, theorists and activists" presented over 100 concepts of war in 20-minute segments. *Dictionary of War* is a resource originally performed with the intent that through online documentation and book publication, the concepts will continue to develop and inform.

35. All quotes are from the video of *Resist, Refuse, Rebel*.

36. Stegan Kaegi, quoted in Blaser, "I Try to Speak About Reality."

37. Blaser, "I Try to Speak About Reality."

38. Robert Leach, "Mother Courage and Her Children," in *The Cambridge Companion to Brecht* (Cambridge: Cambridge Univeristy Press, 2006), 132–42, here 135; see also Bertolt Brecht, *Brecht on Theatre* (London: Methuen, 1964).

39. Frankfurter Allgemeine Sonntagszeitung (FAS), "Real-Life Drama: Rimini Protokoll Creates Progressive Theatre without Actors and Costumes," 5 June 2006, http://www.rimini-protokoll.de/website/en/article_2700.html, accessed 12 March 2008.

40. Daniel Mufson, "Berlin's Holy of Holies," *Performing Arts Journal* 29.1 (2007): 53–64, here 62.

41. For a colorful history, see Rene North, *Military Uniforms 1686–1918* (London: Hamlyn, 1969); also see Jennifer Craik's *Uniforms Exposed: From Conformity to Transgression* (Oxford and New York: Berg, 2005) for a cultural history of the uniform in general.

42. See Guy Hartcup, *Camouflage: The History of Deception and Concealment in War* (London: Pen & Sword, [1979] 2008). Roy Behrens is an expert on camouflage and its sociocultural/political history; see his *False Colors: Art, Design and Modern Camouflage* (Bobolinks, 2002) for helpful context on the interaction among military, artists, and fashion designers on the form.

43. Tim Newark, *Camouflage* (London: Imperial War Museum; and New York: Thames & Hudson, 2007), 54.

44. Ibid., 92, 96–7.

45. Ibid., 72.

46. Ibid., 38.

47. Ibid., 164.
48. See ibid., 146–89.
49. Coco Fusco, "Artist Statement," *TDR: The Drama Review* 52.1 (Spring 2008): 140–53, here 140.
50. *A Room of One's Own* premiered at the Victoria and Albert Museum in London in 2006 and toured subsequently to New York, Philadelphia, Miami, New Haven, and Auckland, New Zealand. The documentary *Operation Atropos* premiered in Los Angeles and was screened at the 2008 Whitney Biennial.
51. José Muñoz, "Performing the State of Exception: Coco Fusco's *Operation Atropos*," *TDR: The Drama Review* 52.1 (Spring 2008): 136–9, here 138.
52. Ibid., 138.
53. "When wearing by persons not on active duty authorized." 10 U.S.C. § 772(f).
54. Black's opinion quotes the Court of Appeals: "The skit was composed of three people. There was Schacht who was dressed in a uniform and cap. A second person was wearing 'military colored' coveralls. The third person was outfitted in typical Viet Cong apparel. The first two men carried water pistols. One of them would yell, 'Be an able American,' and then they would shoot the Viet Cong with their pistols. The pistols expelled a red liquid which, when it struck the victim, created the impression [398 U.S. 58, 61] that he was bleeding. Once the victim fell down the other two would walk up to him and exclaim, 'My God, this is a pregnant woman.' Without noticeable variation this skit was reenacted several times during the morning of the demonstration." 414 F.2d 630, 632. http://caselaw.lp.findlaw.com/scripts/getcase.pl?navby=case&court=us&vol=398&invol=58, accessed 27 April 2011.
55. Thomas Paine, *The American Crisis* (London: James Watson [1776] 1835), 3.
56. Al Hubbard quoted in "The real story of the ... Vietnam Veterans Against the War," 14 September 2004, http://socialistworker.org/2004-2/512/512_08_VVAW.shtml, accessed 15 May 2010.
57. Associated Press, "Chaplain Guilty for Wearing Uniform at Protest: Navy Officer Convicted of Disobeying Order Over White House Demonstration," 13 September 2006, http://www.msnbc.msn.com/id/14824097, accessed 24 May 2010.
58. Paul Vercammen and Thelma Gutierrez, "State's New Immigration Law Worries Arizona Soldier," CNN online, 27 April 27 2010, http://edition.cnn.com/2010/US/04/25/arizona.soldier.immigration.vigil/index.html, accessed 24 May 2010.
59. See Kerry Eleveld and Andrew Harmon, "Choi Arrested at White House Gates," *The Advocate* online, 18 March 2010, http://www.advocate.com/News/Daily_News/2010/03/18/Dan_Choi_Protests_in_Front_of_WH/, accessed 30 June 2010.
60. See www.warep.com
61. Drew Cameron, quoted in "Combat Paper Project: About Combat Paper," http://www.combatpaper.org/about.html, accessed 27 May 2010.
62. Geoff Millard, email correspondence with author, 1 July 2010.
63. For images from the first Operation First Casualty visit, http://www.ivaw.org/photos/gallery/Operation+First+Casualty%2C+Washington+DC%2C+March+19%2C+2007.
64. Adam Kokesh, quoted in "Pentagon Cracks Down on Anti-War Iraq War Veterans For Protesting in Uniform," 12 June 2007, *Democracy Now* online.

http://www.democracynow.org/2007/6/12/pentagon_cracks_down_on_
anti_war, accessed 19 June 2007.

65. Geoff Millard, "Operation First Casualty," Iraq Veterans Against the War website, http://www.ivaw.org/node/460, accessed 27 May 2010.

66. http://www.zombietime.com/operation_first_casualty/.

67. For video of the New York OFC, see Meerkat Media's coverage of the event at
http://www.meerkatmedia.org/movies/gis-take-manhattan-operation-first-
casualty/.

68. Stephen Duncombe, "Bringing the War Home: IVAW's Operation First
Casualty," *In Media Res* website, http://mediacommons.futureofthebook.org/
imr/2009/09/10/bringing-war-home-ivaw-s-operation-first-casualty, accessed
27 May 2010; Stephen Duncombe interviewed by Stephen Sherman,
"'A Politics about Performing Dreams': An Interview with Stephen
Duncombe," *Monthly Review* online, http://mrzine.monthlyreview.org/2007/
sherman230207.html, accessed 27 May 2010.

69. Duncombe, "Bringing the War Home," and Duncombe interviewed by
Stephen Sherman, "A Politics about Performing Dreams."

70. Duncombe interviewed by Stephen Sherman, "A Politics about Performing
Dreams."

71. David Montgomery, "Antiwar to the Corps: Marine Reservist-Protestors Face
Discipline," *The Washington Post*, 31 May 2007, http://www.washingtonpost.
com/wp-dyn/content/article/2007/05/30/AR2007053002627.html, accessed
28 June 2010.

72. http://dyingwarriors.blogspot.com/2007/06/iraq-veteran-begins-weeklong-
tower.html.

73. See "Pentagon Cracks Down on Anti-War Iraq War Veterans For Protesting
in Uniform," 12 June 2007, *Democracy Now*, http://www.democracynow.
org/2007/6/12/pentagon_cracks_down_on_anti_war, accessed 19 June
2007.

74. Evan Knappenberger, email correspondence with author, 24 June 2010.

75. Nina B. Huntemann, "Interview with Colonel Casey Wardynski," in Nina B.
Huntemann and Thomas Matthew Payne, eds, *Joystick Soldiers: The Politics
of Play in Military Video Games* (New York: Routledge, 2010), 178–88, here
181.

76. Joseph DeLappe, "dead-in-iraq" page, http://www.unr.edu/art/delappe/
DeLappe%20Main%20Page/DeLappe%20Online%20MAIN.html, accessed
17 March 2011.

77. DeLappe cites casualty statistics from icasualties.org.

78. Irene Chien, "Playing Against the Grain: Machinima and Military Gaming,"
in Huntemann and Payne, *Joystick Soldiers: The Politics of Play in Military
Video Games* (New York: Routledge, 2010), 239–51, here 240.

79. Ibid., 240.

80. Ibid.

81. DeLappe, "dead-in-iraq" page.

82. See http://www.unr.edu/art/delappe/DeLappe%20Main%20Page/DeLappe%
20Online%20MAIN.html.

83. Li C. Kuo, "A New Kind of Art Form Leads to a New Kind of Protest," *GameSpy*,
23 May 2006, http://www.gamespy.com/pc/americas-army/709854p2.html,
accessed 17 March 2011.

84. Dean Chan, *"Dead-in-Iraq*: The Spatial Politics of Digital Game Art Activism and the In-Game Protest," in Huntemann and Payne, *Joystick Soldiers: The Politics of Play in Military Video Games* (New York: Routledge, 2010), 272–86, here 278.
85. Ibid., 275.
86. See "'Nightline' to Honor 'The Fallen': Ted Koppel to Read Names of Over 900 Servicemen and Women Killed in Iraq, Afghanistan in Memorial Day Broadcast," *ABC News*, http://abcnews.go.com/Nightline/story?id=786279&page=1, accessed 17 March 2011; and "Sinclair Stations Pull Nightline Iraq Casualties Report," *PBS Online NewsHour Update*, http://www.pbs.org/newshour/updates/abc_04-30-04.html, accessed 17 March 2011.

Chapter 3   War, the Video Game

1. Nicholas Mirzoeff, "War Is Culture: Global Counterinsurgency, Visuality, and the Petraeus Doctrine," *PMLA* 124.5: 1737–8, 1741.
2. *Full Spectrum Warrior*, Pandemic Studios, 2004.
3. "The Story Behind the Army Experience Center," *The Army Experience Center* webpage, http://www.thearmyexperience.com/about-the-army-experience-center/the-story-of-the-center, accessed 10 February 2010.
4. Pat Elder, quoted in "US army uses video games as part of recruitment drive," *Al Jazeera English*, 12 November 2009, http://www.youtube.com/watch?v=IvMZHrjfC_c, viewed 10 February via *youtube.com*.
5. Richard Schechner, *Performance Theory* (London: Routledge, 1977), 107–8.
6. See Mike Pattenden, "Why Army Recruitment Is Still Soaring," *TimesOnline*, 7 October 2009, http://www.timesonline.co.uk/tol/life_and_style/men/article6863641.ece#, accessed 7 October 2009.
7. According to its most recent fact sheet, accessed on 12 May 2010 at http://www.shannonwatch.org/docs/Mar2010factsheet.pdf, Shannonwatch reports that between 2002 and late 2009, over 1.7 million US military personnel have stopped over at Shannon Airport in County Clare, Ireland.
8. Slavoj Žižek, *First as Tragedy, Then as Farce* (London: Verso, 2009), 39.
9. Mirzoeff, "War Is Culture," 1740.
10. Ibid., 1737–8.
11. Ibid., 1739.
12. Ibid., 1740.
13. Bea Jauregui, "Military Communitas? Re-Centering the Citizen-Soldier Interface at the Army Experience Center," paper presented at the Reconsidering American Power Conference, 23–25 April 2009, University of Chicago. Abstract at http://cis.uchicago.edu/events/08-09/reconsidering-american-power/abstracts.shtml#jauregui, accessed 2 March 2011.
14. Huntemann and Payne, "Introduction," in *Joystick Soldiers*, 1–18, here 3.
15. See Kai Ryssdal, "The Army Experience Center: Mission accomplished?," NPR *Marketplace*, 30 July 2010, http://marketplace.publicradio.org/display/web/2010/07/30/pm-the-army-experience-center-mission-accomplished/, accessed 31 July 2010.
16. George Orwell, *1984* (New York: Penguin, 1950); Ken Coates, ed., *War is Peace*, *The Spokesman* 73 (2001); Paul Virilio and Sylvère Lotringer, *Pure War*

(Los Angeles: Semiotext(e)), [1983] 2008); Arundhati Roy, "War Is Peace," *OutlookIndia.com*, 18 October 2001.

17. George W. Bush, "Transcript of President Bush Address," 20 September 2001, http://articles.cnn.com/2001-09-20/us/gen.bush.transcript_1_joint-session-national-anthem-citizens?_s=PM:US, accessed 28 March 2011.

18. US Department of the Army, *Counterinsurgency Manual*.

19. Paul Virilio, *Landscape of Events*, trans. Julie Rose (Cambridge, MA: MIT Press, 2000), 18–19.

20. Mirzoeff, "War Is Culture," 1740.

21. James P. Carse, *Finite and Infinite Games: A Vision of Life as Play and Possibility* (New York: Ballantine Books, 1986).

22. Ibid., 3, 9, 19, 67, quoted in Schechner, *Performance Studies: An Introduction*, 97.

23. Elaine Scarry, *The Body in Pain: The Making and Unmaking of the World* (Oxford: Oxford University Press, 1985), 83.

24. Der Derian, "War as Game", 37–48, here 37.

25. This quote is by Julian Assange, Wikileaks co-founder, in an interview with *Democracy Now*'s Amy Goodman about the April 2010 revelation that US soldiers killed Iraqi civilians and journalists. See "Massacre Caught on Tape: US Military Confirms Authenticity of Their Own Chilling Video Showing Killing of Journalists," *Democracy Now*, 6 April 2010, http://www.democracynow.org/2010/4/6/massacre_caught_on_tape_us_military, accessed 12 May 2010.

26. Der Derian, "War as Game," 38.

27. Schechner, *Performance Studies*, 89–90.

28. Zach Whitman Gill, "Rehearsing the War Away: Perpetual Warrior Training in Contemporary US Army Policy," *TDR: The Drama Review* 53.3 (T203) (Fall 2009): 139–55; Robertson Allen, "The Unreal Enemy of America's Army," Draft of essay appearing in *Games and Culture* 6.1: 38–60, http://washington.academia.edu/RobertsonAllen/Papers/166126/The_Unreal_Enemy_of_Americas_Army, accessed 14 February 2011.

29. Richard Schechner, conversation with author, 17 September 2010.

30. Der Derian, "War as Game," 39.

31. Ibid.

32. Gill, "Rehearsing the War Away, " 141.

33. Jean Baudrillard, *The Gulf War Did Not Take Place*, trans. and intro. Paul Patton (Bloomington: Indiana University Press, 1995).

34. Der Derian, "War as Game," 44–5.

35. See Sebastian Junger, *War* (New York: Twelve, 2010), and Sebastian Junger and Tim Hetherington, *Restropo* (Documentary Film), Outpost Films, 2010.

36. www.goarmy.com.

37. Jean Baudrillard, "War Porn," *International Journal of Baudrillard Studies* 2.1 (January 2005), trans. of "Pornographie de la guerre," *Liberation*, Wednesday 19 May 2004, by Paul Taylor, http://www.ubishops.ca/baudrillardstudies/vol2_1/taylor.htm#_edn1, accessed 4 March 2011.

38. Ibid.

39. See "One Soldier's Opinion About Being In Iraq," 19 August 2007, http://www.liveleak.com/view?i=e90_1187514955, accessed 12 February 2010.

40. See "Life as a Marine Grunt in Afghanistan," 16 April 2007, http://www.liveleak.com/view?i=6c4_1176720508, accessed 12 February 2010.

41. Joint Publication 1-02, Department of Defense Dictionary of Military and Associated Terms, 8 November 2010, as amended through 31 January 2011, JP 1-02 395. Cited in Tim Lenoir and Henry Lowood, "Theaters of War: The Military-Entertainment Complex," http://www.stanford.edu/class/sts145/Library/Lenoir-Lowood_TheatersOfWar.pdf, 2, accessed 25 March 2011.

42. For a detailed history of war games that relates to digital wargaming, see Sebastian Deterding, "Living Room Wars: Remediation, Boardgames, and the Early History of Video Wargaming," in Huntemann and Payne, *Joystick Soldiers*, 21–38.

43. For a detailed history of the war game as it relates to the late twentieth-century development of virtual reality and computer simulation, see Tim Lenoir and Henry Lowood, "Theaters of War: The Military-Entertainment Complex," in Jan Lazardzig, Helmar Schramm, and Ludger Schwarte, eds, *Collection, Laboratory, Theater: Scenes of Knowledge in the 17th Century* (Berlin: Walter de Gruyter, 2003), 427–56.

44. Ian Bogost, Foreword to Huntemann and Payne, *Joystick Soldiers*, xi–xvi, here xiii.

45. Tim Lenoir, "All But War Is Simulation: The Military-Entertainment Complex," *Configurations* 8 (2000), 289–435.

46. Ibid., 308.

47. Ibid., 309.

48. Platoni, Kara, "The Pentagon Goes to the Video Arcade," *The Progressive* 63.7 (1999): 27–30, here 28.

49. Deterding, "Living Room Wars," 29.

50. Platoni, "The Pentagon Goes to the Video Arcade," 28.

51. Lenoir, "All But War Is Simulation," 314.

52. Ibid., 316, citing US Department of Defense, Office of the Inspector General, Requirements Planning for Development, Test, Evaluation, and Impact on Readiness of Training Simulators and Devices (a draft proposed audit report), Project No. 5AB-0070.00, 10 January 1997, Appendix D.

53. Platoni, "The Pentagon Goes to the Video Arcade," 29.

54. Clive Thompson, "The Making of an Xbox Warrior," *New York Times Magazine*, 22 August 2002, 32–7.

55. See Platoni, "The Pentagon Goes to the Video Arcade," 27.

56. Lenoir, "All But War Is Simulation," 328.

57. Ibid.

58. Ibid., 329.

59. The name 73 Easting comes from the map line location of the battle in the southern Iraqi desert.

60. Lenoir, "All But War Is Simulation," 329–30.

61. Bruce Sterling, "War Is Virtual Hell," *Wired* 1.1 (March/April 1993), http://www.wired.com/wired/archive/1.01/virthell_pr.html, accessed 3 March 2011.

62. Ibid.

63. Lenoir, "All But War Is Simulation," 330.

64. Sterling, "War Is Virtual Hell."

65. See Schechner, *Performance Studies*, 225–7.

66. Ian Bogost and Cindy Poremba, "Can Games Get Real? A Closer Look at Documentary Games," in Andreas Jahn-Sudmann and Ralf Stockmann, eds,

Computer Games as a Sociocultural Phenomenon: Games without Frontiers – War without Tears (Basingstoke: Palgrave Macmillan, 2008), 12–21, here 12.
67. Ibid., 12–13.
68. Bill Werde, "The War at Home," *Wired* 12.3 (March 2004), http://www.wired.com/wired/archive/12.03/wargames_pr.html, accessed 24 March 2011.
69. www.kumawar.com.
70. Werde, "The War at Home."
71. Colin Freeman, "Battles Re-Enacted in Video Arcades," *San Francisco Chronicle*, 16 January 2005: A-4, http://www.sfgate.com/cgi-bin/article.cgi?f=/c/a/2005/01/16/MNG5LAR6KU1.DTL&type=printable, accessed 24 March 2011.
72. See Elizabeth Losh, "A Battle for Hearts and Minds: The Design Politics of ELECT BiLAT," in Huntemann and Payne, *Joystick Soldiers*, 160–77, here 160–1.
73. Jamin Brophy-Warren, "Iraq, the Videogame," *The Wall Street Journal*, 6 April 2009, http://online.wsj.com/article/SB123902404583292727.html, accessed 28 June 2010.
74. Ibid.
75. See Larry Frum, "Playing as 'Taliban' Removed from 'Medal of Honor' Fame," *CNN*, 1 October 2010, http://articles.cnn.com/2010-10-01/tech/medal.of.honor.taliban_1_medal-of-honor-game-taliban-military-families?_s=PM:TECH, accessed 25 March 2011.
76. See, e.g., Brophy-Warren's article about *Six Days in Fallujah* in which the author describes all three games as part of the "serious games" movement.
77. Bogost and Poremba, "Can Games Get Real?" 16.
78. Ibid., 15.
79. See Thompson, "The Making of an Xbox Warrior," 32–7.
80. Randy Nichols, "Target Acquired: *America's Army* and the Video Games Industry," in Huntemann and Payne, *Joystick Soldiers*, 39–52, here 40.
81. See Jacob Hodes and Emma Ruby-Sachs, "'America's Army' Targets Youth," *The Nation*, 2 September 2002, http://www.thenation.com/article/americas-army-targets-youth, accessed 23 March 2011.
82. Colonel Casey Wardynski, interviewed by Nina B. Huntemann, in Huntemann and Payne, *Joystick Soldiers*, 178–88, here 179.
83. "America's Army," *America's Army* official website, http://www.americasarmy.com/about/, accessed 28 February 2011.
84. Henry Lowood (2008, 84) traces work on other games around the same time, "Impotence and Agency: Computer Games as a Post-9/11 Battlefield," in Jahn-Sudmann and Stockmann, *Computer Games as a Sociocultural Phenomenon* 78–86, here 84. Also part of this trend, he explains, is Full Spectrum Warrior, developed by the University of Southern California's Institute for Creative Technologies "with help from the Army" and Tom Clancy's Rogue Spear (2001). The commercial version of Rogue Spear was modified by "LB&B Associates, a military contractor in Maryland [who] obtained the right from Ubi Soft" to adapt the game for a military training contract specific to "soldiers in urban warfare, focusing on small-unit decision-making skills in keeping with the game's design." The Rogue Spear project was eventually taken over by the ICT for further development. The ICT also began work in the fall of 2001 with "C-Force, a squad-based game, and Combat System XII, a command simulator for company commanders." He cites Noah Schachtman, "New Army Soldiers: Game Gamers," Wired News, 29 October 2001,

http://www.wired.com/news/conflict/0,2100,47931,00.html; William Trotter, "The Power of Simulation: Transforming Our World," *PCGamer*, February (2003), pp. 24–8; and Harold Kennedy, "Computer Games Liven Up Military Recruiting, Training," *National Defense*, November (2002), http://www.nationaldefensemagazine.org/issues/2002/Nov/Computer_Games.htm. According to Lowood:

> These games became *Full Spectrum Command*, a PC-based training game that modeled Military Operations in Urban Terrain (MOUT) in Eastern Europe, delivered to the Army in early 2003, and *Full Spectrum Warrior*, developed with Pandemic Studios for the Army, but also published in commercial versions for consoles and PCs between March and September 2004. *Full Spectrum Warrior* depicted scenarios set in the Middle East. Destineer Studios and Atomic Games released *Close Combat: First to Fight*, based on military training tools, doctrine and input from the US Marine Corps. It continued the *Close Combat* series of military simulation games begun in 1996, spinning off from Atomic's *Close Combat: Marine*, developed for the Marine Corps. (84)

For a list of video games used by the US military, see Randy Nichols, "Target Acquired," 39–52, here 42.

85. See Wardynski interviewed by Nina B. Huntemann, 182.
86. Randy Nichols, "The Games People Play: A Political Economic Analayist of Video Games and Their Production," PhD dissertation, University of Oregon, 2005.
87. See Nieborg, "Training Recruits and Conditioning Youth," 57; and Huntemann and Payne, "Introduction," in Huntemann and Payne, *Joystick Soldiers*, 3.
88. Nina B. Huntemann and Matthew Thomas Payne, "Interview with James F. Dunnigan," in Huntemann and Payne, *Joystick Soldiers*, 67–72, here 68–9.
89. Robertson Allen cites *America's Army* developer Michael Zyda's lecture on the game, in which he lists retention as one of the "results" of *America's Army*. See Michael Zyda, "Crossing the Chasm." Presented at the Serious Game Workshop, Game Developers Conference, San Jose, 23 March 2004, http://archive.gdconf.com/gdc_2004/zyda_michael.pdf, accessed via docstoc.com on 28 February 2011.
90. Robertson Allen, "The Unreal Enemy of America's Army," 3.
91. Wardynski interviewed by Nina B. Huntemann, 184.
92. Daphnée Rentfrow, "S(t)imulating War: From Early Films to Military Games," in Jahn-Sudmann and Stockman, *Computer Games as a Sociocultural Phenomenon* (Basingstoke: Palgrave, 2008), 87–96, here 94.
93. James Der Derian, "Virtuous War," *Dictionary of War* performance-documentation project, 26 September 2009, http://dictionaryofwar.org/concepts/Virtuous_War, accessed 28 March 2011.
94. Carl Schmitt, *The Concept of the Political*, trans. George Schwab (Chicago: University of Chicago Press, [1927] 1996), 26.
95. Here I refer to Robertson Allen's "unreal enemy."
96. Jacques Derrida, *The Politics of Friendship*, trans. George Collins (New York: Verso, 1997), 84.

97. Allen Feldman, "The Structuring Enemy and Archival War," *PMLA* 124.5 (2009): 1704–13, here 1705.

98. Wardynski interviewed by Nina B. Huntemann, 181.

99. David Nieborg, "Training Recruits and Conditioning Youth," 53–66, here 61.

100. Wardynski interviewed by Nina B. Huntemann, 179.

101. Hussein Haj Hassan, quoted in "Children play Israeli-killers in bloody new computer game," 17 August 2007, http://www.dailymail.co.uk/news/article-475966/Children-play-Israeli-killers-bloody-new-game.html#ixzz1IC5voB3W, accessed 31 March 2011.

102. "Under Siege," http://www.afkarmedia.com/index.php?PageTitle=Under%20Siege&Type=games&Status=Details&ID=4, accessed 31 March 2011.

103. Mark L. Sample, "Virtual Torture: Videogames and the War on Terror," *Game Studies: The International Journal of Computer Game Research* 8.2 (2008), http://www.gamestudies.org/0802/articles/sample, accessed 16 February 2011.

104. Lenoir, "All But War Is Simulation."

105. James Walsh, quoted in Mark Weiner, "House panel OKs $10.4M for drones at Hancock," *Syracuse Post-Standard*, 25 June 2008, http://www.syracuse.com/news/index.ssf/2008/06/hancock_in_line_for_drones.html, accessed 3 March 2001.

106. Platoni, "The Pentagon Goes to the Video Arcade," 30.

107. Department of Defense, "Operation Urban Warrior," http://www.defense.gov/specials/urbanwarrior/, accessed 28 February 2011. This website has video clips of the event on 16 March 1999.

108. Ibid.

109. Ed Halter, *From Sun Tsu to Xbox: War and Video Games* (New York: Thunder's Mouth Press, 2006), vii–viii.

110. Robertson Allen, citing Erik Larkin, "U.S. Army Invades E3," *PC World*, 21 May 2005, http://www.pcworld.com/article/120929/us_army_invades_e3.html, accessed 28 February 2011.

111. Allen, "The Unreal Enemy of America's Army," 23. See also Robertson Allen, "The Army rolls through Indianapolis: Fieldwork at the Virtual Army Experience," *Transformative Works and Cultures* 1.2 (2009), http://journal.transformativeworks.org/index.php/twc/article/viewArticle/80, accessed 28 February 2011.

112. Virtual Army Experience Fact Sheet: Bravo and Charlie, http://vae.americasarmy.com/pdf/vae_factsheet.pdf, accessed 23 March 2011.

113. The VAE fact sheet lists the size as 9750 square feet; other reports describe it as 19,500 square feet.

114. Ibid.

115. Ibid.

116. The VAE fact sheet lists the weight as 2700 pounds. See Virtual Army Experience Fact Sheet.

117. Huntemann and Payne, "Introduction," in Huntemann and Payne, *Joystick Soldiers*, 1–18, here 1.

118. Ibid.

119. Caroline Loizos, "Play Behavior in Higher Primates: A Review," 1969, 228–9, quoted in Richard Schechner, *Performance Theory*, 100.

120. Loizos quoted in Schechner, *Performance Theory*, 101.

121. Gregory Bateson, *Steps to an Ecology of Mind* (Chicago: University of Chicago Press, 1972); quoted in Schechner, *Performance Studies*, 103. Bateson continues:

> Finally, in the dim region where art, magic, and religion meet and over-lap, human beings have evolved the "metaphor that is meant," the flag which men will die to save, and the sacrament that is felt to be more than "an outward and visible sign, given to us." [...] We face, then, two peculiarities of play: (a) that the messages or signals exchanged in play are in a certain sense untrue or not meant; and (b) that that which is denoted by these signals is nonexistent. These two peculiarities some-times combine strangely to reverse a conclusion reached above. It was stated that the playful nip denotes the bite, but does not denote that which would be denoted by the bite. But there are other instances where an opposite phenomenon occurs. A man experiences the full intensity of subjective terror when a spear is flung at him out of the 3D screen or when he falls headlong from some peak created in his own mind in the intensity of nightmare. At the moment of terror there was no question-ing of 'reality,' but still there was no spear in the movie house and no cliff in the bedroom." (180, 182–3).

122. Schechner, *Performance Studies*, 103.
123. Ibid.
124. Jeffrey Lesser and James Sterrett, "A Battle in Every Classroom: Gaming and the U.S. Army Command & General Staff College," in Huntemann and Payne, *Joystick Soldiers*, 146–59, here 146.
125. Scarry, *The Body in Pain*, 82.
126. Nick Wadhams, "Troops Stationed in Iraq Turn to Gaming," *Associated Press/ USA Today*, 3 January 2005, http://www.usatoday.com/tech/news/2005-01-03-iraq-gaming_x.htm, accessed 22 March 2011.
127. Nina B. Huntemann, "Playing with Fear: Catharsis and Resistance in Military-Themed Video Games," in Huntemann and Payne, *Joystick Soldiers*, 223–36, here 233.
128. Ibid., 231.
129. Ibid., 233.
130. See Press Release, "One In Five Iraq and Afghanistan Veterans Suffer from PTSD or Major Depression," Rand Corporation website, 17 April 2008, http://www.rand.org/news/press/2008/04/17/, accessed 25 September 2010.
131. Jay Dixit, "The War on Terror: Shell-shocked troops are coming back from Iraq with snakes in their heads. A new virtual reality treatment offers hope for vets," *Wired* 14.8 (August 2006), http://www.wired.com/wired/archive/14.08/warterror.html, accessed 8 July 2010.
132. See B. O. Rothbaum, L. Hodges, R., Alarcon, D. Ready, F. Shahar, K. Graap, J. Pair, P. Hebert, D. Gotz, B. Wills, and D. Baltzell, "Virtual Reality Exposure Therapy for PTSD Vietnam Veterans: A Case Study," *Journal of Traumatic Stress* 12 (1999): 263–71.
133. See VA National Center for PTSD, "What Is PTSD?" U.S. Department for Veterans Affairs, February 2010, http://www.ptsd.va.gov/public/pages/handouts-pdf/handout_What_is_PTSD.pdf, accessed 2 September 2010.

134. John J. Kruzel, "'Virtual Iraq' Combats Horrors of War for Troops with PTSD," American Forces Press Service, http://www.defense.gov/news/newsarticle.aspx?id=51297, accessed 14 March 2011.

135. Albert "Skip" Rizzo and Jarrell Pair, "A Virtual Reality Exposure Therapy Application for Iraq War Veterans with Post Traumatic Stress Disorder: From Training to Toy to Treatment," http://www.apa.org/divisions/div46/Amp%20Summer%202005/RizzoArticle.pdf, accessed 10 September 2010.

136. See Schechner, *Performance Studies*, 95.

137. Rizzo and Pair, "A Virtual Reality Exposure Therapy."

138. Albert A. Rizzo, Joann Difede, Barbara O. Rothbaum, Scott Johnston, Robert N. McLay, Greg Reger, Greg Gahm, Thomas Parsons, Ken Graap, and Jarrell Pair, "VR PTSD Exposure Therapy Results with Active Duty OIF/OEF Combatants," *Medicine Meets Virtual Reality* 17 (J. D. Westwood et al., eds., IOS Press (2009)): 277–82, here 278.

139. Rizzo, Difede, et al., citing L. H. Jaycox, E. B. Foa and A. R. Morral, "Influence of Emotional Engagement and Habituation on Exposure Therapy for PTSD," *Journal of Consulting and Clinical Psychology* 66 (1998): 186–92.

140. Bateson, *Steps to an Ecology of Mind*, 183. See note 121.

141. Dan Leopard quotes "a Brigadier General" who "demonstrat[ed] the ICT virtual reality headgear for [...] CBS *Sunday Morning*, 7 July 2002. Dan Leopard, "Mobilizing Affect: The Politics of Performative Realism in Military New Media," in Huntemann and Payne, *Joystick Soldiers*, 131–45, here 133.

142. Ibid.

143. Ibid., 139.

144. "Elect BiLAT," Institute for Creative Technologies (ICT) website, http://ict.usc.edu/projects/elect_bilat1/, accessed 24 March 2011.

145. Ibid.

146. Julia Kim interviewed by LabTV, USCICT, at http://ict.usc.edu/projects/elect_bilat1/, video accessed 24 March 2011.

147. Sample, "Virtual Torture."

148. Ibid.

Chapter 4   Torture Simulated and Real

1. Steve Powers, phone interview with author, 2008.

2. Steve Powers, quoted in Creative Time, "Steve Powers' *The Waterboarding Thrill Ride*," 2008, 2.

3. The 14 September 2001 Declaration of National Emergency by Reason of Certain Terrorist Attacks has been extended every year since President George W. Bush issued the proclamation, including the Obama Administration years.

4. Barack Obama quoted in Jeff Mason, "Obama says Bush-Approved Waterboarding Was Torture," *Reuters*, 30 April 2009, http://www.reuters.com/article/2009/04/30/us-obama-torture-idUSTRE53T16O20090430, accessed 8 April 2011.

5. Diana Taylor, "Double-Blind: The Torture Case," *Critical Inquiry* 33 (Summer 2007): 710–33, here 733.

6. "Jack Bauer," Wikiality: The Truthiness Encyclopedia, http://wikiality.wikia.com/Jack_bauer, accessed 7 April 2011.

7. Ibid.

8. Republican presidential candidate debate, South Carolina, 15 May 2007. Video available at http://www.foxnews.com/story/0,2933,272672,00.html.

9. *New York Times*, "Republican Presidential Debate in South Carolina," 15 May 2007, Federal News Service Transcript, *New York Times* online, http://www.nytimes.com/2007/05/15/us/politics/16repubs-text.html, accessed 14 August 2007.

10. Ibid. Interestingly, although neither Hume nor the other candidates ever mentioned nuclear bombs, Tancredo responded with a scenario involving "nuclear devices."

11. Schechner, *Performance Studies*, 35.

12. Kipling Buis, "Mrs. Trollope's America," *Vanity Fair* (June 2007): 116–17.

13. John Bell, "Performance Studies in an Age of Terror," *TDR: The Drama Review* 47.2 (2003): 6–8, here 7.

14. Janelle Reinelt, "Toward a Poetics of Theatre and Public Events," *TDR: The Drama Review* 50.3 (2006): 69–87, here 71.

15. Ibid.

16. Debra Watson, "Fox's *24*: Propaganda thinly disguised as television programming," *World Socialist* website, 5 April 2005, http://www.wsws.org/articles/2005/apr2005/2424-a05.shtml#top, accessed 28 September 2007.

17. Quoted in Philippe Sands, "The Green Light," *Vanity Fair* (April 2008): 218–26, 278–82, here 279.

18. Democracy Now, "The Green Light: Attorney Philippe Sands Follows the Bush Administration Torture Trail," *Democracy Now online*, 3 April 2008, http://www.democracynow.org/2008/4/3/the_green_light_attorney_philippe_sands, accessed 23 July 2008.

19. Sands, "The Green Light," 279.

20. Anthony Kubiak, *Stages of Terror: Terrorism, Ideology, and Coercion as Theatre History* (Bloomington: Indiana University Press, 1991), 157.

21. Taylor, "Double-Blind," 713. Taylor refers readers to Slavoj Žižek, *Welcome to the Desert of the Real: Five Essays on September 11 and Related Dates* (London: Verso, 2002); and Steven Lukes, "Liberal Democratic Torture," *British Journal of Political Science* 36 (January 2006): 1–16.

22. Marc Cooper, "Lights! Camera! Attack! Hollywood Enlists," *The Nation*, 10 December 2001, http://www.thenation.com/doc/20011210/cooper, accessed 14 August 2007.

23. "Kiefer Sutherland has won a Best Actor Emmy, Golden Globe and SAG Awards for his acting work on 24. He has also won an Emmy as Co-Executive Producer of the show." (*24* page of Fox Website); *24* won Best Drama in the 2006 Emmys.

24. Jack began, interestingly, as an English major. See his CV on Fox's website dedicated to *24* at http://www.fox.com/24/profiles/.

25. Slavoj Žižek, "The Depraved Heroes of 24 Are the Himmlers of Hollywood," *The Guardian online*, 10 January 2006, www.guardian.co.uk/print/0,,5370717-103677,00.html, accessed 8 August 2007.

26. Ibid.

27. Democracy Now, "More Health Care Professionals Involved in Design, Structuring of Torture than in Providing Care for Survivors," *Democracy Now*, 28 September 2007, http://www.democracynow.org/article.pl?sid=07/09/28/1353248, accessed 30 September 2007.

28. Martin Miller, "*24* Gets a Lesson in Torture from the Experts," *Los Angeles Times*, 13 February 2007, E1.

29. Jane Mayer, "Letter from Hollywood: Whatever It Takes," *New Yorker*, 19 February 2007, http://www.newyorker.com/reporting/2007/02/19/070219fa_fact_mayer, accessed 4 May 2007.

30. Jean Baudrillard, "Simulation and Simulacra," in *Selected Writings*, ed. Mark Poster (Stanford, CA: Stanford University Press, 1988), 166–84, here 167.

31. Ibid.

32. Human Rights First, "Torture on TV Rising and Copied in the Field," *Human Rights First* online, http://www.humanrightsfirst.org/us_law/etn/primetime/index.asp, accessed 27 September 2007.

33. Cable News Network (CNN), "Are Saudis Aiding Iraqi Insurgents?: Deep Freeze," *The Situation Room*, 14 February 2007, http://transcripts.cnn.com/TRANSCRIPTS/0702/14/sitroom.03.html, accessed 27 September 2007.

34. Ibid.

35. George W. Bush, "Memorandum: Humane Treatment of al Queda and Taliban Detainees," 7 February 2002, in Mark Danner, *Torture and Truth: America, Abu Ghraib, and the War on Terror* (New York: New York Review of Books, 2004), 105–6.

36. Ibid., 106.

37. Tim Golden, quoted in Alex Gibney, *Taxi to the Dark Side*, directed and written by Alex Gibney, Feature Documentary, Jigsaw Productions, 2007.

38. Juan Cole, "Former US Interrogator Recounts Torture Cases in Afghanistan and Iraq," *Informed Comment*, 15 December 2007, http://www.juancole.com/2007/12/former-us-interrogator-recounts-torture.html, accessed 7 October 2008.

39. Quoted in Gibney, *Taxi to the Dark Side*.

40. See Mayer. "Letter from Hollywood"; and Kirk Semple, "G.I.s Deployed in Iraq Desert with Lots of American Stuff," *New York Times*, 13 August 2005, http://www.nytimes.com/2005/08/13/international/middleeast/13soldier.html, accessed 14 March 2008.

41. Public Broadcasting Service (PBS), "The Torture Question: Interview with Tony Lagouranis," *Frontline*, 25 September 2005, http://www.pbs.org/wgbh/pages/frontline/torture/interviews/lagouranis.html, accessed 12 March 2008.

42. Tony Lagouranis interviewed on *Democracy Now*, "Is Torture on Hit Fox TV Show '24' Encouraging US Soldiers to Abuse Detainees?" *Democracy Now*, 22 February 2007, http://www.democracynow.org/article.pl?sid=07/02/22/1448252, accessed 14 August 2007.

43. His appearances on *Hardball* and *Frontline* was met with an Army statement and contradicting testimony. See MSNBC, "Official Response to Abuse Allegations: U.S. Army and Marines Respond to Former Interrogator Tony Lagouranis Statements," *Hardball with Chris Matthews*, 17 January 2006, http://www.msnbc.msn.com/id/10895558/, accessed 7 October 2008.

44. David Danzig, quoted in *Democracy Now*, "Is Torture on Hit Fox TV Show '24' Encouraging US Soldiers to Abuse Detainees?"

45. Coco Fusco, "Theatre as Discipline: Performing Military Interrogation: An Interview with Mike Ritz," *TDR: The Drama Review* 52.1 (Spring 2008): 153–9, here 158.

46. Danzig quoted in *Democracy Now*, "Is Torture on Hit Fox TV Show '24' Encouraging US Soldiers to Abuse Detainees?"

47. Human Rights First, "Torture on TV Rising and Copied in the Field."
48. Seasons 7 and 8, which aired after much of the "torture" controversy, attempted to either play down torture, or, as in the beginning of Season 7, justify Jack's past actions and even see him continue to use questionable techniques. His anti-torture colleague, Renee Walker, quickly succumbs to Jack Bauer's tough-guy mentality, telling him in the second episode to do "whatever it takes" to get information.
49. A "Research" section of the show's website supports this blurring of fiction and reality with "real" information about the conflicts faced and tactics used on each episode.
50. Senator John McCain, quoted in "Republican Presidential Debate in South Carolina."; Human Rights First (HRF), "What Can Be Done: Human Rights First's Primetime Torture Project," *Human Rights First*, http://www.human rightsfirst.org/us_law/etn/primetime/project.asp, accessed 27 September 2007.
51. Meet the Press, "Meet the Press Transcript for September 30, 2007," http://www.msnbc.msn.com/id/21065954, accessed 10 October 2007.
52. Ibid.
53. Ben Saul, "Torture Degrades Us All," *Foreign Policy in Focus Policy Report*, 5 December 2007 (Silver City, NM and Washington, DC: Foreign Policy In Focus), http://www.fpif.org/pdf/papers/0512torture.pdf, 3, accessed 25 November 2007.
54. For an extensive analysis of the Dershowitz and Parry arguments, and an overall discussion of the ticking-bomb debate, see Vittorio Bufacchi and Jean Maria Arrigo, "Torture, Terrorism and the State: A Refutation of the Ticking-Bomb Argument," *Journal of Applied Philosophy* 23.3 (2006): 355–73.
55. Quoted in Bill Moyers, "Transcript, *Bill Moyers Journal*, 26 October 2007," http://www.pbs.org/moyers/journal/10262007/transcript4.html, accessed 26 November 2007.
56. See Diana Taylor, *Disappearing Acts*.
57. Darius Rejali, "Torture Makes the Man," *South Central Review* 24.1 (2007): 151–69, here 151.
58. Ibid., 153.
59. Ibid., 154.
60. Ibid.
61. Ibid.
62. Žižek, "The Depraved Heroes of *24* Are the Himmlers of Hollywood"; see also Giorgio Agamben, *Homo Sacer*.
63. See Jean Baudrillard, *The Gulf War Did Not Take Place*.
64. Taylor, "Double-Blind," 716.
65. Ibid., 733.
66. Dahlia Lithwick, "The Bauer of Suggestion: OUR TORTURE POLICY HAS DEEPER ROOTS IN FOX TELEVISION THAN THE CONSTITUTION." *Slate.com*, 26 July 2008, http://www.slate.com/id/2195864/, accessed 8 October 2008.
67. See "Afghans free US 'bounty hunter,'" *BBC News*, http://news.bbc.co.uk/2/hi/south_asia/6749677.stm, accessed 11 April 2011.
68. Heritage Foundation, Transcript of "'24' and America's Image in Fighting Terrorism: Fact, Fiction, or Does it Matter?," 23 June 2006, accessed 28 September 2007, http://www.rushlimbaugh.com/home/rush_photos_main/panel_discussion___24_and_america_s_image_in_fighting_terrorism.guest.html.

69. Ibid.

70. Quoted in ibid.

71. Christopher Hitchens, "Believe Me, It's Torture," *Vanity Fair*, August 2008.

72. *This Week* Transcript: Former Vice President Dick Cheney, ABC News, 14 February 2010, http://abcnews.go.com/ThisWeek/week-transcript-vice-president-dick-cheney/story?id=9818034, accessed 9 April 2011.

73. José Muñoz, "Performing the State of Exception: Coco Fusco's *Operation Atropos* and *A Room of One's Own*," *TDR: The Drama Review* 52.1 (T197) Spring 2008): 137–9, here 137.

74. See Neal Desai, Andre Pineda, Majken Runquist, and Mark Fusunyan, "Torture at Times: Waterboarding in the Media," Joan Shorenstein Center on the Press, Politics and Public Policy, Harvard Student Paper, April 2010, http://www.hks. harvard.edu/presspol/publications/papers/torture_at_times_hks_students. pdf, , p. 3, accessed 8 April 2011.

75. See William Safire's analysis of the word "waterboarding," which he cites as coined in 2004 by *New York Times* journalists James Risen, David Johnston, and Neil Lewis. "On Language: Waterboarding," *New York Times*, 9 March 2008, http://www.nytimes.com/2008/03/09/magazine/09wwlnSafire-t.html?_r=3, accessed 7 April 2011.

76. Jill Lane, "Exceptional Bodies: Performance and the Law," *e-misférica* 3.1 (June), 2006, http://hemi.nyu.edu/journal/home.php?issue=april%202006, accessed 21 December 2007.

77. Agamben, *State of Exception*, 3.

78. Ibid., 3–4.

79. Ibid., 4; see also Judith Butler, "Indefinite Detention," in Judith Butler, *Precarious Life: The Powers of Mourning and Violence* (London: Verso, 2004), 50–100.

80. Ibid., 64.

81. Slavoj Žižek, "Knight of the Living Dead," *New York Times*, 24 March 2007, http://www.nytimes.com/2007/03/24/opinion/24zizek.html, accessed 14 August 2008.

82. Agamben, *Homo Sacer*, 99.

83. See David Johnston and Scott Shane, "Debate Erupts on Techniques Used by C.I.A.," *New York Times*, 5 October 2007, http://www.nytimes.com/2007/10/05/washington/05interrogate.html, accessed 14 August 2008.

84. Jean Baudrillard, "Simulacra and Simulations."

85. Leonard Doyle, "Waterboarding Is Torture – I Did It Myself, Says U.S. Advisor," *The Independent Online*, 1 November 2007, http://news.independent.co.uk/world/americas/article3115549.ece, accessed 21 December 2007.

86. Alfred McCoy, quoted in "Historian Alfred McCoy: Obama Reluctance on Bush Prosecution Affirms Culture of Impunity," *Democracy Now*, 1 May 2009, http://www.democracynow.org/2009/5/1/torture_expert_alfred_mccoy_obama_reluctance, accessed 20 July 2009.

87. See the website for the program *Unbreakable* at http://unbreakable.five.tv. See also Aislinn Simpson, *Telegraph* online, "Channel Five reality TV show featuring waterboarding torture is 'unacceptable,' http://www.telegraph.co.uk/news/3142352/Channel-Five-reality-TV-show-featuring-waterboarding-torture-is-unacceptable.html, accessed 24 August 2009.

88. Desai, et al., "Torture at Times," 15.

89. Darius Rejali, quoted in Safire, "Waterboarding."

90. Examples include Nathan Bockelman's "reperformance" of *Drinking of Water* after Raša Todosijević in Los Angeles on 14 July 2010; and *Water Board: A Play About Torture*, which premiered in Boston in 2009, included two performers, Nadeem Mazen and Stephanie Skier waterboarding each other.

91. By media I mean news and other popular entertainment. One example not fully investigated in this chapter is the presence on-screen of waterboarding in the 2007 film *Rendition*, involving a "North African" interrogator and an Egyptian-American victim of extraordinary rendition.

92. Muñoz, "Performing the State of Exception," 137.

93. See Brian Ross and Richard Esposito, "CIA's Harsh Interrogation Techniques Described," ABC News, 18 November 2005, http://abcnews.go.com/Blotter/Investigation/story?id=1322866, accessed 16 April 2011; Democracy Now, "The 9/11 Commission and Torture: How Information Gained Through Waterboarding and Harsh Interrogations Form Major Part of 9/11 Commission Report," *Democracy Now*, 7 February 2008, http://www.democracynow.org/2008/2/7/the_9_11_commission_torture_how, accessed 19 February 2008; see also Mark Tran, "CIA admit 'waterboarding' al-Qaeda suspects," *Guardian Online*, 5 February 2008, http://www.guardian.co.uk/world/2008/feb/05/india.terrorism, accessed 14 August 2008.

94. Jan Crawford Greenburg and Ariane de Vogue, "Bush Administration Blocked Waterboarding Critic: Former DOJ Official Tested the Method Himself, in Effort to Form Torture Policy," *ABC News Online*, 2 November 2007, http://abcnews.go.com/WN/DOJ/story?id=3814076, accessed 2 January 2008.

95. Christopher Hitchens, "Believe Me, It's Torture," 70–3, here 71.

96. Creative Time, "Steve Powers' *The Waterboarding Thrill Ride*."

97. Office of Legal Counsel memo, 1 August 2002, U.S. Department of Justice, accessed 11 April 2011 via http://luxmedia.com.edgesuite.net/aclu/IG_Report.pdf.

98. See Democracy Now, "The 9/11 Commission and Torture"; see also Tran, "CIA admit 'waterboarding' al-Qaeda suspects."

99. James Risen, David Johnston, and Neil A. Lewis, "The Struggle for Iraq: Detainees: Harsh C.I.A. Methods Cited in Top Qaeda Interrogations," *New York Times*, 13 May 2004, http://www.nytimes.com/2004/05/13/politics/13DETA.html, accessed 11 April 2011.

100. Michael Hayden, quoted in *Democracy Now*, "The 9/11 Commission and Torture."

101. Diana Taylor, "Double-Blind," 733.

102. Michael B. Mukasey, Letter to Senate Judiciary Committee, 30 October 2007, http://www.nytimes.com/packages/pdf/national/20071031_Mukasay.pdf, accessed 14 August 2007.

103. For an extensive analysis of the Dershowitz and Parry arguments, and an overall discussion of the ticking-bomb debate, see Bufacchi and Arrigo, "Torture, Terrorism and the State": 355–73.

104. Office of Legal Council memo, 10 August 2005, U.S. Department of Justice quoted in OIG Report, "Counterterrorism Detention and Interrogation Activities, September 2001–October 2003 (CIA Office of the Inspector General Special Review, 7 May 2004), http://luxmedia.com.edgesuite.net/aclu/IG_Report.pdf, 21, accessed 11 April 2011.

105. Mark Danner cites the Senate Armed Services Committee's description of SERE:

> During the resistance phase of SERE training, US military personnel are exposed to physical and psychological pressures [...] designed to simulate conditions to which they might be subject if taken prisoner by enemies that *did not abide by the Geneva Conventions*. As one JPRA instructor explained, SERE training is *"based on illegal exploitation (under the rules listed in the 1949 Geneva Convention Relative to the Treatment of Prisoners of War) of prisoners over the last 50 years."*

> The techniques used in SERE school, based, in part, on Chinese Communist techniques used during the Korean War to elicit false confessions, include stripping students of their clothing, placing them in stress positions, putting hoods over their heads, disrupting their sleep, treating them like animals, subjecting them to loud music and flashing lights, and exposing them to extreme temperatures. It can also include face and body slaps and until recently, for some who attended the Navy's SERE school, it included waterboarding.

> *Senate Armed Services Committee Inquiry into the Treatment of Detainees in US Custody*, "Executive Summary and Conclusions," released 11 December 2008, p. xiii (emphasis added). Quoted in "The Red Cross Torture Report: What it Means," *New York Review of Books*, 30 April 2009, http://www.markdanner. com/articles/show/153, accessed 24 August 2009.
106. Sands, "The Green Light," 278.
107. OIG Report, "Counterterrorism Detention and Interrogation Activities, September 2001 – October 2003 (CIA Office of the Inspector General Special Review, May 7, 2004), http://luxmedia.com.edgesuite.net/aclu/IG_Report. pdf, p. 14, accessed 11 April 2011.
108. Greenburg and de Vogue, "Bush Administration Blocked Waterboarding Critic."
109. Ibid.
110. Maboud Ebrahimzadeh, quoted in *Democracy Now*, "Headlines for November 6, 2007," *Democracy Now* online, http://www.democracynow. org/2007/11/6/headlines, accessed 21 December 2007. Video of the protest performance is available on Youtube.com at http://www.youtube.com/ watch?v=OaQ1Eryjq9I.
111. For video footage visit: http://www.youtube.com/watch?v=meErDDSlKX8& feature=related.
112. C. Clark Kissinger, "Water Boarding Is Torture!," 8 November 2007 (from *Revolution* newspaper), http://revolutionaryfrontlines.wordpress.com/ 2010/03/24/, accessed 13 April 2011.
113. Text from permit, quoted in David Swanson, "U.S. Govt. Threatens to Prosecute Waterboarding," *World Can't Wait*, 20 June 2009, http://www. worldcantwait.net/index.php?option=com_content&view=article&id=5672: us-govt-threatens-to-prosecute-waterboarding&catid=117:homepage& Itemid=289, accessed 13 April 2011.
114. Hitchens, "Believe Me, It's Torture," 70–3, here 70.
115. Ibid, 71.

116. Ibid.
117. Ibid.
118. Creative Time, "Steve Powers' *The Waterboarding Thrill Ride.*"
119. Steve Powers, quoted in ibid.
120. "About Team Delta," *Team Delta* website, http://www.teamdelta.net/about. htm, accessed 11 March 2011.
121. "Programs," *Team Delta* website, http://www.teamdelta.net/programs.htm, accessed 11 March 2011.
122. See the Team Delta website for more on both films: *We Can Make You Talk*, Tiger/Tigress Productions, 2003, and *Torture: Guantanamo Guidebook*, Channel 4, 2005, http://www.teamdelta.net, accessed 11 March 2011.
123. Fusco, "Theatre as Discipline," 153–9, here 153.
124. See, for example, "Former Interrogators Debate Harsh Tactics," *Tell Me More*, Michel Martin, host, NPR, 21 May 2009, accessed 11 March 2011, http:// www.npr.org/templates/story/story.php?storyId=104378628.
125. Fusco, "Theatre as Discipline," 154.
126. Ibid.
127. Ritz in Fusco, "Theatre as Discipline," 155.
128. Ritz in Fusco, "Theatre as Discipline," 157.
129. Gill, "Rehearsing the War Away," 139–55.
130. Scott Magelssen, "Rehearsing the 'Warrior Ethos': 'Theatre Immersion' and the Simulation of Theatres of War," *TDR* 53.1 (Spring 2009): 47–72.
131. Mihaly Csikszentmihalyi, *Flow: The Psychology of Optimal Experience* (New York: HarperCollins, 1990).
132. Henri Alleg, *The Question* (Lincoln: University of Nebraska Press, [1958] 2006).
133. See Danner "The Red Cross Torture Report"; and International Committee of the Red Cross (ICRC), "ICRC Report on the Treatment of Fourteen 'High Value Detainees' in CIA Custody" (Washington, DC: ICRC, 2007).
134. Zubaydah, in ICRC, 10.

Chapter 5   Obamania

1. Barack Obama, quoted in Andy Greenberg, "Video of Obama on Bradley Manning: 'He Broke The Law,'" *Forbes*, 22 April 2011, http://blogs.forbes. com/andygreenberg/2011/04/22/video-of-obama-on-bradley-manning-he-broke-the-law/, accessed 9 May 2011.
2. Karen Greenberg, *The Least Worst Place*, 1.
3. Barack Obama, *The Audacity of Hope: Thoughts on Reclaiming the American Dream* (New York: Crown, 2006), 11.
4. Nicholas Mirzoeff, "An End to the American Civil War?" *Journal of Visual Culture* 8.2 (2009): 228–33, here 231–2. Citing Joseph Roach, *Cities of the Dead: Circum-Atlantic Performance* (New York: Columbia University Press, 1996).
5. "Contact the White House," White House website, http://www.whitehouse. gov/contact, accessed 9 May 2011.
6. "'I Am Willing to Give My Life': Bahraini Human Rights Activists Risk Lives to Protest U.S./Saudi-Backed Repression," *Democracy Now*, 12 April 2011, http://

www.democracynow.org/2011/4/12/i_am_willing_to_give_my, accessed 13 April 2011.

7. Tavis Smiley, quoted in "Tavis Smiley: If At First You Don't Succeed, 'Fail Up,'" *All Things Considered*, NPR, 4 May 2011, http://www.wbur.org/npr/135985392/ tavis-smiley-if-at-first-you-dont-succeed-fail-up, accessed 8 May 2011.

8. See Barbara Ehrenreich, *Smile or Die: How Positive Thinking Fooled America and the World* (London: Granta, 2009). Barbara Ehrenreich's book was originally published in the United States in 2009 under the title *Bright-Sided: How the Relentless Promotion of Positive Thinking Has Undermined America* (New York: Metropolitan Books/Henry Holt).

9. Žižek, *Welcome to the Desert of the Real*.

10. *America: A Tribute to Heroes* was a telethon/benefit concert held ten days after 9/11 and its recording available on Warner Bros records captures the post-9/11 *zeitgeist* well, with practically impromptu performances by Bruce Springsteen, Jon Bon Jovi, Sheryl Crow, Bono, and others.

11. For a critical performance studies analysis of the visual responses to 9/11, see Barbara Kirshenblatt-Gimblett, "Kodak Moments, Flashbulb Memories: Responses to 9/11," *TDR* 47.1 (T177) (Spring 2003): 11–48.

12. "Transcript of President Bush's Address," CNN online.

13. See Naomi Klein, *The Shock Doctrine*.

14. Žižek, *First as Tragedy*, 39.

15. Slavoj Žižek, "From Joyce-the-Symptom ... to the Symptom of Power," *Lacanian Ink* 11, http://www.plexus.org/lacink/lacink11/zizek.html, accessed 30 may 2010.

16. Ibid.

17. "President Bush's Speech," *Online News Hour*, 7 October 2001, http://www.pbs.org/newshour/terrorism/combating/bush_10-7.html, accessed 28 May 2010.

18. Murphy, Jarrett, "Text of Bush Speech: President Declares End to Major Combat Operations in Iraq," *CBS News* online, 1 May 2003, http://www.cbsnews.com/stories/2003/05/01/iraq/main551946.shtml, accessed 28 May 2010.

19. Truthiness was Merriam-Webster's #1 Word of the Year for 2006:

    > 1. truthiness (noun)
    > 1 : "truth that comes from the gut, not books" (Stephen Colbert, Comedy Central's "The Colbert Report," October 2005)
    > 2 : "the quality of preferring concepts or facts one wishes to be true, rather than concepts or facts known to be true" (American Dialect Society, January 2006)

    See "Merriam-Webster's Word of the Year 2006," http://www.merriam-webster.com/info/06words.htm, accessed 5 June 2010.

20. www.wikiality.wikia.com/welcome.

21. http://wikiality.wikia.com/Mission_Accomplished.

22. Colbert, "The Word – Wikiality."

23. See Heidi Collins, Interview with George W. Bush, 11 November 2008, "Transcript: Bush Recalls Regrettable, Most Proud Moments," http://www.cnn.com/2008/POLITICS/11/11/bush.transcript/index.html, accessed 5 June 2010.

24. Colbert, "The Word – Wikiality."
25. "President Calls for Expanding Opportunities for Homeownership," http://georgewbush-whitehouse.archives.gov/news/releases/2002/06/20020617-2.html, accessed 12 February 2010.
26. "President Hosts Conference on Minority Ownership," http://georgewbush-whitehouse.archives.gov/news/releases/2002/10/images/20021015-7-1_homeowners-d10-15-0-515h.html, accessed 12 February 2010.
27. David Hare, *The Power of Yes* (London: Faber & Faber, 2009), 71.
28. Ibid., 13.
29. Ehrenreich, *Smile or Die*, 187.
30. Ibid., 188–9.
31. Ibid., 189.
32. Ibid., 190.
33. "Transcript: Illinois Senate Candidate Barack Obama," *The Washington Post*, 27 July 2004, http://www.washingtonpost.com/wp-dyn/articles/A19751-2004Jul27.html, accessed 9 June 2010.
34. "Nobel Peace Prize for 2009," Press release, Nobel Prize website, http://nobelprize.org/nobel_prizes/peace/laureates/2009/press.html, accessed 12 November 2009.
35. "Award Ceremony Speech, Presentation Speech by Thorbjørn Jagland, Chairman of the Norwegian Nobel Committee," Oslo, 10 December 2009, http://nobelprize.org/nobel_prizes/peace/laureates/2009/presentation-speech.html, accessed 9 June 2010.
36. See www.joelosteen.com.
37. Amy Walter and Devin Dwyer, "Bin Laden Death: Obama Approval Rating Spikes, but Republicans Say Economy More Important," *ABC News*, 3 May 2011, http://abcnews.go.com/Politics/president-obama-approval-rating-spikes-bin-laden-death/story?id=13518704, accessed 10 May 2011.
38. Bill Maher, *Real Time with Bill Maher*, HBO, 6 May 2011, http://www.hbo.com/real-time-with-bill-maher/index.html.
39. Michael Eric Dyson, quoted in "Real Time with Bill Maher," episode 212, HBO, 6 May 2011, http://www.hbo.com/real-time-with-bill-maher/index.html#/real-time-with-bill-maher/episodes/0/212-episode/synopsis/quotes.html, accessed 10 May 2011.
40. See "U.S. Assassination Campaign Continues as CIA Drone Targets U.S.-Born Cleric Anwar al-Awlaki in Yemen," *Democracy Now*, 9 May 2011, http://www.democracynow.org/2011/5/9/us_assassination_campaign_continues_as_cia, accessed 10 May 2011.

References

ABC News (2010) This Week Transcript: Former Vice President Dick Cheney, *ABC News*, 14 February, http://abcnews.go.com/ThisWeek/week-transcript-vice-president-dick-cheney/story?id9818034, accessed 9 April 2011.

—— (2011) Dick Cheney, interview with Jonathan Karl, "Transcript: Cheney Defends Hard Line Tactics," *ABC News*, 16 December, http://abcnews.go.com/Politics/story?id6464697&page1, accessed 5 May 2011.

—— (2011) "'Nightline' to Honor 'The Fallen': Ted Koppel to Read Names of Over 900 Servicemen and Women Killed in Iraq, Afghanistan in Memorial Day Broadcast," *ABC News*, http://abcnews.go.com/Nightline/story?id786279&page1, accessed 17 March.

Agamben, Giorgio ([1995] 1998) *Homo Sacer: Sovereign Power and Bare Life* (Stanford, CA: Stanford University Press).

—— ([2003] 2005) *State of Exception* (Chicago: University of Chicago Press).

Al Jazeera (2009) "US army uses video games as part of recruitment drive," *Al Jazeera English* 12 November, viewed 10 February via youtube.com, http://www.youtube.com/watch?vIvMZHrjfC_c.

Alleg, Henri ([1958] 2006) *The Question* (Lincoln: University of Nebraska Press).

Allen, Joe (2004) "The real story of the...Vietnam Veterans Against the War," 14 September, http://socialistworker.org/2004-2/512/512_08_VVAW.shtml, accessed 15 May 2010.

Allen, Robertson (2009) "The Army rolls through Indianapolis: Fieldwork at the Virtual Army Experience," *Transformative Works and Cultures*, 1, 2, http://journal.transformativeworks.org/index.php/twc/article/viewArticle/80, accessed 28 February 2011.

—— (2011) "The Unreal Enemy of America's Army," Draft of essay appearing in *Games and Culture* 6.1: 38–60, http://washington.academia.edu/RobertsonAllen/Papers/166126/The_Unreal_Enemy_of_Americas_Army, accessed 14 February 2011.

Artaud, Antonin (1958) *Theatre of Cruelty* (New York: Grove Press).

Associated Press (2006) "Chaplain Guilty for Wearing Uniform at Protest: Navy Officer Convicted of Disobeying Order Over White House Demonstration," 13 September, http://www.msnbc.msn.com/id/14824097, accessed 24 May 2010.

Bateson, Gregory (1972) *Steps to an Ecology of Mind* (Chicago: University of Chicago Press).

Baudrillard, Jean (1995) *The Gulf War Did Not Take Place*, trans. and intro. Paul Patton (Bloomington: Indiana University Press).

—— (1988) "Simulation and Simulacra," in *Selected Writings*, ed. Mark Poster (Stanford, CA: Stanford University Press), 166–84.

—— (2004) "War Porn," *International Journal of Baudrillard Studies* 2.1 (2005), trans. of "Pornographie de la guerre," *Liberation*, Wednesday 19 May 2004 by Paul Taylor, http://www.ubishops.ca/baudrillardstudies/vol2_1/taylor.htm#_edn1, accessed 4 March 2011.

BBC (2007) "Afghans free US 'bounty hunter,'" *BBC News*, 13 June, http://news. bbc.co.uk/2/hi/south_asia/6749677.stm, accessed 11 April 2011.

Behrens, Roy (2002) *False Colors: Art, Design and Modern Camouflage* (Bobolinks Books online).

Bell, John (2003) "Performance Studies in an Age of Terror," *TDR: The Drama Review* 47.2: 6–8.

Berghaus, Günter, ed. (1996) *Fascism and Theatre: Comparative Studies on the Aesthetics and Politics of Performance in Europe 1925–1945* (Oxford: Berghahn Books).

Blaser, Patrice (2004) "I Try to Speak About Reality," Interview with Helgard Haug, Stefan Kaegi, and Daniel Wetzel. Vienna, http://www.rimini-protokoll. de/misc_frontend.php?misc_id29, accessed 3 June 2007.

Boenisch, Peter (2008) "Other People Live: Rimini Protokoll and Their Theatre of Experts," *Contemporary Theatre Review* 18.1: 107–13.

Bogost, Ian (2010) Foreword to Nina B. Huntemann and Matthew Thomas Payne, eds *Joystick Soldiers: The Politics of Play in Military Videogames* (New York: Routledge), xi–xvi.

Bogost, Ian, and Cindy Poremba (2008) "Can Games Get Real? A Closer Look at Documentary Games," in Andreas Jahn-Sudmann and Ralf Stockmann, eds, *Computer Games as a Sociocultural Phenomenon: Games without Frontiers – War without Tears* (Basingstoke: Palgrave Macmillan), 12–21.

Brecht, Bertolt (1964) *Brecht on Theatre* (London: Methuen).

Brophy-Warren, Jamin (2009) "Iraq, the Videogame," *The Wall Street Journal*, 6 April, http://online.wsj.com/article/SB123902404583292727.html, accessed 28 June 2010.

Bufacchi, Vittorio, and Jean Maria Arrigo (2006) "Torture, Terrorism and the State: A Refutation of the Ticking-Bomb Argument," *Journal of Applied Philosophy* 23.3: 355–73.

Buis, Kipling (2007) "Mrs. Trollope's America," *Vanity Fair*, June, 116–17.

Bush, George W. (2001) "President Urges Readiness and Patience: Remarks by the President, Secretary of State Colin Powell and Attorney General John Ashcroft, Camp David, Thurmont, Maryland," Office of the Press Secretary, September 15, 2001, http://georgewbush-whitehouse.archives.gov/news/releases/2001/09/20010915-4.html, accessed 5 May 2011.

—— (2001) "Transcript of President Bush Address," 20 September, http:// articles.cnn.com/2001-09-20/us/gen.bush.transcript_1_joint-session-national-anthem-citizens?_sPM:US, accessed 28 March 2011.

—— (2002) "Memorandum: Humane Treatment of al Queda and Taliban Detainees," 7 February, in Mark Danner, *Torture and Truth: America, Abu Ghraib, and the War on Terror* (New York: New York Review of Books, 2004), 105–6.

—— (2002) "President Calls for Expanding Opportunities for Homeownership," http://georgewbush-whitehouse.archives.gov/news/releases/2002/06/2002061 7-2.html, accessed 12 February 2010.

—— (2002) "President Hosts Conference on Minority Ownership," October, http://georgewbush-whitehouse.archives.gov/news/releases/2002/10/ images/20021015-7-1_homeowners-d10-15-0-515h.html, accessed 12 February 2010.

—— (2010) *Decision Points* (New York: Crown Publishing).

Butler, Judith (2004) "Indefinite Detention," in *Precarious Life: The Powers of Mourning and Violence* (London: Verso), 50–100.

Carse, James P. (1986) *Finite and Infinite Games: A Vision of Life as Play and Possibility* (New York: Ballantine Books).

CBS (2008) "What Really Happened to Pat Tillman?" *60 Minutes*, CBS, 4 May, http://www.cbsnews.com/stories/2008/05/01/60minutes/main4061656.shtml, accessed 5 May 2011.

Chan, Dean (2010) "Dead-in-Iraq: The Spatial Politics of Digital Game Art Activism and the In-Game Protest," in Nina B. Huntemann and Thomas Matthew Payne, eds, *Joystick Soldiers: The Politics of Play in Military Video Games* (New York: Routledge), 272–86.

Chien, Irene (2010) "Playing Against the Grain: Machinima and Military Gaming," in Nina B. Huntemann and Thomas Matthew Payne, eds, *Joystick Soldiers: The Politics of Play in Military Video Games* (New York: Routledge), 239–51.

Chomsky, Noam (2010) Interview with Amy Goodman, *Democracy Now*, 15 March, http://www.democracynow.org/2010/3/15/noam_chomsky_on_obamas_foreign_policy, accessed 22 March 2010.

Chulack, Christopher, dir. (2009) *Southland*, Season 1, episode 1, NBC.

CNN (2001) "Bush: Bin Laden 'Wanted Dead or Alive,'" *CNN* online, 17 September 2001, http://articles.cnn.com/2001-09-17/us/bush.powell.terrorism_1_bin-qaeda-terrorist-attacks?_sPM:US, accessed 8 May 2011.

—— (2001) "Transcript of President Bush's Address," *CNN* online, http://archives.cnn.com/2001/US/09/20/gen.bush.transcript/, accessed 28 May 2010.

—— (2001) "Transcript of President Bush's Address," *CNN* online, 21 September, http://articles.cnn.com/2001-09-20/us/gen.bush.transcript_1_joint-session-national-anthem-citizens?_sPM:US, accessed 2 February 2011.

—— (2003) "Cities jammed in worldwide protest of war in Iraq," *CNN* online, 15 February, http://articles.cnn.com/2003-02-15/us/sprj.irq.protests.main_1_anti-war-rallies-anti-war-movement-police-use-pepper-spray?_sPM:US, accessed 13 April 2011.

—— (2007) "Are Saudis Aiding Iraqi Insurgents?; Deep Freeze," *The Situation Room*, CNN, 14 February, http://transcripts.cnn.com/TRANSCRIPTS/0702/14/sitroom.03.html, accessed 27 September 2007.

Coates, Ken ed. (2001) *War is Peace*, The Spokesman 73.

Colbert, Stephen (2006) "The Word – Wikiality," *The Colbert Report*, 31 July, http://www.colbertnation.com/the-colbert-report-videos/72347/july-31-2006/the-word—wikiality, accessed 6 June 2010.

Cole, Juan (2007) "Former US Interrogator Recounts Torture Cases in Afghanistan and Iraq," *Informed Comment*, 15 December, http://www.juancole.com/2007/12/former-us-interrogator-recounts-torture.html, accessed 7 October 2008.

Collins, Heidi (2008) Interview with George W. Bush, 11 November, "Transcript: Bush Recalls Regrettable, Most Proud Moments," http://www.cnn.com/2008/POLITICS/11/11/bush.transcript/index.html, accessed 5 June 2010.

"Combat Paper Project: About Combat Paper," http://www.combatpaper.org/about.html, accessed 27 May 2010.

Cooper, Marc (2001) "Lights! Camera! Attack! Hollywood Enlists," *The Nation* 10 December, http://www.thenation.com/doc/20011210/cooper, accessed 14 August 2007.

Cos, Grant C. (2007) "Dissent and the Rhetoric of Reflection: Barbara Lee's September 14, 2001, Speech," *Rhetor: Revue de la Société canadienne pour l'étude de la rhétorique* 2, www.cssr-scer.ca/rhetor, accessed 4 May 2011.

Craik, Jennifer (2005) *Uniforms Exposed: From Conformity to Transgression* (Oxford and New York: Berg).

Creative Time, "Steve Powers' *The Waterboarding Thrill Ride*," Creativetime.org. http://www.creativetime.org/programs/archive/2008/democracy/powers.php, accessed 10 August 2008.

Croft, Stuart (2006) *Culture, Crisis and America's War on Terror* (Cambridge: Cambridge University Press).

Csikszentmihalyi, Mihaly (1990) *Flow: The Psychology of Optimal Experience* (New York: HarperCollins).

Daily Mail (2007) "Children play Israeli-killers in bloody new computer game," *Daily Mail*, 17 August, http://www.dailymail.co.uk/news/article-475966/Children-play-Israeli-killers-bloody-new-game.html#ixzz1IC5voB3W, accessed 31 March 2011.

Danner, Mark (2006) *The Secret Way to War: The Downing Street Memo and the Iraq War's Buried History* (New York: New York Review of Books).

—— (2008) "Frozen Scandal," *New York Review of Books*, 4 December, http://www.nybooks.com/articles/archives/2008/dec/04/frozen-scandal/#fn1-649488691, accessed 5 May 2011.

—— (2009) "The Red Cross Torture Report: What it Means," *New York Review of Books*, 30 April, http://www.markdanner.com/articles/show/153, accessed 24 August 2009.

DeLappe, Joseph (2011) "dead-in-iraq" page, http://www.unr.edu/art/delappe/DeLappe%20Main%20Page/DeLappe%20Online%20MAIN.html, accessed 17 March.

Democracy Now (2001) "Thousands Take to the Streets in San Francisco and Washington, D.C. to Call for Peace and Justice," *Democracy Now*, 1 October, http://www.democracynow.org/2001/10/1/thousands_take_to_the_streets_in, accessed 13 April 2011.

—— (2007) "Is Torture on Hit Fox TV Show '24' Encouraging US Soldiers to Abuse Detainees?" *Democracy Now*, 22 February, http://www.democracynow.org/article.pl?sid07/02/22/1448252, accessed 14 August 2007.

—— (2007) "Pentagon Cracks Down on Anti-War Iraq War Veterans For Protesting in Uniform," 12 June, *Democracy Now*, http://www.democracynow.org/2007/6/12/pentagon_cracks_down_on_anti_war, accessed 19 June 2007.

—— (2007) "More Health Care Professionals Involved in Design, Structuring of Torture than in Providing Care for Survivors," *Democracy Now*, 28 September, http://www.democracynow.org/article.pl?sid07/09/28/1353248, accessed 30 September 2007.

—— (2007) "Headlines for November 6, 2007," *Democracy Now* online, http://www.democracynow.org/2007/11/6/headlines, accessed 21 December 2007.

—— (2008) "The 9/11 Commission and Torture: How Information Gained Through Waterboarding and Harsh Interrogations Form Major Part of 9/11 Commission Report," *Democracy Now*, 7 February, http://www.democracynow.org/2008/2/7/the_9_11_commission_torture_how, accessed 19 February 2008.

—— (2008) "The Green Light: Attorney Philippe Sands Follows the Bush Administration Torture Trail," *Democracy Now*, 3 April, http://www.democracynow.org/2008/4/3/the_green_light_attorney_philippe_sands, accessed 23 July 2008.

—— (2009) "Historian Alfred McCoy: Obama Reluctance on Bush Prosecution Affirms Culture of Impunity," *Democracy Now*, 1 May, http://www.democracynow.

org/2009/5/1/torture_expert_alfred_mccoy_obama_reluctance, accessed 20 July 2009.

—— (2010) "Massacre Caught on Tape: US Military Confirms Authenticity of Their Own Chilling Video Showing Killing of Journalists," *Democracy Now*, 6 April, http://www.democracynow.org/2010/4/6/massacre_caught_on_tape_us_military, accessed 12 May 2010.

—— (2010) "Michael Moore on His Life, His Films and His Activism," *Democracy Now*, 6 September, http://www.democracynow.org/2010/9/6/michael_moore_on_his_life_hisv, accessed 31 January 2011.

—— (2011) "'I Am Willing to Give My Life': Bahraini Human Rights Activists Risk Lives to Protest U.S./Saudi-Backed Repression," *Democracy Now*, 12 April, http://www.democracynow.org/2011/4/12/i_am_willing_to_give_my, accessed 13 April 2011.

—— (2011) "U.S. Assassination Campaign Continues as CIA Drone Targets U.S.-Born Cleric Anwar al-Awlaki in Yemen," *Democracy Now*, 9 May, http://www.democracynow.org/2011/5/9/us_assassination_campaign_continues_as_cia, accessed 10 May 2011.

Der Derian, James (2003) "War as Game," *Brown Journal of World Affairs*, 37–48.

—— (2009) "Virtuous War," *Dictionary of War* performance-documentation project, 26 September, http://dictionaryofwar.org/concepts/Virtuous_War, accessed 28 March 2011.

Derrida, Jacques (1997) *The Politics of Friendship*, trans. George Collins (New York: Verso).

Desai, Neal, Andre Pineda, Majken Runquist, and Mark Fusunyan (2010) "Torture at Times: Waterboarding in the Media," Joan Shorenstein Center on the Press, Politics and Public Policy, Harvard Student Paper, April, http://www.hks.harvard.edu/presspol/publications/papers/torture_at_times_hks_students.pdf, accessed 8 April 2011.

Deterding, Sebastian (2010) "Living Room Wars: Remediation, Boardgames, and the Early History of Video Wargaming," in Nina B. Huntemann and Thomas Matthew Payne, eds, *Joystick Soldiers: The Politics of Play in Military Videogames* (New York: Routledge), 21–38.

Dixit, Jay (2006) "The War on Terror: Shell-shocked troops are coming back from Iraq with snakes in their heads. A new vitual reality treatment offers hope for vets," *Wired* 14.8 (August), http://www.wired.com/wired/archive/14.08/warterror.html, accessed 8 July 2010.

Doyle, Leonard (2007) "Waterboarding Is Torture – I Did It Myself, Says U.S. Advisor," *The Independent Online*, 1 November, http://news.independent.co.uk/world/americas/article3115549.ece, accessed 21 December 2007.

Dublin Airport Authority (2011) "History of Shannon Airport," Shannon Airport website, http://www.shannonairport.com/gns/about-us/media-centre/history-of-shannon-airport.aspx, accessed 12 April 2011.

Duncombe, Stephen (2010) "Bringing the War Home: IVAW's Operation First Casualty," *In Media Res* website, http://mediacommons.futureofthebook.org/imr/2009/09/10/bringing-war-home-ivaw-s-operation-first-casualty, accessed 27 May.

Dvorak, P. (2002) "Like Protestors, Chief Hit the Streets of D.C.: Being Close to the Action Was Key," *Washington Post*, 24 April, B1.

Ehrenreich, Barbara (2009) *Smile or Die: How Positive Thinking Fooled America and the World* (London: Granta).

Eleveld, Kerry, and Andrew Harmon (2010) "Choi Arrested at White House Gates," *The Advocate* online, 18 March, http://www.advocate.com/News/Daily_News/2010/03/18/Dan_Choi_Protests_in_Front_of_WH/, accessed 30 June 2010.

Feldman, Allen (2009) "The Structuring Enemy and Archival War," *PMLA* 124.5: 1704–13.

Frankfurter Allgemeine Sonntagszeitung (FAS) (2006) "Real-Life Drama: Rimini Protokoll Creates Progressive Theatre without Actors and Costumes," 5 June, http://www.rimini-protokoll.de/website/en/article_2700.html, accessed 12 March 2008.

Freeman, Colin (2005) "Battles Re-enacted in Video Arcades," *San Francisco Chronicle*, 16 January, A-4, http://www.sfgate.com/cgi-bin/article.cgi?f/c/a/2005/01/16/MNG5LAR6KU1.DTL&typeprintable, accessed 24 March 2011.

Frum, Larry (2010) "Playing as 'Taliban' Removed from 'Medal of Honor' Fame," *CNN* online, 1 October, http://articles.cnn.com/2010-10-01/tech/medal.of.honor.taliban_1_medal-of-honor-game-taliban-military-families?_sPM:TECH, accessed 25 March 2011.

Full Spectrum Warrior, Pandemic Studios, 2004.

Fusco, Coco (2008) "Artist Statement," *TDR: The Drama Review* 52.1: 140–53.

—— (2008) "Theatre as Discipline: Performing Military Interrogation. An Interview with Mike Ritz," *TDR: The Drama Review* 52.1 (Spring): 153–9.

Gibney, Alex (2007) *Taxi to the Dark Side*, directed and written by Alex Gibney, Feature Documentary, Jigsaw Productions.

Gill, Zach Whitman (2009) "Rehearsing the War Away: Perpetual Warrior Training in Contemporary US Army Policy," *TDR: The Drama Review* 53.3: 139–55.

Giroux, Henry (2010) *Hearts of Darkness: Torturing Children in the War on Terror* (Paradigm), excerpted in "Torturing Democracy," *Truthout*, http://www.truth-out.org/torturing-democracy67570, accessed 5 May 2011.

Greenberg, Andy (2011) "Video of Obama on Bradley Manning: 'He Broke The Law,'" *Forbes*, 22 April, http://blogs.forbes.com/andygreenberg/2011/04/22/video-of-obama-on-bradley-manning-he-broke-the-law/, accessed 9 May 2011.

Greenberg, Karen (2009) *The Least Worst Place: Guantánamo's First 100 Days* (New York: Oxford University Press).

Greenburg, Jan Crawford, and Ariane de Vogue (2007) "Bush Administration Blocked Waterboarding Critic: Former DOJ Official Tested the Method Himself, in Effort to Form Torture Policy," *ABC News online*, 2 November, http://abcnews.go.com/WN/DOJ/story?id3814076, accessed 2 January 2008.

Halter, Ed (2006) *From Sun Tsu to Xbox: War and Video Games* (New York: Thunder's Mouth Press).

Hare, David (2009) *The Power of Yes* (London: Faber & Faber).

Hartcup, Guy ([1979] 2008) *Camouflage: The History of Deception and Concealment in War* (London: Pen and Sword).

Heritage Foundation (2006) Transcript of "'24' and America's Image in Fighting Terrorism: Fact, Fiction, or Does it Matter?," 23 June, http://www.rushlimbaugh.com/home/rush_photos_main/panel_discussion___24__and_america_s_image_in_fighting_terrorism.guest.html, accessed 28 September 2007.

Hitchens, Christopher (2008) "Believe Me, It's Torture," *Vanity Fair*, August, 70–3.

Hodes, Jacob, and Emma Ruby-Sachs (2002) "'America's Army' Targets Youth," *The Nation*, 2 September, http://www.thenation.com/article/americas-army-targets-youth, accessed 23 March 2011.

Human Rights First (2007), "What Can Be Done: Human Rights First's Primetime Torture Project," *Human Rights First*, http://www.humanrightsfirst.org/us_law/etn/primetime/project.asp, accessed 27 September 2007.

—— (2007) "Torture on TV Rising and Copied in the Field," *Human Rights First*, http://www.humanrightsfirst.org/us_law/etn/primetime/index.asp, accessed 27 September 2007.

Huntemann, Nina B. (2010) "Interview with Colonal Casey Wardynski," in Nina B. Huntemann and Thomas Matthew Payne, eds, *Joystick Soldiers: The Politics of Play in Military Video Games* (New York: Routledge), 178–88.

—— (2010) "Playing with Fear: Catharsis and Resistance in Military-Themed Video Games," in Nina B. Huntemann and Thomas Matthew Payne, eds, *Joystick Soldiers: The Politics of Play in Military Videogames* (New York: Routledge), 223–36.

Huntemann, Nina B., and Matthew Thomas Payne, eds (2010) *Joystick Soldiers: The Politics of Play in Military Videogames* (New York: Routledge), 67–72.

—— (2010) "Interview with James F. Dunnigan," in Nina B. Huntemann and Thomas Matthew Payne, eds, *Joystick Soldiers: The Politics of Play in Military Videogames* (New York: Routledge), 67–72.

—— (2010) "Introduction," in Nina B. Huntemann and Thomas Matthew Payne, eds, *Joystick Warriors: The Politics of Play in Military Videogames* (New York: Routledge), 1–18.

Institute for Creative Technologies (ICT) (2011) "Elect BiLAT," Institute for Creative Technologies (ICT) website, http://ict.usc.edu/projects/elect_bilat1/ accessed 24 March 2011.

International Committee of the Red Cross (ICRC) (2007) "ICRC Report on the Treatment of Fourteen 'High Value Detainees' in CIA Custody" (Washington, DC: ICRC).

"Jack Bauer," Wikiality: The Truthiness Encyclopedia, http://wikiality.wikia.com/Jack_bauer, accessed 7 April 2011.

Jagland, Thorbjørn (2009) "Award Ceremony Speech, Presentation Speech by Thorbjørn Jagland, Chairman of the Norwegian Nobel Committee," Oslo, 10 December, http://nobelprize.org/nobel_prizes/peace/laureates/2009/presentation-speech.html, accessed 9 June 2010.

Jahn-Sudmann, Andreas and Ralf Stockmann, eds, 2008. *Computer Games as a Sociocultural Phenomenon: Games Without Frontiers – War Without Tears* (Basingstoke: Palgrave Macmillan).

Jauregui, Bea (2009) "Military Communitas? Re-centering the Citizen-Soldier Interface at the Army Experience Center," paper presented at the Reconsidering American Power Conference, April 23–25, University of Chicago. Abstract, http://cis.uchicago.edu/events/08-09/reconsidering-american-power/abstracts.shtml#jauregui, accessed 2 March 2011.

Jaycox, L. H., E. B. Foa and A. R. Morral (1998) "Influence of Emotional Engagement and Habituation on Exposure Therapy for PTSD," *Journal of Consulting and Clinical Psychology* 66: 186–192.

Johnston, David, and Scott Shane (2007) "Debate Erupts on Techniques Used by C.I.A.," *New York Times*, 5 October, http://www.nytimes.com/2007/10/05/washington/05interrogate.html, accessed 14 August 2008.

Junger, Sebastian (2010) *War* (New York: Twelve).

Junger, Sebastian, and Tim Hetherington (2010) *Restropo* (Documentary Film), Outpost Films.

Karl, Jonathan (2008) "Transcript: Cheney Defends Hard Line Tactics," *ABC News*, 16 December, http://abcnews.go.com/Politics/story?id6464697&page1, accessed 5 May 2011.

Kennedy, Harold (2002) "Computer Games Liven Up Military Recruiting, Training," *National Defense*, November, http://www.nationaldefensemagazine.org/archive/2002/November/Pages/Computer_Games6621.aspx, accessed 21 May 2011.

Kirshenblatt-Gimblett, Barbara (2003) "Kodak Moments, Flashbulb Memories: Responses to 9/11," *TDR: The Drama Review* 47.1 (Spring): 11–48.

Kissinger, C. Clark (2007) "Water Boarding Is Torture!," *Revolution* newspaper, 8 November, http://revolutionaryfrontlines.wordpress.com/2010/03/24/, accessed 13 April 2011.

Klein, Naomi (2004) "The Year of the Fake," *The Nation*, 9 January, http://www.naomiklein.org/articles/2004/01/year-fake, accessed 5 May 2011.

—— (2008) *The Shock Doctrine: The Rise of Disaster Capitalism* (New York: Metropolitan Books).

Knappenberger, Evan (2010) Email correspondence with author, 24 June.

Kruzel, John J. (2011) "'Virtual Iraq' Combats Horrors of War for Troops with PTSD," American Forces Press Service, http://www.defense.gov/news/news article.aspx?id51297, accessed 14 March.

Kubiak, Anthony (1991) *Stages of Terror: Terrorism, Ideology, and Coercion as Theatre History* (Bloomington: Indiana University Press).

Kuo, Li C. (2006) "A New Kind of Art Form Leads to a New Kind of Protest," *GameSpy*, 23 May, http://www.gamespy.com/pc/americas-army/709854p2.html, accessed 17 March 2011.

Lane, Jill (2006) "Exceptional Bodies: Performance and the Law," *e-misférica*, 3.1 (June), http://hemi.nyu.edu/journal/home.php?issueapril%202006, accessed 21 December 2007.

Larkin, Erik (2005) "U.S. Army Invades E3," *PC World*, 21 May, http://www.pcworld.com/article/120929/us_army_invades_e3.html, accessed 28 February 2011.

Leach, Robert (2006) "Mother Courage and Her Children," in *The Cambridge Companion to Brecht* (Cambridge: Cambridge University Press), 132–42.

Lenoir, Tim (2000) "All But War Is Simulation: The Military-Entertainment Complex," *Configurations* 8: 289–35.

Lenoir, Tim, and Henry Lowood (2003) "Theaters of War: The Military-Entertainment Complex," http://www.stanford.edu/class/sts145/Library/Lenoir-Lowood_TheatersOfWar.pdf, 2, accessed 25 March 2011.

—— (2003) "Theaters of War: The Military-Entertainment Complex," in Jan Lazardzig, Helmar Schramm, and Ludger Schwarte, eds, *Collection, Laboratory, Theater: Scenes of Knowledge in the 17th Century* (Berlin: Walter de Gruyter), 427–56.

Leopard, Dan (2010) "Mobilizing Affect: The Politics of Performative Realism in Military New Media," in Nina B. Huntemann and Thomas Matthew Payne, eds, *Joystick Soldiers: The Politics of Play in Military Videogames* (New York: Routledge), 131–45.

Lesser, Jeffrey, and James Sterrett (2010) "A Battle in Every Classroom: Gaming and the U.S. Army Command & General Staff College," in Nina B. Huntemann and Thomas Matthew Payne, eds, *Joystick Soldiers: The Politics of Play in Military Videogames* (New York: Routledge), 146–59.

Lithwick, Dahlia (2008) "The Bauer of Suggestion: OUR TORTURE POLICY HAS DEEPER ROOTS IN FOX TELEVISION THAN THE CONSTITUTION." *Slate.com*, 26 July, http://www.slate.com/id/2195864/, accessed 8 October 2008.

Liu, Alec, and Jeremy A. Kaplan (2011) "Arkansas May Be Man-Made, Experts Warn," 1 March, *FoxNews.com*, http://www.foxnews.com/scitech/2011/03/01/fracking-earthquakes-arkansas-man-experts-warn/, accessed 26 July 2011.

LiveLeak (2007) "Life as a Marine Grunt in Afghanistan," LiveLeak.com, 16 April, http://www.liveleak.com/view?i6c4_1176720508, accessed 12 February 2010.

—— (2007) "One Soldier's Opinion About Being In Iraq," LiveLeak.com, 19 August, http://www.liveleak.com/view?ie90_1187514955, accessed 12 February 2010.

Losh, Elizabeth (2010) "A Battle for Hearts and Minds: The Design Politics of ELECT BiLAT," in Nina B. Huntemann and Thomas Matthew Payne, eds, *Joystick Soldiers: The Politics of Play in Military Videogames* (New York: Routledge), 160–77.

Lowood, Henry (2008) "Impotence and Agency: Computer Games as a Post-9/11 Battlefield," in Andreas Jahn-Sudmann and Ralf Stockmann, eds, *Computer Games as a Sociocultural Phenomenon: Games Without Frontiers – War Without Tears* (Basingstoke: Palgrave Macmillan, 2008), 78–86.

Lukes, Steven (2006) "Liberal Democratic Torture," *British Journal of Political Science* 36 (January): 1–16.

Magelssen, Scott (2009) "Rehearsing the 'Warrior Ethos': 'Theatre Immersion' and the Simulation of Theatres of War," *TDR: The Drama Review* 53.1 (Spring): 47–72.

Maher, Bill (2011) "Real Time with Bill Maher," episode 212, HBO, 6 May, http://www.hbo.com/real-time-with-bill-maher/index.html#/real-time-with-bill-maher/episodes/0/212-episode/synopsis/quotes.html, accessed 10 May 2011.

Martin, Carol (2006) "Bodies of Evidence," *TDR: The Drama Review* 50.3: 8–15.

Mason, Jeff (2009) "Obama says Bush-Approved Waterboarding Was Torture," Reuters, 30 April, http://www.reuters.com/article/2009/04/30/us-obama-torture-idUSTRE53T16O20090430, accessed 8 April 2011.

Matthews, Chris (2006) "Official Response to Abuse Allegations: U.S. Army and Marines Respond to Former Interrogator Tony Lagouranis Statements," *Hardball with Chris Matthews*, MSNBC, 17 January, http://www.msnbc.msn.com/id/10895558/, accessed 7 October 2008.

Mayer, Jane (2007) "Letter from Hollywood: Whatever It Takes," *New Yorker*, 19 February, http://www.newyorker.com/reporting/2007/02/19/070219fa_fact_mayer, accessed 4 May 2007.

—— (2008) *The Dark Side: The Inside Story on How the War on Terror Turned into a War on American Ideals* (New York: Random House).

McCoy, Alfred (2006) *A Question of Torture: CIA Interrogation from the Cold War to the War on Terror* (New York: Metropolitan Books).

McKenzie, Jon (2001) *Perform or Else* (London: Routledge).

McKenzie, Jon (2003) "Democracy's Performance," *TDR: The Drama Review* 47.2 (T178): 117–28.

Media Matters (2009) "Four Major Papers, 9–12 March – But Not Iraq War Protest – Warranted Front-Page Coverage," 15 September, http://mediamatters. org/research/200909150037, accessed 13 April 2011.

—— (2009) "Fox Promotion of Tea Parties Follows Years of Attacking Progressive Demonstrators," 17 April, http://mediamatters.org/research/200904170036, accessed 13 April 2011.

Meet the Press (2007) "Meet the Press Transcript for September 30, 2007," http://www.msnbc.msn.com/id/21065954, accessed 10 October 2007.

Millard, Geoff (2010) Email correspondence with author, 1 July.

—— (2010) "Operation First Casualty," Iraq Veterans Against the War website, http://www.ivaw.org/node/460, accessed 27 May 2010.

Miller, Martin (2007) "*24* Gets a Lesson in Torture from the Experts," *Los Angeles Times*, 13 February, E1.

Mirzoeff, Nicholas (2005) *Watching Babylon: The War in Iraq and Global Visual Culture* (London: Routledge).

—— (2009) "An End to the American Civil War?" *Journal of Visual Culture* 8.2: 228–33.

—— (2009) "War Is Culture: Global Counterinsurgency, Visuality, and the Petraeus Doctrine," *PMLA* 124.5: 1737–8, here 1741.

Mitchell, Don, and Lynn A. Staeheli (2005) "Permitting Protest: Parsing the Fine Geography of Dissent in America," *International Journal of Urban and Regional Research*, 29.4: 796–813.

Montgomery, David (2007) "Antiwar to the Corps: Marine Reservist-Protestors Face Discipline," *The Washington Post*, 31 May, http://www.washingtonpost. com/wp-dyn/content/article/2007/05/30/AR2007053002627.html, accessed 28 June 2010.

Moyers, Bill (2007) "Takin' It to the Streets – A Bill Moyers Essay," *Bill Moyers Journal*, 2 November, http://www.pbs.org/moyers/journal/11022007/profile3. html, accessed 13 April 2011.

—— (2007) "Transcript, Bill Moyers Journal, 26 October 2007," http://www. pbs.org/moyers/journal/10262007/transcript4.html, accessed 26 November 2007.

Mufson, Daniel (2007) "Berlin's Holy of Holies," *Performing Arts Journal* 29.1: 53–64.

Mukasey, Michael B. (2007) Letter to Senate Judiciary Committee, 30 October, http://www.nytimes.com/packages/pdf/national/20071031_Mukasay.pdf, accessed 14 August 2007.

Multitude e.V. and Unfriendly Takeover, (2007) "A to Z: The Precarious Alphabet of War," Dictionary of War, http://dictionaryofwar.org/en-dict/node/644, accessed 27 September 2007.

Muñoz, José (2008) "Performing the State of Exception: Coco Fusco's Operation Atropos," *TDR: The Drama Review* 52.1: 136–9.

Murphy, Jarrett (2003) "Text of Bush Speech: President Declares End to Major Combat Operations in Iraq," *CBS News* online, 1 May, http://www.cbsnews. com/stories/2003/05/01/iraq/main551946.shtml, accessed 28 May 2010.

Newark, Tim (2007) *Camouflage* (London: Imperial War Museum; New York: Thames & Hudson).

New York Times (2007) "Republican Presidential Debate in South Carolina," 15 May, Federal News Service Transcript, *New York Times* online, http://www.nytimes.com/2007/05/15/us/politics/16repubs-text.html, accessed 14 August 2007.

Nichols, Randy (2005) "The Games People Play: A Political Economic Analysist of Video Games and Their Production," PhD dissertation, University of Oregon.

—— (2010) "Target Acquired: America's Army and the Video Games Industry," in Nina B. Huntemann and Thomas Matthew Payne, eds, *Joystick Soldiers: The Politics of Play in Military Videogames* (New York: Routledge), 39–52.

Nieborg, David (2010) "Training Recruits and Conditioning Youth: The Soft Power of Military Games," in Nina B. Huntemann and Thomas Matthew Payne, eds, *Joystick Soldiers: The Politics of Play in Military Videogames* (New York: Routledge), 53–66.

Nobel Prize (2009) "Nobel Peace Prize for 2009," Press release, Nobel Prize website, http://nobelprize.org/nobel_prizes/peace/laureates/2009/press.html, accessed 12 November 2009.

North, Rene (1969) *Military Uniforms 1686–1918* (London: Hamlyn).

NPR (2009) "Former Interrogators Debate Harsh Tactics," *Tell Me More*, Michel Martin, host, NPR, 21 May, http://www.npr.org/templates/story/story.php?storyId104378628, accessed 11 March 2011.

—— (2011) "Tavis Smiley: If At First You Don't Succeed, 'Fail Up,'" *All Things Considered*, NPR, 4 May, http://www.wbur.org/npr/135985392/tavis-smiley-if-at-first-you-dont-succeed-fail-up, accessed 8 May 2011.

Obama, Barack (2006) *The Audacity of Hope: Thoughts on Reclaiming the American Dream* (New York: Crown).

Office of the Inspector General (2004) OIG Report, "Counterterrorism Detention and Interrogation Activities, September 2001-October 2003 (CIA Office of the Inspector General Special Review, 7 May), http://luxmedia.com.edgesuite.net/aclu/IG_Report.pdf, 21, accessed 11 April 2011.

Office of Legal Counsel (2002) Office of Legal Counsel memo, 1 August, U.S. Department of Justice, accessed 11 April 2011 via http://luxmedia.com.edge-suite.net/aclu/IG_Report.pdf.

Office of the Press Secretary (2001) "President Urges Readiness and Patience: Remarks by the President, Secretary of State Colin Powell and Attorney General John Ashcroft, Camp David, Thurmont, Maryland," Office of the Press Secretary, 15 September, http://georgewbush-whitehouse.archives.gov/news/releases/2001/09/20010915-4.html, accessed 5 May 2011.

Orwell, George (1950) *1984* (New York: Penguin).

Paglen, Trevor (2009) *Blank Spots on the Map: The Dark Geography of the Pentagon's Secret World* (New York: Dutton).

Paine, Thomas ([1776] 1835) *The American Crisis* (London: James Watson).

Pattenden, Mike (2009) "Why Army Recruitment Is Still Soaring," *TimesOnline* 7 October, http://www.timesonline.co.uk/tol/life_and_style/men/article6863641.ece#, accessed 7 October.

PBS (2001) "President Bush's Speech," *Online NewsHour*, 7 October, http://www.pbs.org/newshour/terrorism/combating/bush_10-7.html, accessed 28 May 2010.

—— (2005) "The Torture Question: Interview with Tony Lagouranis," *Frontline*, 25 September, http://www.pbs.org/wgbh/pages/frontline/torture/interviews/lagouranis.html, accessed 12 March 2008.

—— (2007) "Bin Laden's Fatwa," *PBS NewsHour* online, http://www.pbs.org/newshour/terrorism/international/fatwa_1996.html, accessed 26 January 2011.

—— (2011) "Sinclair Stations Pull Nightline Iraq Casualties Report," *PBS NewsHour Update*, http://www.pbs.org/newshour/updates/abc_04-30-04.html, accessed 17 March.

Phillips, Dougal (2007) "The Self-Torment of the White House Screen: Language, Lyotard and Looking Back at the War on Terror," *Colloquy* 13: 5–19.

Pilkington, Ed (2011) "Colin Powell demands answers over Curveball's WMD lies," *Guardian*, 16 February, http://www.guardian.co.uk/world/2011/feb/16/colin-powell-cia-curveball, accessed 5 May 2011.

Platoni, Kara (1999) "The Pentagon Goes to the Video Arcade," *The Progressive* 63.7: 27–30.

Powers, Steve (2008) Phone interview with author, August.

Rancière, Jacques (2010) "Ten Theses on Politics," in *Dissensus: On Politics and Aesthetics*, ed. and trans. Steven Corcoran (London: Continuum).

Rand Corporation (2008) Press Release, "One In Five Iraq and Afghanistan Veterans Suffer from PTSD or Major Depression," Rand Corporation website, 17 April, http://www.rand.org/news/press/2008/04/17/, accessed 25 September 2010.

Raphael, Tim (2009) "The Body Electric: GE, TV, and the Reagan Brand," *TDR: The Drama Review* 53.2: 113–38.

—— (2009) *The President Electric: Ronald Reagan and the Politics of Performance* (Ann Arbor: University of Michigan Press).

Reinelt, Janelle (2005) Review of *Stuff Happens, Theatre Journal* 57.2: 303–6.

—— (2006) "Toward a Poetics of Theatre and Public Events," *TDR: The Drama Review* 50.3: 69–87.

Rejali, Darius (2007) "Torture Makes the Man," *South Central Review* 24.1: 151–69.

Rentfrow, Daphnée (2008) "S(t)imulating War: From Early Films to Military Games," in Andreas Jahn-Sudmann and Ralf Stockmann, eds, *Computer Games as a Sociocultural Phenomenon: Games without Frontiers – War without Tears* (Basingstoke: Palgrave), 87–96.

Rimini Protokoll (2007) "Helgard Haug," Rimini Protokoll website, http://www.rimini-protokoll.de/artist_frontend.php?artist_id3, accessed 11 June 2007.

Risen, James, David Johnston, and Neil A. Lewis (2004) "The Struggle for Iraq: Detainees: Harsh C.I.A. Methods Cited in Top Qaeda Interrogations," *New York Times*, 13 May, http://www.nytimes.com/2004/05/13/politics/13DETA.html, accessed 11 April 2011.

Rizzo, Albert "Skip," and Jarrell Pair (2010) "A Virtual Reality Exposure Therapy Application for Iraq War Veterans with Post Traumatic Stress Disorder: From Training to Toy to Treatment," http://www.apa.org/divisions/div46/Amp%20Summer%2005/RizzoArticle.pdf, accessed 10 September.

Rizzo, Albert A., Joann Difede, Barbara O. Rothbaum, Scott Johnston, Robert N. McLay, Greg Reger, Greg Gahm, Thomas Parsons, Ken Graap, and Jarrell Pair (2009) "VR PTSD Exposure Therapy Results with Active Duty OIF/OEF Combatants," *Medicine Meets Virtual Reality* 17 (J. D. Westwood et al., eds, IOS Press), 277–82.

Roach, Joseph (1996) *Cities of the Dead: Circum-Atlantic Performance* (New York: Columbia University Press, 1996).

Ross, Brian, and Richard Esposito (2005) "CIA's Harsh Interrogation Techniques Described," *ABC News*, 18 November, http://abcnews.go.com/Blotter/Investigation/story?id1322866, accessed 16 April 2011.

Rothbaum, B.O., L. Hodges, R., Alarcon, D. Ready, F. Shahar, K. Graap, J. Pair, P. Hebert, D. Gotz, B. Wills, and D. Baltzell (1999) "Virtual Reality Exposure Therapy for PTSD Vietnam Veterans: A Case Study," *Journal of Traumatic Stress* 12: 263–71.

Roy, Arundhati (2001) "War Is Peace," *OutlookIndia.com*, 18 October.

Russert, Tim (2001) *Meet the Press*, NBC, 16 September.

Ryssdal, Kai (2010) "The Army Experience Center: Mission accomplished?," *NPR Marketplace*, 30 July, http://marketplace.publicradio.org/display/web/2010/07/30/pm-the-army-experience-center-mission-accomplished/, accessed 31 July 2010.

Safire, William (2008) "On Language: Waterboarding," *New York Times*, 9 March, http://www.nytimes.com/2008/03/09/magazine/09wwlnSafire-t.html?_r3, accessed 7 April 2011.

Sample, Mark L. (2008) "Virtual Torture: Videogames and the War on Terror," *Game Studies: The International Journal of Computer Game Research* 8.2, http://www.gamestudies.org/0802/articles/sample, accessed 16 February 2011.

Sands, Philippe (2008) "The Green Light," *Vanity Fair*, April, 218–26, 278–82.

Saul, Ben (2007) "Torture Degrades Us All," *Foreign Policy in Focus Policy Report*, 5 December (Silver City, NM and Washington, DC: Foreign Policy In Focus), http://www.fpif.org/pdf/papers/0512torture.pdf, accessed 25 November 2007.

Scarry, Elaine (1985) *The Body in Pain: The Making and Unmaking of the World* (Oxford: Oxford University Press).

Schacht v. United States (1970) 398 U.S. 58.

Schachtman, Noah (2001) "New Army Soldiers: Game Gamers," *Wired News*, 29 October, http://www.wired.com/news/conflict/0,2100,47931,00.html, accessed 1 April 2011.

Schechner, Richard (1977) *Performance Theory* (London: Routledge), 107–8.

—— (2006) *Performance Studies: An Introduction*, 2nd edn (London: Routledge).

—— (2009) "9/11 as Avant-Garde Art?" *PMLA* 124.5: 1820–9.

—— (2010) Conversation with author, 17 September.

Schemo, D. (2002) "Mideast Turmoil: Demonstrations: Thousands Hold Rally in Capital to Back Israel," *New York Times*, 16 April, A18.

Schmitt, Carl ([1927] 1996) *The Concept of the Political*, trans. George Schwab (Chicago: University of Chicago Press).

Semple, Kirk (2005) "G.I.s Deployed in Iraq Desert with Lots of American Stuff," *New York Times* 13 August 2005, http://www.nytimes.com/2005/08/13/international/middleeast/13soldier.html, accessed 14 March 2008.

Shannon Watch (2010) Fact Sheet, http://www.shannonwatch.org/docs/Mar2010factsheet.pdf, accessed 2 April 2011.

Sherman, Stephen (2010) "'A Politics about Performing Dreams': An Interview with Stephen Duncombe," *Monthly Review* online, http://mrzine.monthlyreview.org/2007/sherman230207.html, accessed 27 May 2010.

Simpson, Aislinn (2008) "Channel Five reality TV show featuring waterboarding torture is 'unacceptable,'" *Telegraph* online, 6 October, http://www.telegraph.co.uk/news/3142352/Channel-Five-reality-TV-show-featuring-waterboarding-torture-is-unacceptable.html, accessed 24 August 2009.

Spillius, Alex (2007) "George Bush the Texan Is 'Scared of Horses,'" *Daily Telegraph*, 21 September, http://www.telegraph.co.uk/news/worldnews/1563773/George-Bush-the-Texan-is-scared-of-horses.html, accessed 8 May 2011.

Steinhauser, Paul (2011) "Obama's Record-Breaking Campaign Haul," *CNN*, 13 July, http://politicalticker.blogs.cnn.com/2011/07/13/obama-and-dnc-raise-more-than-86-million/, accessed 26 July 2011.

Sterling, Bruce (1993) "War Is Virtual Hell," *Wired* 1.1 (March/April), http://www.wired.com/wired/archive/1.01/virthell_pr.html, accessed 3 March 2011.

Swanson, David (2009) "U.S. Govt. Threatens to Prosecute Waterboarding," *World Can't Wait*, 20 June, http://www.worldcantwait.net/index.php?optioncom_content&viewarticle&id5672:us-govt-threatens-to-prosecute-waterboarding&catid117:homepage&Itemid289, accessed 13 April 2011.

Tarrow, Sidney (2010) Preface, *The World Says No to War: Demonstrations Against the War on Iraq* (Minneapolis, MN: University of Minnesota Press), viii.

Taylor, Diana (1997) *Disappearing Acts: Spectacles of Gender and Nationalism in Argentina's "Dirty War"* (Durham, NC: Duke University Press).

—— (2003) *The Archive and the Repertoire: Performing Cultural Memory in the Americas* (Durham, NC: Duke University Press).

—— (2004) "Editorial Remarks: The New Radical Performance Artists: Staging Democracy in the Americas," *e-misférica* 1.1, http://hemisphericinstitute.org/journal/1_1/editorial_eng.html, accessed 26 January 2011.

—— (2007) "Double-Blind: The Torture Case," *Critical Inquiry* 33 (Summer): 710–33.

Team Delta (2011) "About Team Delta," Team Delta website, http://www.teamdelta.net/about.htm, accessed 11 March 2011.

—— (2011) "Programs," Team Delta website, http://www.teamdelta.net/programs.htm, accessed 11 March 2011.

Thompson, Clive (2002) "The Making of an Xbox Warrior," *New York Times Magazine*, 22 August, 32–7.

Time (2011) "Top Ten Bushisms," *Time* online, http://www.time.com/time/specials/packages/completelist/0,29569,1870938,00.html, accessed 26 January 2011.

Tran, Mark (2008) "CIA admit 'waterboarding' al-Qaida suspects," *Guardian* online, 5 February, http://www.guardian.co.uk/world/2008/feb/05/india.terrorism, accessed 14 August 2008.

Trotter, William (2003) "The Power of Simulation: Transforming Our World," *PCGamer*, February, 24–8.

"Under Siege," http://www.afkarmedia.com/index.php?PageTitleUnder%20Siege&Typegames&StatusDetails&ID4, accessed 31 March 2011.

United for Peace and Justice, "History," http://unitedforpeace.org/about/history/, accessed 13 April 2011.

US Department of the Army (2006) *Counterinsurgency Manual*, FM 3-24, MCWP 3–33.5, December.

—— (2010) "The Story Behind the Army Experience Center," Army Experience Center webpage, http://www.thearmyexperience.com/about-the-army-experience-center/the-story-of-the-center, accessed 10 February.

—— (2011) "America's Army," America's Army official website, http://www.americasarmy.com/about/, accessed 28 February 2011.

—— (2011) Virtual Army Experience Fact Sheet: Bravo and Charlie, http://vae.americasarmy.com/pdf/vae_factsheet.pdf, accessed 23 March 2011.

US Department of Defense (1997) Office of the Inspector General, Requirements Planning for Development, Test, Evaluation, and Impact on Readiness of

Training Simulators and Devices (a draft proposed audit report), Project No. 5AB-0070.00, January 10, Appendix D.

—— (2010) Joint Publication 1-02, Department of Defense, *Dictionary of Military and Associated Terms*, 8 November 2010, as amended through 31 January 2011, JP 1-02 395.

—— (2011) "Operation Urban Warrior," http://www.defense.gov/specials/urban-warrior/, accessed 28 February.

VA National Center for PTSD (2010) "What Is PTSD?" U.S. Department for Veterans Affairs, February, http://www.ptsd.va.gov/public/pages/handouts-pdf/handout_What_is_PTSD.pdf, accessed 2 September 2010.

Vercammen, Paul, and Thelma Gutierrez (2010) "State's New Immigration Law Worries Arizona Soldier," *CNN* online, 27 April, http://edition.cnn.com/2010/US/04/25/arizona.soldier.immigration.vigil/index.html, accessed 24 May 2010.

Virilio, Paul (2000) *Landscape of Events*, trans. Julie Rose (Cambridge, MA: MIT Press).

Virilio, Paul, and Sylvère Lotringer ([1983] 2008) *Pure War* (Los Angeles, CA: Semiotext(e)).

Wadhams, Nick (2005) "Troops Stationed in Iraq Turn to Gaming," *Associated Press/USA Today*, 3 January, http://www.usatoday.com/tech/news/2005-01-03-iraq-gaming_x.htm, accessed 22 March 2011.

Walter, Amy, and Devin Dwyer (2011) "Bin Laden Death: Obama Approval Rating Spikes, but Republicans Say Economy More Important," *ABC News*, 3 May 2011, http://abcnews.go.com/Politics/president-obama-approval-rating-spikes-bin-laden-death/story?id13518704, accessed 10 May 2011.

Washington Post (2004) "Transcript: Illinois Senate Candidate Barack Obama," *The Washington Post*, 27 July, http://www.washingtonpost.com/wp-dyn/articles/A19751-2004Jul27.html, accessed 9 June 2010.

Watson, Debra (2005) "Fox's *24*: Propaganda thinly disguised as television programming," *World Socialist* website, 5 April, http://www.wsws.org/articles/2005/apr2005/2424-a05.shtml#top, accessed 28 September 2007.

Weiner, Mark (2008) "House panel OKs $10.4M for drones at Hancock," *Syracuse Post-Standard*, 25 June, http://www.syracuse.com/news/index.ssf/2008/06/hancock_in_line_for_drones.html, accessed 3 March 2011.

Werde, Bill (2004) "The War at Home," *Wired* 12.3 (March), http://www.wired.com/wired/archive/12.03/wargames_pr.html, accessed 24 March 2011.

"When wearing by persons not on active duty authorized," Title 10 U.S. Code, Pts. 772(f).

White House (2002) "President Bush, Colombia President Uribe Discuss Terrorism," White House Press Release, 25 September, http://www.whitehouse.gov/news/releases/2002/09/print/20020925-1.html, accessed 14 August 2007.

—— (2010) "Letter from the President on the Continuation of the National Emergency with Respect to Certain Terrorist Attacks," 10 September, http://www.whitehouse.gov/the-press-office/2010/09/10/letter-president-continuation-national-emergency-with-respect-certain-te, accessed 26 January 2011.

Woodward, Bob (2002) *Bush at War* (New York: Simon & Schuster).

Žižek, Slavoj (2002) *Welcome to the Desert of the Real* (London: Verso).

—— (2006) "The Depraved Heroes of 24 Are the Himmlers of Hollywood," *The Guardian* online, 10 January, www.guardian.co.uk/print/0,,5370717-103677,00. html, accessed 8 August 2007.

—— (2007) "Knight of the Living Dead," *New York Times*, 24 March, http://www. nytimes.com/2007/03/24/opinion/24zizek.html, accessed 14 August 2008.

—— (2009) *First as Tragedy, Then as Farce* (London: Verso).

—— (2010) "From Joyce-the-Symptom ... to the Symptom of Power," *Lacanian Ink* 11, http://www.plexus.org/lacink/lacink11/zizek.html, accessed 30 May.

Zombietime, http://www.zombietime.com/operation_first_casualty/.

Zyda, Michael (2004) "Crossing the Chasm," paper presented at the Serious Game Workshop, Game Developers Conference, San Jose, 23 March, http:// archive.gdconf.com/gdc_2004/zyda_michael.pdf, accessed via docstoc.com on 28 February 2011.

Index